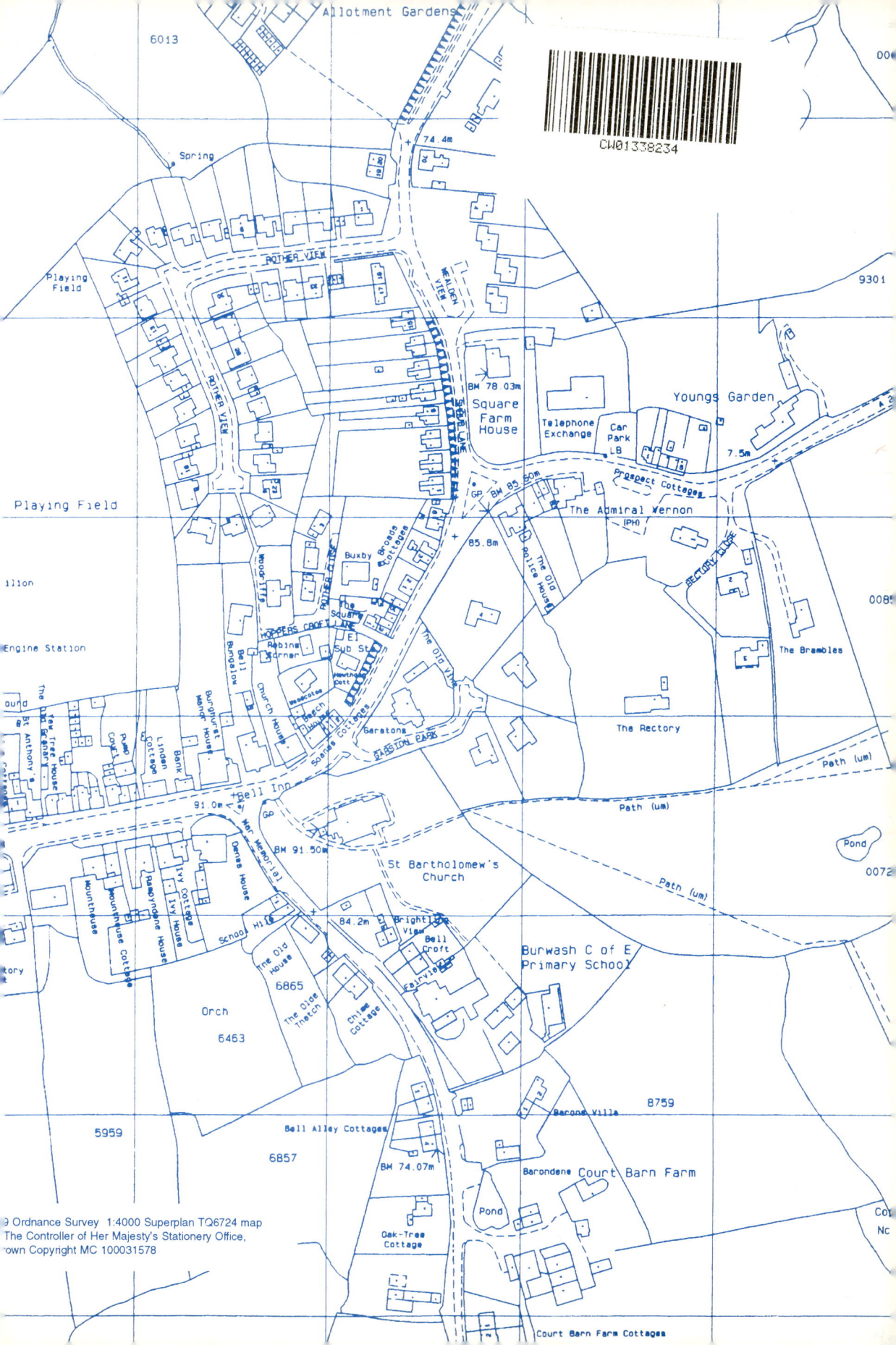

BURWASH
Domesday to Millennium

John Barkshire

© John Barkshire 2000

Published by John Barkshire
Denes House, High Street, Burwash TN19 7EH

ISBN 0 9538259 0 6

Typeset by David Brown, Maynards Green, Sussex 01435 812506
Index by Keyword Enterprises, Aylesford, Kent 01622 717903
Printed by Windmill Press, Hadlow Down, Sussex 01825 830319

Contents

Preface	v
Prologue	vii
Chapter One: **Domesday to Civil War (1086 – 1659)**	1
Chapter Two: **St Bartholomew's Church**	31
Chapter Three: **Restoration and Georgian (1660 – 1836)**	39
Chapter Four: **Denes House and its inhabitants**	71
Chapter Five: **Victoria to World War (1837 – 1918)**	77
Chapter Six: **Modern Burwash (1919 – 2000)**	123
Sources and Acknowledgements	171
Index	175

Preface

When I decided to embark on writing a history of Burwash I soon found that there were a number of preliminary decisions to be made which would collectively dictate the shape and character of this work. These decisions were the geographical area to be covered, the period of the history, the standard of accuracy and the general nature and ethos of the story.

I started with the decision that the ethos would put the emphasis on people, their work and lifestyle and how the village and its inhabitants have evolved over the centuries rather than producing a purely architectural catalogue. This dictated that the book would be divided into periods of historical relevance and that the logical starting date was 1086, being about the time of the first reference to the modern village. The geographical decision was a difficult one as people, families and living patterns ignore artificial administrative boundaries such as a village or parish. It was tempting to cover a wide geographical area but in the interests of conciseness and coherence I decided to concentrate on the main centre of the village and bring in surrounding properties and people only wherever they had an influence on village life. In order to assist with the identification of houses referred to in the text the endpapers are maps of the village (1999) and surrounding district (1910). A question of accuracy may seem a curious one in an historical work but if I had included only totally provable facts many interesting and probably true incidents would have been omitted; if however I included every rumour and tale the authenticity of the work would be undermined. I have therefore tried to strike a balance and to make it quite clear in the text where I am including indisputable fact or where there are degrees of uncertainty. I also decided to use the actual spelling of names, houses and other words as they appear in my sources without adding *sic*. This can result in different spellings occurring close together.

Having arrived at the general shape I then divided the book into periods. I would have liked each chapter to cover similar lengths of period and to contain identical detail but unfortunately the information available varies considerably with only general or occasional information being available for the early periods. Parish records only started in 1538, and those of Burwash only survive from 1558; from then on the amount of detail available steadily increases. I have tried to meet this by successively decreasing the length of the period each chapter covers but there is still more interesting information available for the later chapters. I decided to put in two short chapters on specific subjects. The first is on St Bartholomew's Church because it is the oldest building in the parish and the only one which has stood through the whole of this history. The second is on Denes House and its inhabitants because this is where my research started and I could not bear to waste the information I had collected. I have also included a short prologue on early pre-Norman Sussex in order to provide a background to the main work.

The last problem was the timescale of producing the book. It would have been very tempting to spend many years on research as there is a mass of information that can be unearthed by diligent digging but this would have delayed publication indefinitely. I felt this would have been unfair to the many people who have sent me information and I therefore set myself a deadline of the millennium year. I do however intend to return to the subject and I expect to produce a second, supplementary, volume which will also give me the opportunity to correct the inevitable mistakes.

Finally, some thankyou's. First to the large number of people, too numerous to mention individually, who lent me deeds, photographs, extracts of titles and other information about their homes and some of whom spent a considerable amount of time doing personal research. I apologise for not being able to include all this information and I also ask for forgiveness when I have accepted a different version of events from the one you believed: I have followed the weight of evidence and I hope that nobody will be offended. Second, I must thank Christopher Whittick for his advice and for reading and correcting a proof, and all the staff at East Sussex Record Office in Lewes for their patience and support during my three years of visiting their search room. David and Barbara Martin deserve a special mention. They have researched and produced booklets on a large number of individual properties in Burwash as well as writing on many relevant topics. Without their work my research would have been both more difficult and less complete and I have drawn extensively on their various publications. My last thankyou is to my wife Audrey who typed and corrected six drafts and whose constructive comments helped improve the flow of the text.

John Barkshire

Denes House, June 2000

Prologue

EARLY SUSSEX

It is likely that early man first inhabited Sussex at the time of the palaeolithic (Old Stone) age (30,000 BC) as flint implements of this time have been found on several sites, including one near Heathfield. These inhabitants would have led a primitive forest life of fishing and hunting. The last Ice Age then produced arctic conditions that drove any population to warmer southern lands but when the ice cap retreated in the Mesolithic Age (10,000 BC) the sea level dropped, man returned, and gradually the English Channel was formed separating England and its inhabitants from the Continent. Some of these people certainly spent their nomadic life in the Weald as their tools and weapons have been found, particularly at Selmeston and near Uckfield and Robertsbridge. A few thousand years later in about 3000 BC a series of invasions started to take place including some from darker haired people from southern Europe who introduced settled stable communities and the Neolithic colonisation of Southern England, including the South Downs, had begun. These were the people who built the temple at Avebury and later Stonehenge. One of their causeway camps was built at Coombe Hill above Eastbourne with accompanying burial mounds or barrows. The Bronze Age (1000-400 BC) was punctuated by a wave of invasions by Celts from the south east over a period of several hundred years. These hardy invaders were not afraid to live in the Wealden forests and in the coming Iron Age (400 BC) were probably also charcoal burners creating fuel for their new iron workings. There is evidence of Iron Age workings as near as Ashburnham and the Burwash ridge might well have contained pockets of habitation.

After a few hundred years of stability, an invasion by the Belgae in 75 BC was soon followed by the first Roman expedition twenty years later. Their extensive building programme demonstrated the importance of Sussex, but the Roman inhabitation was mainly to the west with their principal fortification in the east being at the port of Anderida (Pevensey). Villas and a bathhouse were located at Eastbourne and ironworks at Ticehurst, Dallington and almost certainly at Burwash Common. Iron was an important product of the area and was taken to the port of Bodiam from where it was shipped downstream, across the shallow waters of Romsey Marsh, to the naval base at Dover. This continued until about 230 AD when the Classis Britannica was disbanded and Dover port

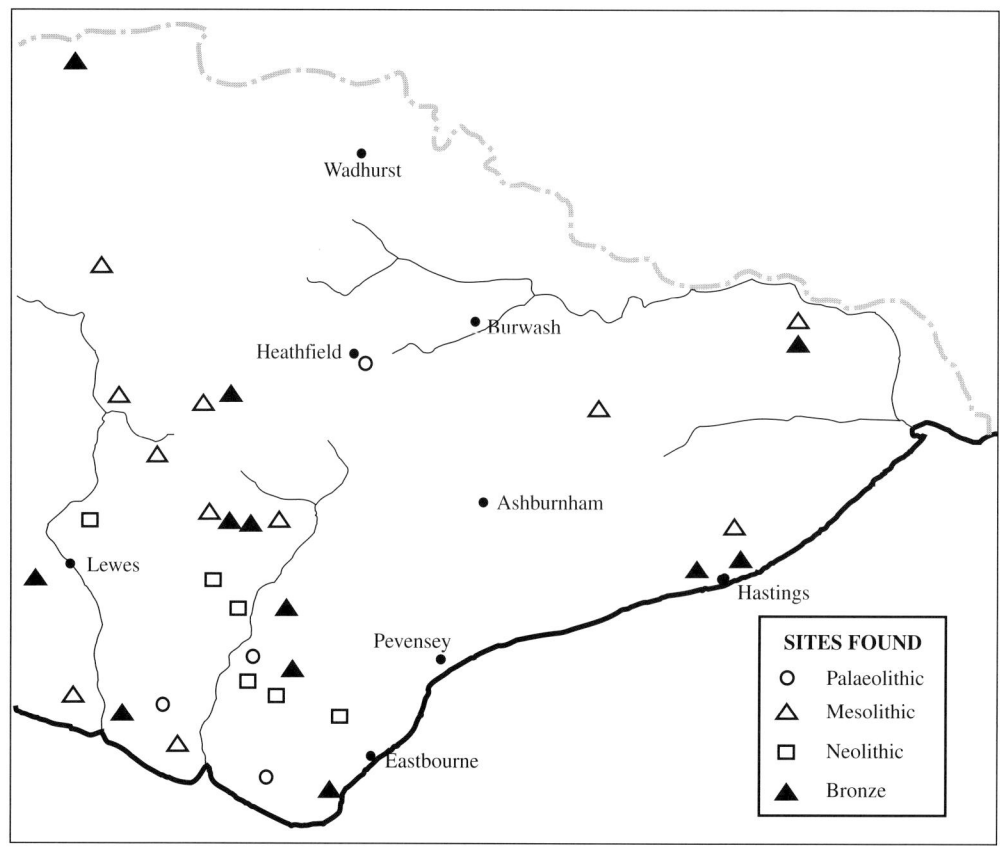

Early Sussex

dismantled. One of the Romans' most impressive features was their road network and in addition to the main roads they had a huge network of minor roads of which the most important were numbered tracks. Track IV ran along the Hurst Green to Heathfield ridgeway, probably following the route of an older Celtic way. This would have been improved and straightened by the Romans. Along the routes were a series of posting stations placed at convenient intervals to break up the journey. Being halfway between Heathfield and Hurst Green, Burwash was almost certainly one of these stations, which normally consisted of small rectangular enclosures providing the necessities for travellers. A small settlement would probably have grown up round this posting station, especially as another, smaller, trackway is thought to have gone north to Stonegate and Wadhurst and Burwash was therefore at a minor crossroads.

After the Romans left Britain, in about 400 AD, their civilisation gradually fell into

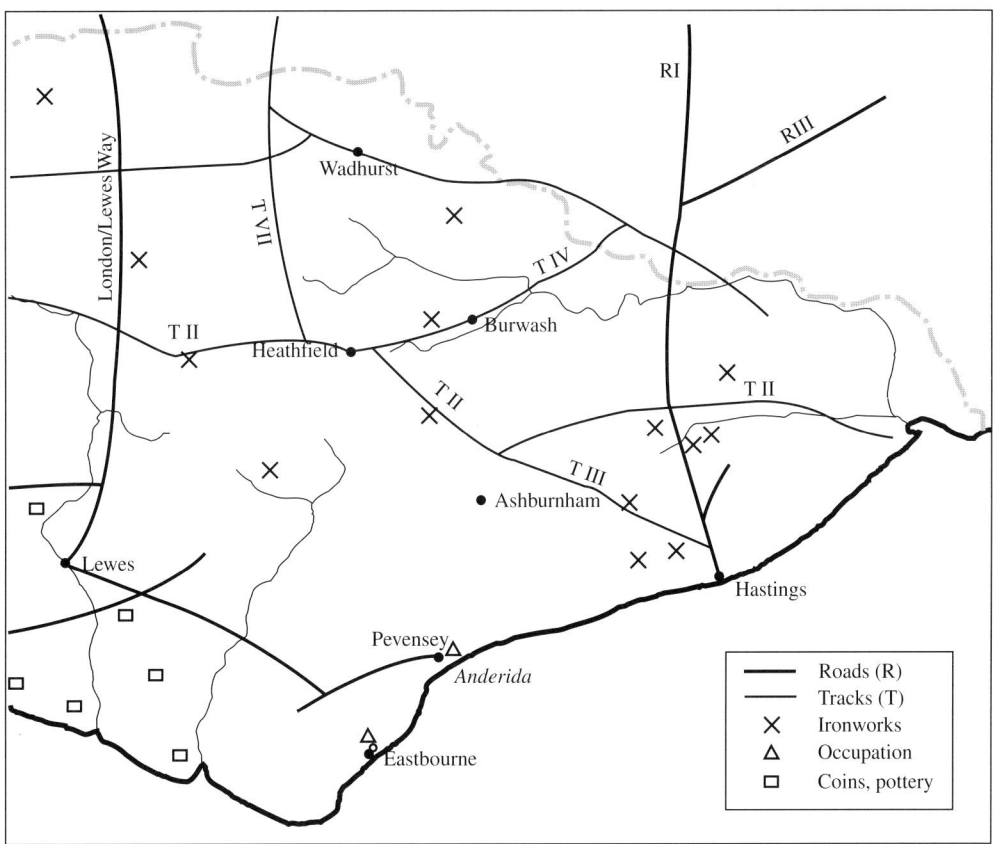

Roman Sussex

decay and we entered the long period about which little is known and during which England lost touch with the continent and slipped back into obscurity. East Sussex, which had seen only relatively minor Roman influence, quickly went back to a sparse population surviving again by hunting and fishing; many were nomads and any hamlets were small and basic. The Wealden forest formed an unfriendly and impenetrable barrier that discouraged travel or even settlement. It was during this period, around 450 AD, that the Saxons started their raids into England which led to an invasion of Sussex in 471 and conquest by 491. It was then that the county received its name as the Kingdom of the South Saxons. The Saxons were sturdy farmers, using oxen ploughs and creating communal fields as they started to clear the forests. They built in wood however and no remains of Saxon buildings have therefore survived. The other event of this period was the arrival of St Wilfred in 681 and his conversion of the South Saxons to Christianity. Wilfred

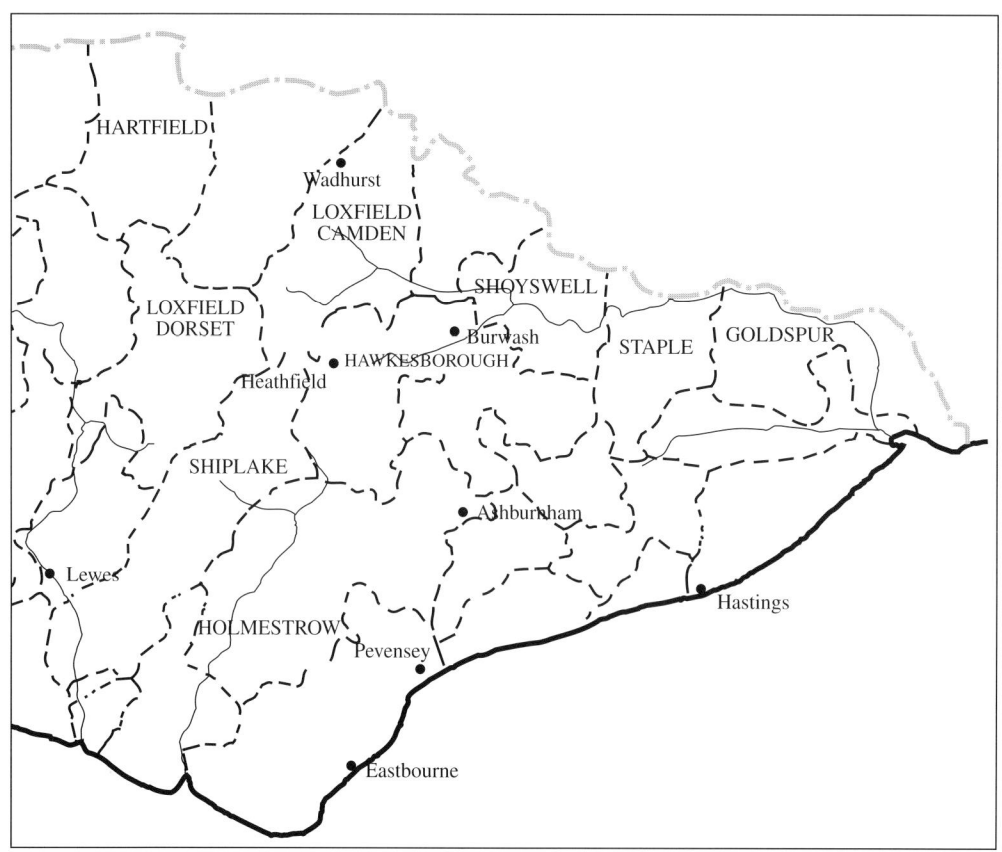

Saxon Hundreds

made his See at Selsey and the boundaries of his diocese were those of modern Sussex. These are unique in England in that they have remained unaltered since their foundation, with the only change being the move of the Bishop's seat from Selsey to Chichester in 1076.

The long period of Saxon rule ended with the Norman Conquest of 1066 but lasting features of this earlier period were the introduction of civil areas known as Hundreds and the beginnings of ecclesiastical parishes. The Hundreds were administrative regions, which from the 10th Century provided justice and other such functions that were the predecessors of petty sessional divisions and local government. There were sixty-one hundreds in Sussex, varying considerably in size. Burwash was largely in the Hawkesborough Hundred and, although there is no evidence, it is easy to conjecture that there could have been a simple wooden Saxon church on the current site of St. Bartholomews, surrounded by equally simple early dwellings.

Chapter One

DOMESDAY TO CIVIL WAR
1086 – 1659

Once their conquest of England was complete the Normans set about organising and administering the country and to achieve this they introduced the feudal system. Under this the King owned virtually the whole country. He then divided it up and granted much of it to his principal Norman supporters who became Barons in return for rendering services to the King. These services were generally to provide men and horses properly equipped when needed for war. The Barons then subdivided their land among lesser Lords on the same sort of terms and the system cascaded down through local Manors until it came to those at the bottom who owned nothing but worked, as villeins, in return for their keep.

Sussex, which was of some strategic importance because it contained the most direct communication routes to Normandy, was divided into five rapes, or administrative divisions. Rapes are peculiar to Sussex, much as Ridings are to Yorkshire and Lathes to Kent. These north-to-south areas were each given to one of King William's most trusted Norman Barons. What is now East Sussex contained the rapes of Lewes, Pevensey and Hastings, and the easterly Hastings rape containing Burwash was granted to the Count of Eu. Norman rule thus began, but it is doubtful if it had much impact on the lives of most of the inhabitants of the county although Sussex's importance led to an expansion of its ports and a further clearing and colonisation of the Weald, extending the pattern begun by the Saxons.

In 1086, just twenty years after the conquest and in the year before he died, William I ordered a comprehensive survey of his kingdom in order to establish the ownership and value of every manor and village, the extent of their woodlands, meadow and pasture, and the number of the population. In enabled the King to know how his realm "was peopled and with what sort of men". This survey was called the Domesday Inquest and it was to establish the facts by means of sworn evidence, as unprejudiced as could be obtained, and

Chapter One

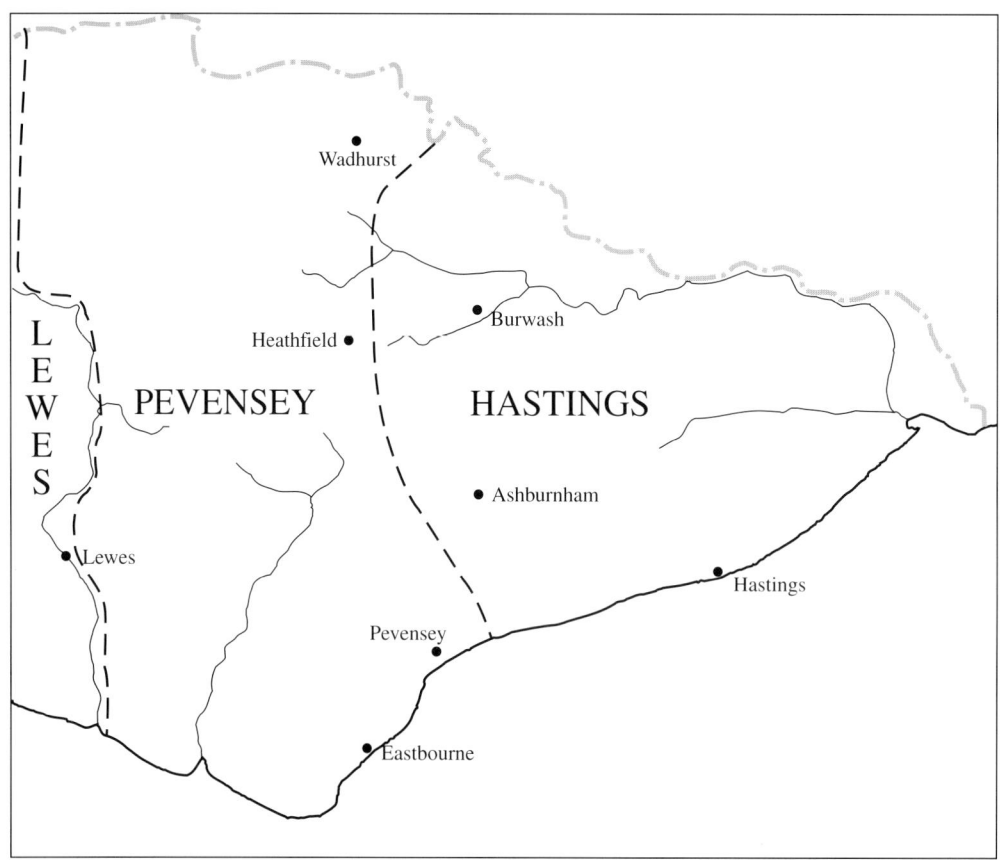

Norman Rapes

from which there could be no appeal, and then to commit them to writing. This was the first such exercise ever undertaken in England and the logistics must have been daunting, but it was completed within eight months and its significance is put into perspective by the fact that the next such nationwide survey was the census of 1801. Burwash was not recorded in the survey which means that it had fewer than ten households, indicating a population of perhaps up to fifty. This tiny community must however have been something of a focal point for the surrounding population as, within ten years of the survey, a stone church was built capable of holding nearly one hundred worshippers. Furthermore it was enlarged a hundred years later and again in 1250 so that it could then accommodate a congregation of about one hundred and fifty. There were no other churches in the area until Heathfield (1250) and Etchingham (1340) were built, which emphasises the relative importance of the hilltop settlement of Burwash. No traces of dwellings remain from this period but they would first have been of simple wood or possibly stone construction progressing to timber frame with wattle and daub panels but only containing a single or, at the most, two rooms with a central fire to give light and heat and on which to do the cooking. Furniture would consist of a trestle table, three-legged stools for the uneven floor, a truckle bed or tiered bunks and a few simple utensils. Shutters or oiled cloth would cover any window spaces and the doorway, and often the animals lived in a stable or lean-to that was part of the house. It is easy to envisage an untidy

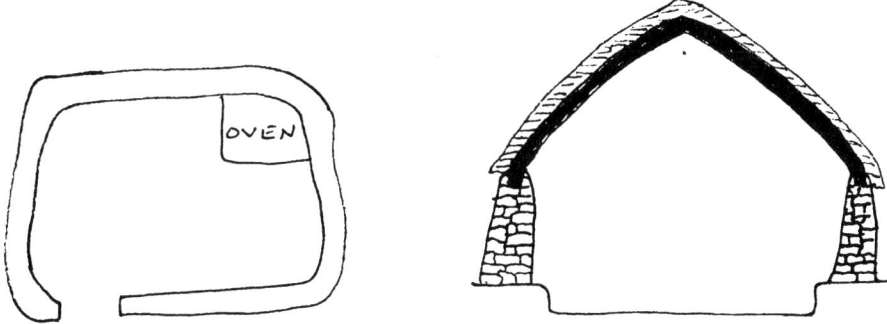

Simple 13th century house with thatching being supported by the cruck frames at each end joined by a ridge pole

straggle of these dwellings clustered near the church along the line of the track that followed the route of the old Roman road. The church, as the major building, was the focal point and it also served as the village meeting place, was used for storage and provided shelter for travellers.

So in the 12th and 13th centuries Burwash was probably slowly growing in size with most of its population scraping a living from the land as they had for hundreds of years. Gradually this changed as Burwash emerged as a minor trading centre with people from the surrounding area coming to sell their simple produce and satisfy their equally simple requirements. In 1252 these arrangements were given official status when a weekly market on Fridays was granted by the King and in the same year an annual three-day fair on the vigil, day and morrow of SS. Philip and James (May 1). In 1310 an additional yearly fair was granted on the feast of St. Bartholomew (August 24) with an extension for the two days following.

During this period a manor house was constructed, again demonstrating the growing status of Burwash, and in 1280 was described "there is there a capital mansion which is worth annually in herbage, garden produce, and a certain area in front of the gate, 7s.6d. Eighty-seven acres of arable land in the demesne as well within as outside the park which are worth annually £1.1s.9d. In the park are twenty acres of wood the herbage of which with the pannage is worth annually 6s.8d. The sale of the underwood in the same park is worth 9s. The sale of the heather 12d. Warren and conies 4s." Thereafter it seems to have deteriorated because when this building was destroyed in about 1310 the crops of its garden were said to have consisted of nettles and fruit and the remains of the building were deemed to be of no value. The manor was, however, rebuilt by John, Earl of Richmond, later Earl of Lancaster, in 1360. There also seems to have been a park connected to this manor as in 1247 four bucks were sent from it for the use of the King's children at Windsor and by 1334 the park extended to 100 acres. The location of this vanished manor house has been the subject of many theories including a site near Batemans, one at Court Barn Farm or one near the Glebe. Of these theories the defendable site on top of a hill away from robbers and wolves in the forest below seems perhaps the most plausible. The flat plateau of the glebe with its ancient row of oaks leading to the church and its surrounding earthworks supports this and the scene can be imaginatively reconstructed.

The origin of the name of the village is also a matter of debate as it evolved from Burhercse in the 12th century to Burghesse in the 13th, Burgherssh or Burwassh in the 15th, Burrishe in the 16th and the modern Burwash in the 17th century. It is said to mean, in old English, a stronghold, BURH, with a stubble field, ERSE, but there are other theories such as "town in the forest" or "fortified hill in the woods" using two different meanings of BURGH and HURST.

In addition to the manor of Burwash there was the second principal manor of Burghurst and minor manors of Brooksmarle, Turzes, Woodknowle, Mottynsden, Fosters and St. Giles. Burwash manor remained largely in royal patronage until it passed to the Pelhams (who were also Dukes of Newcastle), who in 1741 also succeeded to the manor of Burghurst, which had been held by the family of de Burghersh since 1256. The Burghersh family held many distinguished posts: Robert was Constable of Dover Castle and Lord Warden of the Cinque Ports around 1300; Henry was Bishop of Lincoln, Lord Treasurer and Lord Chancellor to Edward III, and his son, Sir Bartholomew Burgersh KG, 3rd Baron, fought at the Battle of Crecy. Bartholomew's son Henry became the 4th Baron and his daughter Joan (1325-1404) married John de Mohun, 5th Lord Dunster, in 1340 at the age of fifteen. After Mohun's death in 1375 she lived in some style in the royal court and her three daughters married William, Earl of Salisbury, Edward, Duke of York who was killed at Agincourt in 1415, and Lord Strange. Joan herself was buried in the crypt of Canterbury Cathedral where her tomb can be seen today inscribed "Johane de Burwasche". The title of Baron Burghersh is held today by the Fane family, who are also Earls of Westmorland. Both these principal manors were sold by the executors of Henry

Pelham to the Ashburnhams around 1800, in which family they remain today. This brought to an end the connection of the Pelhams with Burwash that went back to soon after their arrival in Sussex from Hertfordshire in the 13th century, when they had land at Warbleton before establishing their main residence at Laughton. By the 15th century they were described as Lords of the Rape of Hastings. They were said to be the third oldest Sussex family and they eventually sold the Manors to the oldest, the Ashburnhams.

The manor of Brooksmarle was known as Broxmayle in the 13th century but records cease in the 16th century; likewise Turzes (13th century Tyreshers) was lost in the 18th century, having been owned by the Shoyswell and the Constable families. It had its share of violent history for after Reynold de Tyreshers had robbed his neighbours of their land during the Barons War (1263-65) his sons Reynold and Thomas fought to their death inside the manor house in a dispute over his will. Woodknowle was first held by Reynold de Wokynolle in 1212, staying in this family for over four hundred years, by which time it was in the Lunsford name through a marriage of Joan Woknolle to William Lunsford (or Lonnesford) in about 1340. After the Lunsfords sold it in 1639 it passed later through the Lanes, Frys, and Owen Stones to Henry Lucas in 1869. Mottynsden was held by John Motyn in 1332 but joined with Woodknowle in 1545 through John Lunsford. Fosters (or Forsters) was tenanted by the a Wylie's in the 16th century as in 1508 a John a Wylie occupied "Forsters tenement of the Park" but this manor disappeared over the years. St.Giles was in the possession of Goddard Oxenbridge in 1530, was owned by ironmaster George May in 1569, then Elphicks, Thomas Jenkins, Robert Chandlers and on to the Dyke family. By marriage it passed to Henry Hone Haviland in the 19th century and then in 1869 to Henry Newton. Although these manors have ceased to have any meaning or territorial ownership they all, except Fosters and St. Giles, survive today in properties bearing their names and St.Giles has indeed been revived in a modern house near its original site.

The Norman dynasty was followed by the Plantagenets in 1154 when the weak Stephen was succeeded by Henry II. The next two hundred years of the Plantagenet kings were to contain events that established much of the structure of future English society. Henry II extended his kingdom from Scotland and Ireland to the Mediterranean through conquest and marriage but at home he received humiliation at the hands of the church following the murder of Becket in 1170 at Canterbury. It was he who introduced the concept of government by common law and justice through local assizes.

His successor Richard I (Lionheart) was best known for the Crusades but his brother John then faced the Barons' revolt that led to the signing of the Magna Carta at Runneymede in 1215. This set the foundation for the future democratic government of our country and, following the provisions of Oxford (1258) and Westminster (1259), sowed the beginnings of our parliamentary system.

In the constantly recurring war with France the triumphs of Crecy (1346) and Agincourt (1415) were followed by reversal at the hands of Joan of Arc at Orleans (1429). In 1377 Plantagenets were succeeded by the Houses of York and Lancaster and the long running struggle for power between these rival royal factions culminated in the Wars of the Roses (1455–85).

In Sussex however the most profound and far-reaching event of the period was the Black Death of 1348. The change of Kings, new civil liberties and overseas battles won or lost had only a marginal effect on the people in Sussex and Burwash and the way of life until 1348 had only evolved slowly and changed little since Saxon times. The peasant farmer grew enough to feed his family but was beholden to the Lord of the Manor and owed him service in lieu of rent. Black Death then killed between a quarter and half the population in many areas and destroyed this old social system by creating labour shortages which shifted the balance of power for ever. Landowners tried to keep wages down and the Statute of Labourers (1351) was an effort to fix prices and keep wages low but these ultimately led to the Peasants Revolt under Wat Tyler (1381). Reform and freedom of wages gradually followed as did a society of free men that was to produce the squirearchy and a powerful middle class of farmers and tradesmen who were to dominate village and town life in the centuries ahead. The rise in influence of the yeoman farmer or smallholder which was triggered by this change saw the emergence of some of the Burwash families who were increasingly to play a vital role in the development of the village for many years to come. In addition to those old families owning the Lordships of the Manor, others settled in the parish by 1300 included Ralph de Gotesholle (at Goodsole), and John de Poulesworthe (Poundsford). They were followed by the Colins or Colyns, Bynes, Cruttendens, Conys and Hepdens. All of these had arrived by the 16th century and were starting to accumulate land and wealth.

In the 13th and 14th centuries hunting and poaching were an important occupation for all country folk as the woods and streams were full of game and fish of all sorts to supplement an otherwise frugal diet. This led to a complaint in 1389 that "people keep greyhounds and other dogs and on the holy days when good Christian folk be at church hearing divine service, they go hunting in park, warren and coneyries of lords and others to the very great destruction of the same".

Chaucer (1340–1400) had painted a vivid picture of English characters of this time but perhaps of greater long-term importance was William Caxton (1422–91) who in 1477 brought his printing press to London and set it up in Westminster. He was both translator and printer and produced nearly one hundred books ranging from Chaucer to Cicero, Malory to Aesop. His process laid the foundation for the spread of literature and literacy throughout the country. This aided the gradual spread of schools which were endowed by Kings and Bishops alike and often provided free schooling for the sons of the newly emerging middle class, thus encouraging their growth of influence in trade and society. Against this background of social change there was slow but steady economic growth based on increasing trade. This trading was not just across the seas but between villages and more importantly between different parts of the country. Wool from one area was traded with corn from another, bacon for pottery, mutton for cloth. This trade brought with it a slow rise in the standard of living, an improvement in the roads and an interchange of cultures. So in every village people's minds were broadened as travelling players added to the knowledge of the outside world. Travel was dangerous but inns and monasteries provided shelter and food. The utensils and furniture of many of the population started to improve.

The other significant influences on the life of Sussex were its growth as a centre of shipbuilding, which became its most important industry, and the growth of the iron industry in the Weald. The combination of the effects of Black Death and the rise of these two industries led to a lessening of the relative dominance of the coastal towns and a rise in the importance and population of the Weald. The shipwrights used the oak of the Weald, which was amongst the finest in Europe, and seemed to offer an endless supply of material, and took it to the Cinque Ports and Portsmouth where the ships were built. This industry was to continue over the centuries supplying the material for merchantmen and fighting ships as Britain spread its influence round the world and conducted wars to protect its commercial interests and its growing empire.

Allied to this was the iron industry which, in addition to supplying many domestic, hunting and farming tools and utensils, also produced the cannon that were used aboard the ships. The Wealden iron industry dated back to Roman times and had continued through the medieval period, but it was still small-scale and very locally and family based. It used a simple furnace in which iron and charcoal were placed in layers and burned for several days until a lump of iron formed in the base of the furnace. These lumps were taken away to be moulded in a forge and were known as blooms, thus giving the name of bloomery to the furnace site. In the 15th century a new technique was introduced from France which revolutionised the industry. The power for the vital bellows was now provided by water or oxen driving a wheel and this greatly increased the

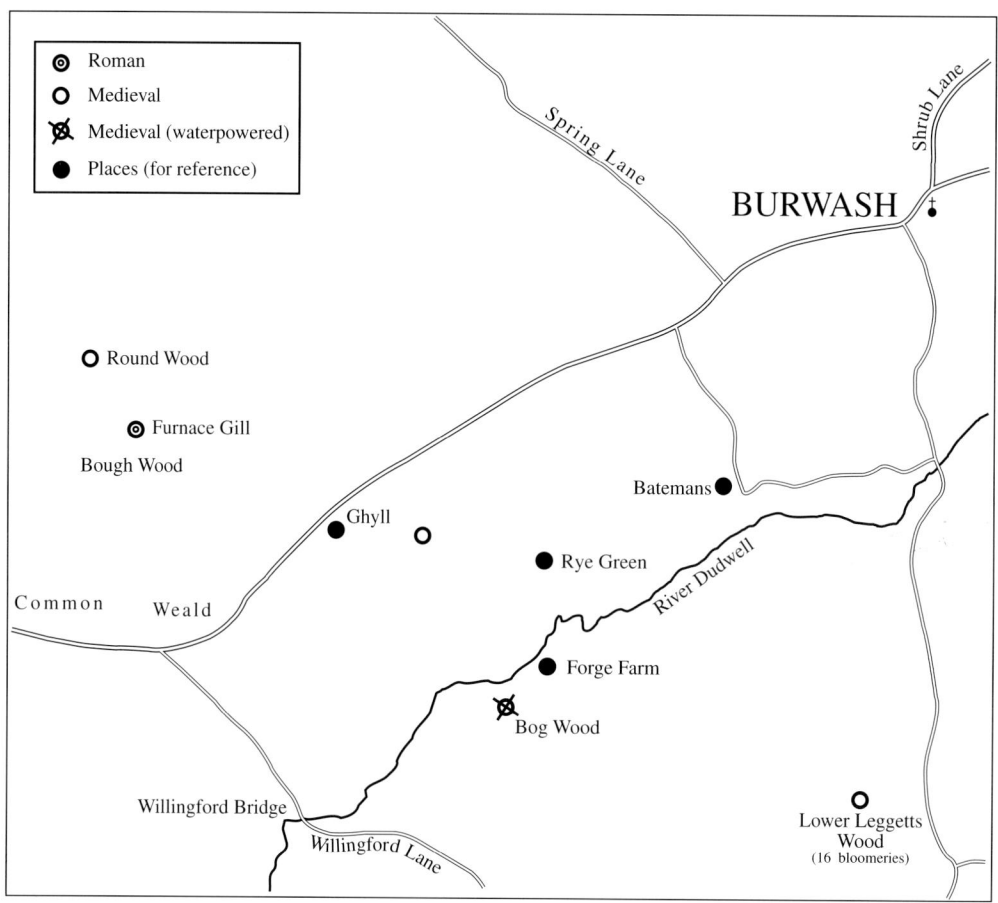

Local ironworks

heat generated. This enabled larger, permanent, furnaces to be built into which ore was fed at the top and poured out in pure liquid form at the bottom. As well as the advantage of a permanent structure this continuous process enormously increased the output and thus the scale of the industry. Wadhurst clay contained rich layers of iron and at that time there was no shortage of local timber for fuel.

There is evidence round Burwash of both the ore bloomeries and the new water-powered furnaces. There had been the possible Roman site at Furnace Gill in Bough Wood north of Burwash Common and medieval bloomeries nearby at Round Wood, another near Keylands, and a group of sixteen bloomeries in Lower Leggetts Wood near Kemland. Forge hammers were reported in Burwash in 1430. Burwash forge itself was between Bogwood and Forgewood on the stream and footpath running from Batemans to

Willingford. There is evidence here of both ponds and scattered cinders and Forge Farm was a short distance away. This site was originally a bloomery which was being operated by John Harvey in 1540 but was taken over the following year by John Collins (or Colyns) who had already introduced water-operated methods to his forge at Socknersh where he employed eight French workers. Collins used the Burwash forge for the specialist refining of pig iron. Collins was probably a descendant of the Colins to whom there is in St Bartholomew's church an iron sepulchral slab of the 14th century with the lettering "ORATE P(RO) ANNEMA JOHNE COLINE". "Pray for the soul of". The slab is said to be the oldest such slab in Sussex and was no doubt made in Collins' own forge. The Colins family had lived at Socknersh for some hundreds of years and built the present manor in about 1600 to replace the older manor house on the site. The original owner had been Sir William de Sokenerish, Knight, and the manor had then been inherited by Sir Alan de Boxhall or Buxhall when he was aged two in 1325. He held office under Edward III and accompanied his kinsman Lord Burghersh to France on a Royal mission in 1364, shortly after which he was made one of the first Knights of the Garter. He transferred his loyalty to John of Gaunt and indeed carried out the murder of two fellow knights for him, within the precincts of Westminster Abbey. He died in 1381 and the property passed to the Batys and then Colins. In John Colyn's will, dated 1541, he left to his three sons, John, Alexander and Bartholomew, Burwash forge with furnace, tools and instruments to be occupied "lovingly and brotherly". His daughter Odyerne was married to John Crotynden. The last of the family at Socknersh, Henry, was to die without issue over two hundred years later.

The other local bloomery forges gradually fell into disuse but Burwash forge continued, passing briefly into Robert Cruttenden's hands before being purchased by Thomas Hepden in 1592. This sale resulted in a chancery suit being filed and performance asked for an "iron forge or ironworks known as Bergherst forge, the inheritance of one Henry Colley, and a certain stack of coal lying at the same forge containing the number of 300 loads, being very necessary and beneficial for such person as should occupy the said iron forge". The Hepdens sold it to Jeffery Glyd (of Glydwish or Gliddish) in 1661 before it was purchased by the Fuller family of Brightling in 1700 and they kept it until it ceased production in 1803. The decline of this Wealden industry was to be steady after reaching its peak towards the end of the 16th century. By 1581 concern was being expressed at the rate of timber destruction and Acts were passed forbidding the use of timber for furnace fuel within fourteen miles of London and twelve miles of the coast, or the erection of ironworks within twenty miles of London. This temporarily concentrated production into the Weald but the use of coking coal instead of timber led to the industry gradually moving to the Midlands. By 1717 only twenty

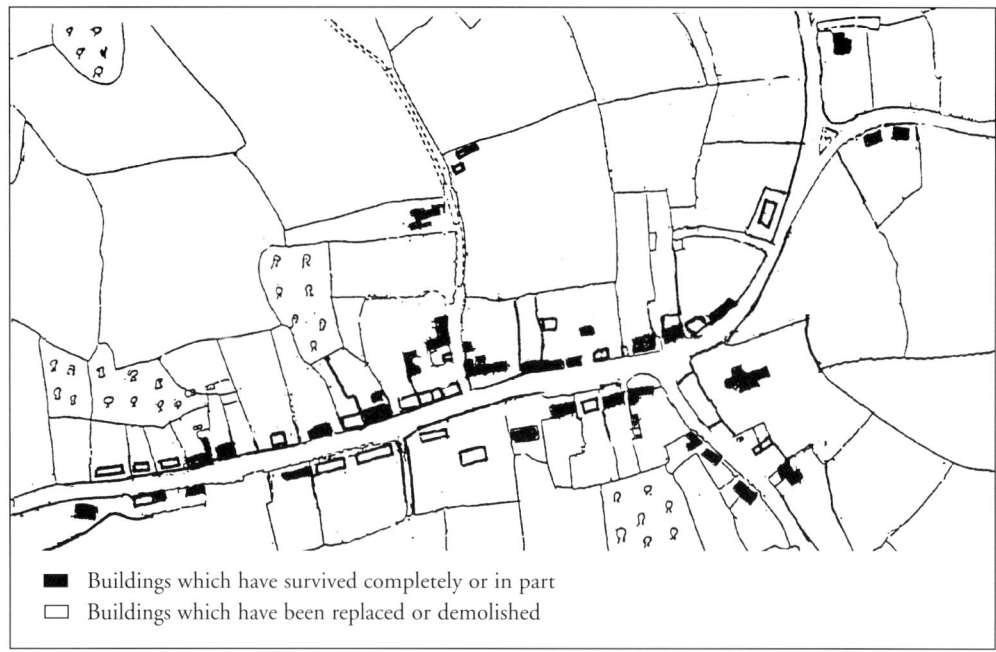

Burwash in about 1625

furnaces were in production in the Weald and in 1809 the last Wealden furnace, at Ashburnham, closed down.

During the long medieval period Burwash had steadily developed in size and importance through its markets, fairs and trade and by the end of this period, when Henry Tudor became King Henry VII after the decisive Battle of Bosworth in 1485, it had largely assumed the shape and size that was to remain unaltered until the Victorian developments four hundred years later. During the Elizabethan and early Stuart period many of the old buildings were rebuilt or dwellings replaced barns so that by about 1625 much of today's High Street existed, although the buildings would generally have been of a timber framed appearance. This remained until it was covered by the tile hanging of the 18th century.

Many of the houses in and around the village were so-called hall houses and collectively they are a fine example of the development of domestic buildings during the later part of the medieval period. In the 14th century most houses, other than the great and grand, consisted of only one or two rooms with a central fire. The fire provided heat and the method of cooking and smoke escaped through vents in the roof. Often the structure consisted of a single room (the hall) or had a second room (the parlour) at one end,

Domesday to Civil War (1086–1659)

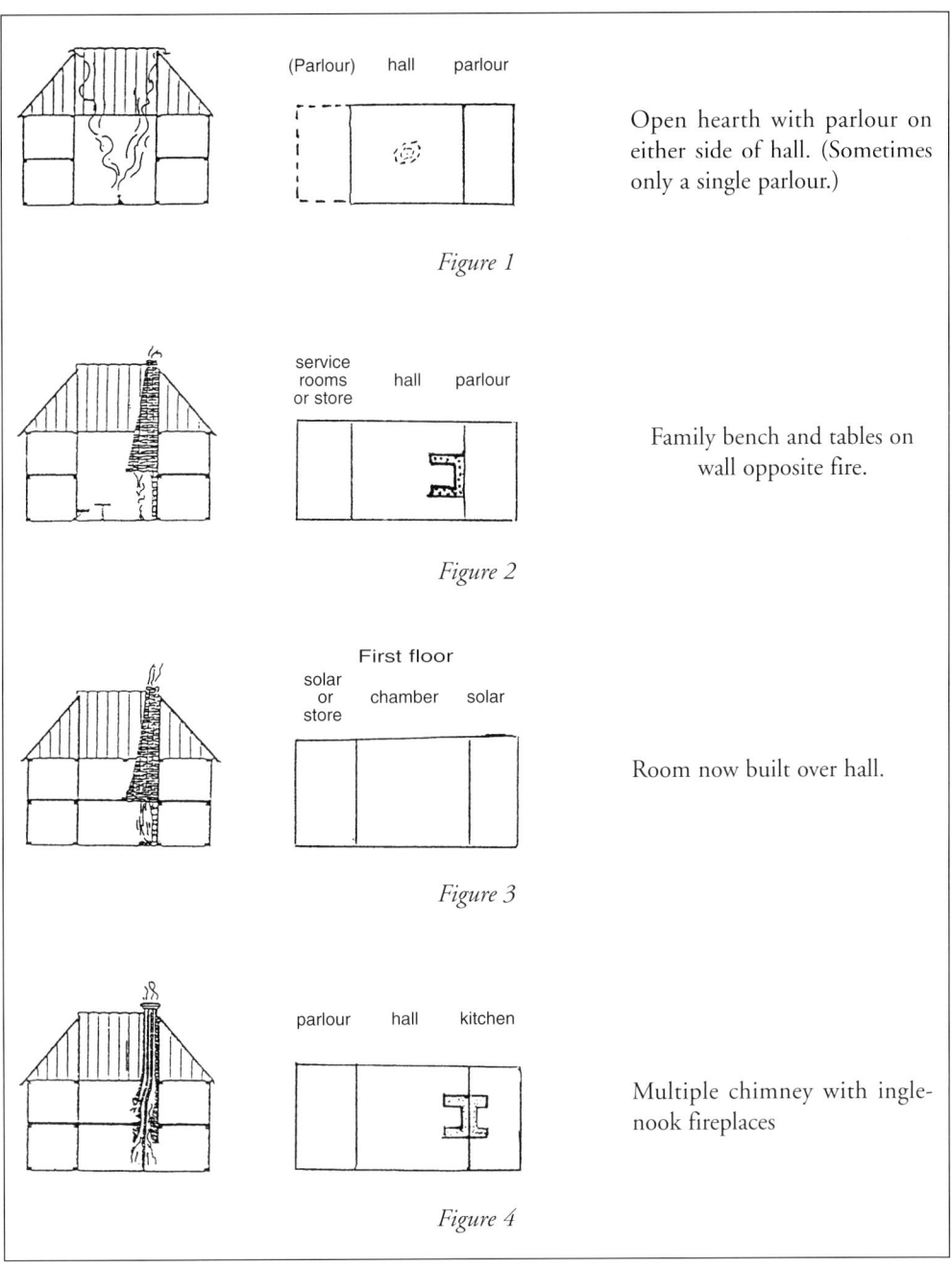

Figure 1 — Open hearth with parlour on either side of hall. (Sometimes only a single parlour.)

Figure 2 — Family bench and tables on wall opposite fire.

Figure 3 — Room now built over hall.

Figure 4 — Multiple chimney with inglenook fireplaces

Development of hall houses

12   Chapter One

Early Hall House

sometimes with a chamber above it. A ladder or single staircase provided access. (fig.1) The next stage of development came towards the end of the 15th century and saw the introduction of a chimney (at first timber then brick or stone) with a canopy to channel the smoke away from the rest of the hall. The fireplace was therefore moved to the lower end of the hall and in many such houses there is evidence of the family bench being fixed to the wall opposite the fire: the table would have been in front of the bench. At the same time a third set of rooms (store or service rooms) was added opposite the parlour. (fig.2) With the smoke now contained the next development was the building of a floor across the hall so increasing the accommodation upstairs. (fig.3) The fireplaces were generally large with space to sit either side and room to include the cooking apparatus and pots. These inglenooks, sometimes with salt cupboards and bread ovens, survive in many houses today. Windows would have been small and in many village houses consisted of bars and sliding shutters. The staircase increased in sophistication (and safety) as the houses themselves developed. The final stage (fig.4) was the more complex chimney system serving several fires on both the ground and first floors.

Down Shrub Lane lies one of the oldest houses in the parish, Crowhurst Bridge Farm. Land at Crowhurst was included in a gift in 1170 by the Count of Eu to Combwell Priory (between Flimwell and Lamberhurst) who owned it until the Abbey was dissolved in 1535. By 1500 it was occupied by the a Wyke family and in 1658 a tenement and

Domesday to Civil War (1086–1659) **13**

Crowhurst Bridge Farm

eighteen acres was rented by James Friends. Having passed through both the Fosters and Oxenbridges it came into the ownership of the Crotynden (Cruttenden) family who later gave it to the Dissenting Church who kept it until the early 20th century when it was sold by trustees into private ownership. It is likely that the house is therefore well over five hundred years old.

Numbers 52 and 53 Shrub Lane also date back to the 16th or 17th centuries as "The Shrub" and these houses all used to be linked to the hamlet of Tottgreene by a road which ran from Crowhurst Bridge to Socknersh. Much of this road can be traced today and lies in a sunken way flanked by trees. In the 16th century the hamlet of Tott lay therefore on a crossroads of this old road and the one from Burwash to Etchingham. The hamlet consisted of between five to ten dwellings grouped round the small green. Tott Farm (Great Tott) itself was possibly built, but more likely

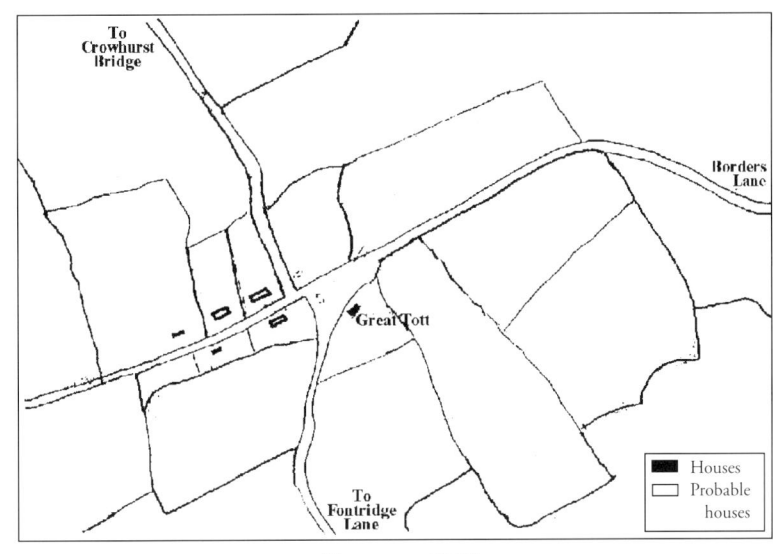
Tottgreene 1550

14   Chapter One

The Shrub

restored, by John Cruttenden in the early part of that century as a quite large jettied house. It is possible that the barn is also of this period but the rest of the hamlet has disappeared although the old houses were on the site of Tott Cottages and of Little Tott (Meadowlands) and may have been incorporated into the later buildings. The Cruttendens were to remain owners of Tott Farm and one hundred and twenty acres for another three hundred years and by 1600 they were already farming from Tott to Fontridge Lane. Their principal residence was to be Fontridge House, another old building which was to be rebuilt in Georgian times.

On the road from Tottgreene was the area that was becoming known as the Square and there may well have been old cottages flanking the road on the slope up to the church. The only one to survive is Sones Cottage, on the north west side, which dates from the 15th century. It was to be joined a little later by Beeches. Next door Hoppers Croft (now Church House) was an earlier building owned in 1621 by Henry Goldsmith and

Beeches and Sones

his wife Faintnot who occupied a house, kitchen, barn and orchard together with Laddes or Swanne Mead, Longe Croft, Rushe Croft and Hoppers Croft. This holding incorporated all the land between the house and Ham Lane, including what is now the playing field. The Goldsmiths gradually increased their wealth and land over the years. In 1639 their son, also Henry, married Margaret Thunder and in 1640 they named their firstborn Thunder Goldsmith.

Oakbeam and Bower

The Bell Inn has some 15th-century work where a few beams from an earlier house have survived in the reconstructions and many extensions that took place in the late 16th and early 17th centuries. Much of what can be seen today in the front room of the pub and the fireplace date from the earlier periods. Adams Strake (Burghurst) has traces of the 15th-century house in its roof while a 16th-century bargeboard carved with a chevron ornament has been re-used as a rafter. It probably got its name from

Lime, Cygnet and Swan Inn

Old Granary and Yew Tree

"Strake" being "a strip of land" belonging to Adams - of whom there is no trace. Oakbeam and Bower comprised a single four-bay house built around 1500 and containing a fine early smoke bay as well as an early example of a balustrade to protect an open stairwell. Dudwell was added later, in the 18th century. Lime Cottage, Cygnet and Swan Inn were also a single dwelling, built in the first half of the 16th century. There was a single central fireplace which survives in Swan Inn House although it protrudes into Cygnet. In the late 17th century the house was divided into two and the fireplace in Lime Cottage was added, as were the extensions at the back. Later this western part was subdivided (Cygnet and Lime Cottage) and further rear extensions were built. Behind these rows of houses lay a number of small simple dwellings including the oldest parts remaining of Pump Court and a long lasting blacksmith's yard.

Yew Tree House was built in about 1420 and almost certainly covered the whole site now occupied by itself and the Old Granary. Only the eastern part of the old house remains and this was slightly altered in the 16th century and again in the 17th century when the Granary was built or altered to replace the western end of the house. The chimney in Yew Tree was added in the 18th century, in the centre of the old house, but, by then, against a party wall. Everton Cottages almost certainly existed by the 17th century and round the

Chateaubriand – the Great Hall

corner in Ham Lane the modernly named Hoppers Croft was a barn dating from the 16th century which was probably converted into two dwellings of sorts in the late 18th century before being modernised in the 20th century. A collection of hovels and barns existed up Ham Lane where both the Rose & Crown and an earlier building at Brooksmarle date to this period, as Brooksmarle was conveyed by Thomas Maye to a Polhill in 1598 with one hundred and ten acres. The Maye (May) family were long standing local landowners and were connected by marriage to the Busbridges, Constables, Polhills, Cruttendens and Lades. Their principal home was later to be at Pashley Manor and they played a considerable role in government, successive generations being Chancellor, Master of the Rolls and Secretary to Parliament. Thomas May (1595-1650) was a well known Cromwellian historian and poet who was buried in Westminster Abbey; after the Restoration his bones and others were dug up and thrown in a pit in nearby St Margarets.

18 Chapter One

Shadwell Row

Perhaps the oldest house in the High Street is Chateaubriand which was built around 1375 as a five-bay house of which only some gothic doorways survive, although it still also has the remains of a detached kitchen at the rear which was very much a feature of the period when it was built. These detached kitchens fell into disuse during the late 16th century when the introduction of brick chimneys made it safe to have large fires for cooking within the main house.

There was a house or building on the site of Villiers and the shop (now Broadview Kitchens) but this was largely or completely rebuilt in the 17th century to form the main part of the house there today. There were subsequent extensions and alterations, one of which was built over the alleyway that ran down the western side and which can still be clearly seen. Shadwell Row consisted of two houses: one of these comprises Timbers and Highway and the other comprises Shadwell and Smugglers. The former is late 14th century and the latter early 15th century with parts of the old buildings having

Tudor House

Lime Tree

survived alterations and renovations over the centuries. Both these houses had timber chimneys that were not rebuilt until around 1730. The fireplaces were then built back to back on the common wall with a single chimney stack above. Revenue was added a little later.

Tudor House, comprising both the ex-Tudor House Restaurant and Tudor Cottage was certainly completed by the early 16th century but may well have been earlier. It was a four bay continuous jettied building with a return jetty (overhang) at the eastern end and is one of the few examples of such a building to have survived in Burwash. The rear western extension was added in the early 17th century and other additions in the 18th, 19th and 20th centuries, but much of the old house remains intact. The house containing Abbots Antiques and Lime Tree dates to about 1639 and further west the remains of an earlier building can be found in the basements of Burwash Home Improvements and Chaplins which were the ground floors when the roadway was at the lower level of Wren's front door.

On the south side Novar, Wayside and Providence date back to the 17th century, again as a single house, and there were medieval houses on the site of Wrenns Cottages, of which only the end one, Cobblers, remains. Cobblers (and also Kestrels which is north of

Old Rectory

Holmshurst) have fireplaces of the early 16th century with traces of an early timber chimney. These timber chimneys were quite common at the time, because of the high cost of bricks, but they were banned in London in the 14th century because of the risk of fire and the practice gradually died out, although remaining for longer in country districts, along with outside kitchens. Willow and part of Chestnut also date to the 16th or 17th centuries.

The Bear has early elements as does Sadlers and there may well have been other, long since demolished, cottages on both sides of the High Street in between those houses which have survived today. The old Rectory was in a street running parallel with the High Street. The original building with its overshot lower bay is thought to have been in existence in the late 14th or early 15th century. By about 1450 it consisted of a five-

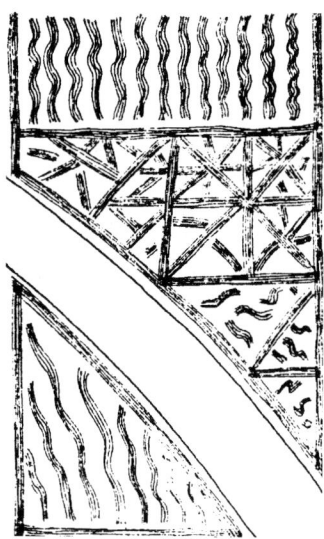

Plaster panel in hall (on the hall/solar partition)

bay, sixty foot long, high class medieval house with appropriate internal decorative panels; one of these was a combed daub with an unusual diamond shaped pattern which is now on display at The Weald & Downland Museum at Singleton. Around 1500 a lathe and plaster chimney was built on top of an existing six foot stone screen to create the main fireplace. In the later 16th century the eastern bay was demolished and at the same time considerable modernisation took place. A huge four-flue fireplace replaced the earlier single-flue, a first floor covered over the central hall and ceilings were put into the first floor. A cellar was added and alterations made to the service rooms. The windows were re-arranged to fit the new structure.

Old Rectory hall

An older building where Mount House now stands had been owned back in 1318 by John de Osyndene then later by William Cokke, then Thomas Glazier who had sold it to Henry a Wick (a Wyke or a Weeke) by 1538. His son or grandson, Edward, married next door neighbour Joan Dawe in 1566, a sister of Thomas Dawe of Roppyden (Rampyndene). It was the a Wicks who built the new Mount House in about 1550 although at that time it was a long lower building of the height and proportions of Mount

House Cottage. It was sold to the Hepdens in 1584 and the brothers Thomas and Goddard may both have lived there. Goddard's first four children were named Hopestill, Fearnot, Thankful and Constant, which implies a strong religious zeal, and the first two girls married brothers Samuel and Thomas Newington in 1618 and 1619 respectively. The Hepdens sold Mount House to Thomas Roper in 1594 and Goddard went on to build Holmshurst, which bears the initials GH and the date 1610. It would have been the Ropers who carried out the first extension of Mount House in about 1620 before selling it to John Stephen in 1668. The adjacent barn was also built in the late 16th century.

There was a house on the site of Rampyndene which was recorded as owned by Richard Jeffreys in 1538 before passing to a long line of Dawes (or Daws) who owned it right through the rest of the 16th and early 17th centuries. There were also houses on the sites of Denes House and The Ivy where in 1594 lived Simon Coney or Conys. Simon's son Mark married Helen Byne in 1602 and this started the Coneys' steady rise in wealth and importance. The Bynes were a rich landowning family and when Helen's father Thomas died in 1620 she inherited one-third of his estate, including the 16th century Bowmans Farm and other land east of Dudwell Bridge. This part of the estate was then inherited by their grandson John Coney around 1680.

The Old House and The Cottages (now 1 and 2 School Hill)

Chime and Old Thatch

Down Bell Alley, The Cottages (now numbers 1 and 2 School Hill), the Old House, Chime and the Old Thatch all date to the 15th or 16th centuries and are unusual in having largely kept their external appearance and dimensions. Beyond the church in the Square was the messuage of Olivers Garden on the south side of the road, consisting of old buildings and land of about one acre where Admiral House, the row of cottages and the Old Police House now stand. Square Farm was opposite and the original Youngs Garden was owned in 1652 by John Bunce on his marriage to Joane Foster and again an older building survives within the later shell.

Further to the south Batemans was built in 1634 on the site of an older house, probably by William Langham who lived there until his death in 1652. He also owned or rented Brooksmarle, Halt Down (Holton), Perrymans, Dudwell (Dudwell Mill), Rye Green and Ashlands, and he left much of his large estate to his daughter Alice who had married Joseph Newington, the son of Samuel and Hopestill (nee Hepden). The Jacobean house of Batemans was then almost certainly an H-shape but some of the wings, and especially the north front wing, were subsequently pulled down. There were references to two mills in the vicinity back in the 13th and 14th centuries. Park Mill was originally constructed around 1250 and, further along the river, Dudwell or Ditlers Mill certainly has its origins in the 14th century. It stopped working around 1900, soon after Thomas Ellis was crushed while greasing the wheels, and was then completely demolished.

At the western end of the then village was St. Nicholas Cottage, built around 1640 with two rooms up and two down and an outside staircase. In 1750 a rear extension was to be added with a catslide roof and the stairs were enclosed. Yeomans Cottage next door must have been added at about that time or soon after. Opposite these was the single building that forms the rear part of Paygate Cottage and contains huge oak beams and timbers of the 16th century.

In Spring Lane were a number of 16th-century houses of which only small traces remain as newer, larger and grander houses have replaced the originals over the centuries. These included Frys (Burwash Place), Brownings (now gone), Southover, Holton (called Halton in 1620) and Frenches (Franchise). Only Mottynsden remains largely unchanged. By 1600 the Lunsfords owned Mottynsden, St. Giles, Frenches and Woodknowle, all of which they sold in 1639. Mottynsden went to Christopher Manser, St. Giles to John Dawe, and Frenches and Woodknowle to the Polhills who became the largest landowners on this side of the village, living at Frenches and renting out many of the surrounding farms.

By the early 17th century, not only was the village and parish assuming a shape that is recognisable today but also many of the families who were to play an important part in the life of Burwash were now well established. The Cruttendens, Bynes, Coneys and Langhams owned most of the land to the south and east of the village and beyond them were the Collins at Socknersh. The Hepdens at Holmshurst and Polhills at Frenches were to the north and west while in between the Newingtons and Goldsmiths, by marriage and acquisition, were expanding their holdings. Other old families included Jeffry, Daw or Dawe, Manser, Foster, Fry, Swane or Swaine, Woodsell, Walker, Weeke (a Wyke), Jarvis, Noakes (Noke or Anoke), Butler, Waterer and Austen. They were now joined by Ellys or Ellis, Blunden, Blundell, Muggeridge, Ticehurst, Wood and Mepham. All of these were to be yeoman farmers, craftsmen, shopkeepers and traders who lived, worshipped, intermarried and provided the life of the village, largely staying within the parish for generation after generation. Their fortunes ebbed and flowed but they provided continuity and they also served as village clerks, churchwardens and other posts of important local responsibilities.

The yeomen farmers amongst them acquired relatively small areas of land and then built houses, or enlarged existing dwellings, and added barns and other farm buildings. In the mid 16th century fifty per cent of farms in Sussex were under fifty acres and thirty-five per cent between fifty and one hundred and fifty acres. Virtually all of the farms round

Burwash fell into these categories: many were to stay the same size and with the same field pattern for centuries and were passed down from father to son in successive generations. Such farms were Borders in Borders Lane to the east; Fontridge (since rebuilt), Fishers, Grandtwizzle, Glydwish (burnt down), Brickhouse, Perrymans and the still largely unaltered Bowmans to the south east along Fontridge Lane. Dudwell (Mill), Glaisyers and Little Worge to the south and in the west Rye Green and the Green (or Green Hill Farm). This lay at the western end of Holton Lane, described in the 16th century as "Whapple Way from Holton House", where it joins the Heathfield road. Green Hill was a 15th century hall house which has been progressively altered and enlarged over the centuries; its most notable feature is an unusual stair turret added in the late 17th century which contains a fine open well staircase giving access to all floors from cellar to attic. Further west was Pounceford (Poundsford), Kyngsdown and Clymhurst. Nearby Henshurst (Parkhill) and Westdown both still had outside kitchens. Henshurst also contains combed daub of the 16th century and rare interwoven hazel rods in partitions through much of the house, all dating back to its construction in the early 15th century. Much of this latter area was later to become Burwash Common and Weald.

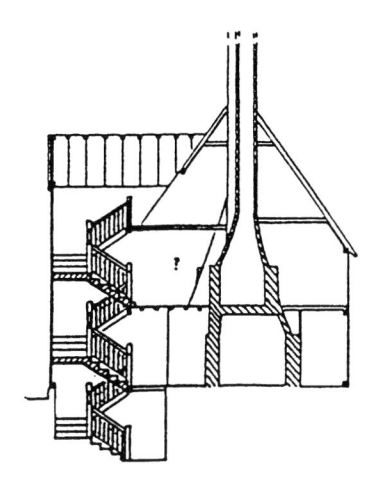

Green Hill stair turret

These farms in the 16th and 17th centuries would primarily have supported the household needs. Most had orchards and kitchen gardens and kept a cow and a pig. The larger ones would have had cattle to fatten, a few would have had sheep and some would have grown wheat (for flour), barley (for malt), oats (cattle feed), peas, beans and tares. Almost all would have had some hay, kept in round thatched stacks. Horses were essential and all but the smallest had waggons and carts. Farm implements would have changed little from medieval times and a lot of the work was done by hand. It was a hard life, offering little more than survival on the smallest farms but a degree of prosperity on the larger ones; above all it bred a fiercely independent population who were totally committed to their land and the community.

Henry VII had been succeeded by his son Henry VIII in 1509 and the country entered one of the significant periods of its history with the split with Rome following Henry's divorce from Catherine of Aragon in 1533, and the subsequent breaking of the centuries-old power and influence of the Church by the dissolution of the monastries starting in 1535. The nearest monastery to Burwash was the strict Cistercian Abbey at Robertsbridge founded in 1176 but this had only eight monks by 1536 and was excluded from the Act. Of more significance to Burwash was the creation of the Church of England and under Edward VI, a pious and scholarly king, who reigned for just six years from 1547-53, a new prayer book was introduced into churches throughout England. Queen Mary (1553-58), a staunch Catholic, reversed everything and restored the Catholic faith, with severe penalties including death for anyone found defaulting. Queen Elizabeth immediately reinstated King Edward's prayer book with the Act of Uniformity (1559) and proclaimed the Church of England as the established church through the Act of Supremacy. Worshippers in country parishes must have been bewildered by these changes especially as in most cases their parson had remained unchanged throughout this period and simply adapted his message according to the requirements of the reigning monarch. In Burwash the last Catholic priest at St.Bartholomew's was David Spencer who succeeded Robert Colson as Rector in 1562. Despite his inner beliefs he nonetheless outwardly conformed and indeed made a good living out of the protestant church, as in addition to Burwash he was the holder of five other preferments or benefices in Sussex parishes. Spencer did however refuse to continue the style of preaching he had done during Queen Mary's reign, and he was a close collaborator of Thomas Stapleton, the well known Catholic theologian, looking after Stapleton's property when he was exiled and ensuring that he received a regular flow of income. The Vicar of Burwash at this time was William Saville (1556-67) and he too absented himself after the re-introduction of the protestant religion and all the work was thus left to the Curate, Robert Allen, who luckily was in sympathy with the new order.

The long reign of Elizabeth (1558-1603) contained important events both at home and abroad. It saw the start of British colonial expansion and the extension of the fruitful partnership of privateers and state. The partnership took the form of privateers operating under the British flag with semi-official status, while capturing Spanish treasure galleons, attacking and robbing their colonies, annexing territory and sinking their warships. In return the privateers such as Drake, Hawkins and Frobisher supplied the Crown with a considerable flow of gold that enabled the Exchequer to balance its budget and finance the growth of trade and commerce. These appropriations of Spanish property combined with the execution of the Catholic Mary Stuart led to the Spanish armada of 1588. Many of the ships involved in Drake's great victory were built of Sussex oak and armed with cannon made from the iron from Sussex forges such as those in Burwash.

Domestically the prime issue was over the policy of enclosure, where landowners had gradually annexed the common land and ploughed or grazed it for their own purposes. This had less effect on the area round Burwash as there were no great landowners other than the Ashburnhams to the south, and the yeoman farmers and minor squires like the Cruttendens and Polhills employed local labour to work the farms they were carving out of the old forests of the Rother and Dudwell valleys. What did affect the whole country were rising prices and in particular rising food prices. This minor agrarian crisis had an impact on Burwash and created an increasing number of poor. This national problem of poverty was addressed in a number of statutes that were brought together in the Poor Law Act of 1601. This statute compelled towns to build stores or stocks of produce such as wool, hemp and flax so that the "honest poor of able body" might be set to work and paid "according to the desert of the work". Rogues were sent to houses of correction and beggars had their ears bored or were whipped. The Vestry Meeting elected panels of "overseers of the poor" whose duties were to raise money "by taxation of every inhabitant" both to pay the poor and manage the workhouses. The Burwash poor rate was set at 2d. in the £. Justices of the Peace were then required to certify the accounts as accurate. Among the Justices many other duties were presiding over local courts which included cases such as the one in 1630 where a Burwash man was accused of causing nuisance as he was "a common sower of discord and debate among his neighbours, full of evil and foul wordes".

The state of 17th-century roads throughout Sussex, and certainly around Burwash, was a constant problem. Although Parishes and Hundreds were actually responsible for their upkeep it was generally the self interest of farmers or landowners which led to some repair and maintenance. The roads were usually narrow, muddy and deeply rutted making travel on anything but horseback hazardous and unpleasant. The situation was exacerbated by the movement of iron and timber although some attempt was made to make these industries responsible for the roads they used and in some areas forge cinders provided better surface than the usual one of chalk which soon dissolved into the mud. In 1640 the forge owner of Snape Furnace in Kent certified that he had laid cinders as required on the road to Burwash Forge. But in the same year the Constable of the Hawkesborough Hundred was unable to hold his annual April meeting to nominate a surveyor into the condition of Burwash roads "by reason of the great inundation of water which caused floods and made the roads unusable". At this time, as well as the roads and lanes we know today, and the ones from Crowhurst to Socknersh, and from Haltdown (Holton) to Green Farm, there must have been a variety of others used regularly by the villagers and those living in the neighbourhood that now only survive as footpaths or bridleways.

The accession of the Stuarts through James I (1603-25) saw little change in English life although the tensions that would lead to the Civil War were starting to appear. Anti-papist feeling was fuelled by the Catholic gunpowder plot (1605) and led to their persecution; the event is commemorated up to this day by bonfires and fireworks and in some areas of Sussex there is still a small anti-papist movement. This feeling helped to polarise the growing split between Anglican and Puritan which focussed on the role of the Bishops and the observance, strict or otherwise, of the Lord's day. An attempt to suppress games, dances and sport led to the King issuing a declaration in 1617 that "all who had already attended divine service might engage in certain lawful recreation afterwards". This led to the so-called Book of Sports which parish priests read from the pulpit and which listed acceptable Sunday activities. A more positive event was the production of the Authorised version of the Bible in 1611, replacing the Geneva and Great Bishops versions. This new translation took fifty scholars seven years to complete and, on sale for 5s.0d., was an immediate success. Virtually unchanged for four hundred years nearly one hundred million copies have been sold of the English version with further translations into hundreds of other languages. One of the editions of the old Geneva bible, printed in 1560, was known as the "breeches" bible because of a translation of Genesis III v.7 which says, referring to Adam and Eve, "they sewed fig leaves together and made themselves breeches", whereas all other versions translate this as "aprons". There is a rare copy of the breeches bible in St. Bartholomew's.

This was the age of Shakespeare, Marlowe and Ben Johnson; an age when travelling players went from village to village entertaining as they went. Burwash, with its markets and fairs, must have been a regular venue for such groups. Medical science and research also progressed. Henry VIII had established professorships of medicine at Oxford and Cambridge and the College of Physicians (1518) was joined by the Company of Barber-Surgeons (1540). In 1565 the Queen allowed the College of Physicians to carry out human dissection for the first time. General advances were however slowed by adherence to the theory that excess of any of the four humours fluids in the body, sanguine, phlegmatic, choleric or melancholic, could only be cured by cupping or bloodletting. It would have been this level of medicine that existed in Burwash for many years to come but the existence of a local doctor or surgeon was evident by 1614 when John Wilmshert's mother was taken sick with pleurisy and received "herbal remedies in conjunction with bloodletting".

Despite the founding of many great schools, following the earlier lead of Edward VI, schooling at this time was almost non-existent in a village such as Burwash. The landed gentry would have private tutors or send their sons to the newish grammar schools, or to Oxford and Cambridge. The local clergy, especially curates, would supplement their meagre income by teaching and this often included the children of the better off shopkeepers and merchants, but for the vast majority of the population there was no form of education unless they were lucky enough to serve an apprenticeship to a trade or craft.

❦

During the eleven years of Charles I's rule without Parliament (1629-40) his subjects were slightly disgruntled by the taxes he imposed and the lack of Parliament but generally the absence of wars, a growing economy and lack of interference by the Crown in the life of most people led to a state of reasonably contented lethargy in country districts. Three incidents changed this. These were the introduction of the long unused Ship Money Tax whereby inland counties had to contribute to the upkeep of the Navy, a further tax on all those who failed to attend church on Sunday as required by the Act of Uniformity but long ignored, and third, an attempt to force the Scots to adopt the English prayer book. These combined to produce war with Scotland and widespread discontent which surfaced when the King, in order to finance this conflict, was forced to recall Parliament in 1640. Parliament was quickly dissolved but when it reassembled later that year the scene was set for the deep-seated divisions that were to rend the nation asunder and led to the Civil War in 1642.

After early Royalist successes in the field the new model army under Fairfax, Ireton and Cromwell triumphed, and the first part of the Civil War ended in the Battle of Naseby in 1645. Negotiations and squabbling were followed by a further outbreak of fighting which in turn led to the King's defeat and his subsequent trial and beheading in 1649. Thus began the eleven years of Parliamentary and puritan rule under Oliver Cromwell and his successors.

In Sussex, as elsewhere, the population was deeply divided in its sympathies both during the war and in the period of parliamentary rule. Of the thirteen Sussex boroughs returning two MPs, three were for the Crown, five for Parliament and five were split in their loyalties. Among the forty-four landowning gentry, four were Royalists, thirteen for Parliament but twenty-seven were neutral. There was little pattern dividing or uniting town or country, landowner or farm labourer and families were often split apart although generally the east of Sussex favoured Parliament. Little fighting took place near Burwash although a minor skirmish was thought to have happened at Willards Hill where a musket ball of the period was found embedded in the roof of Willards Hill House, another 16th century building which has evidence of an earlier timber chimney.

There were however some leading local supporters of Parliament. Anthony Cruttenden (JP 1645-49) married a daughter of fiery puritan Herbert Hay of Glyndebourne, and the son of Edward Polhill (JP from 1646 onwards) married William

Newton's daughter: these were alliances between strong puritan families. Thomas Collins, who married Mary Cruttenden in 1619, was a committee man, a captain in the Parliamentary forces and a member of the Sussex sequestering committee. John Busbridge of Haremere, Etchingham, was also a member of this committee and became a parliamentary colonel during the Civil War after Charles I had sacked him from the Bench in 1642. He was a strict puritan and close friend and ally of Sir Thomas Pelham but Busbridge's brother Robert fought as a Royalist. The Sussex sequestering committee was set up in 1643 and Royalists had to appear and take the oath to avoid having their land confiscated; in addition seventy-six out of two hundred and seventy-two clerical benefices were sequestered. The rector of Burwash, John Swan, had written to Pelham (holder of the benefice) that he "feared nothing from those who questioned his right to Burwash rectory so long as God shall preserve me from malignancy and so long as I shall enjoy the favours and honour of your noble patronage". He was however replaced in 1641 by Joseph Hawkesworth who in turn gave way to Wail Attersole in 1658. Because the Bishops did not function at this time many "intruders were not in Holy Orders and none received Canonical Instruction and therefore had neither mission nor jurisdiction". Attersole fell into this category and therefore appears in italics on the list of Rectors. Similarly the two vicars of this period, William Lancaster (appointed 1657) and then Thomas Goldham (1658) both appear in the same italics in the church records. Fear reigned as neighbours spied on neighbours, Magistrates revoked beer licences, priests were expected to preach positive propaganda and collections were taken for the national covenant. At such a collection in 1642 Burwash contributed £39 to the puritan cause led by Edward Polhill giving £5 and Anthony Cruttenden £3. Only a few larger villages like Burwash retained a beerhouse with a licence although a Burwash man was also convicted of keeping an unlicenced house. So village life would have been quieter, with strict observance of the Sabbath, and a sober hardworking ethos applied to all aspects of the daily routine. This period and the strong puritan convictions it encouraged nurtured the seeds of nonconformity which was to have a continuing influence on Burwash over the next three hundred years.

Chapter Two

ST BARTHOLOMEW'S CHURCH

With the spread of Christianity through Sussex in the 7th century, and the formation of a Bishopric in Selsey in 681, it is possible that a simple early church may have been built in Burwash in Saxon times. If it did exist it would probably have been on or near the same site. No evidence of this survives but the building of a Norman church so soon after the Conquest supports the theory of a small centre of population with such a church already being in existance.

The first part of the current church was built around 1090 and was an aisleless structure consisting of a chancel, nave and tower. The tower and a small portion of the south wall of the nave at the west end survive from this date: the great depth of Norman mortar is still visible. This church probably had glassless slits for windows, a rush covered earth floor, and no seats. Worshippers would have stood or knelt. The first enlargement

The early Norman church

occurred in 1190, presumably to meet the requirements of a growing population, by the addition of a south aisle. This required the building of pillars to support the arches, and these pillars remain today. In 1250 a north aisle was added and again the original pillars remain. Both the north and south arcades have pointed arches of two orders and while the three northern columns are octagonal the two southern columns are different, one being octagonal and the other round. There is no explanation for this.

As part of the 1250 work a larger chancel completely replaced the original: the 13th-century chancel arch with its 14th- century supporting corbels remains as does the arch from the tower into the nave which was built at the same time. In the 14th century both aisles were widened and buttresses were added to the south west corner of the tower. New windows were also installed in the aisles, a porch added to the west door and a vestry built in the north east corner. Some time after this dormer windows were added in the roof of the nave but apart from this the church remained structurally unaltered until 1856. It can be seen clearly in S H Grimm's drawing of 1784 and this was the building the inhabitants of Burwash knew from the 14th to the 19th century, through Reformation and Civil War, as Catholics and as Protestants.

St Bartholomew's in 1784

© Copyright The British Museum

Internally the church would have started introducing seating with a few simple benches, with most of the congregation still standing. Over the centuries more benches, some with backs, were in turn replaced by marginally more comfortable pews. By the 17th century the oak pews were probably enclosed by doors and many will have been square so as to contain complete families. The main pews were certainly owned, rented or appropriated by individual families as in 1688 Edward Collins (on acquiring Tan House, formerly Ringmers, which became known as Square Farm) received a faculty for his own pew ("second on the left") with the Polhills (of Frenches) having the front pew and Brooksmarle Farm having the pew behind. As late as 1851 the inspectors said "many of the pews being square and appropriated the church does not hold as many as it might if better pewed". The pulpit during this time was almost certainly sited by the first north pillar. In the 17th century John Cruttenden (of Fontridge) had built a family gallery in the south aisle "with stairs by a little south door having previously moved the stairs to their present place to create more room". In 1686 the Churchwardens, John Coney and Edward Lawrence provided a poor box, a communion rail and table and it was noticed that one "bell was crackt". In 1685 another gallery was built. This cost £18.10s.0d. to "the carpenter for building the gallery and timber" and £1.1s.11d. for "the masons about the gallery". It is likely that this gallery was over the nave and that it was replaced by a larger gallery in 1720. The later gallery held the organ and was known as the singing gallery which suggests that the choir might also have used it. It was reached from the belfry and was "put out to build for the sum of £30.0s.0d. £17.17s.6d. was raised by a tax of 2d. in the pound on the lands in the parish; the residue was raised and paid by the persons hereunder named viz:" The list was headed by the Vicar, George Jordan, followed by Messrs. Cruttenden, Dyke, Gouldsmith, Hussey and Nepecker, and also included John Lawrence, singing master. The gallery was built by William Taylor.

The font with the Pelham family buckle carving (granted to them by King Edward III in 1356 for service at Poitiers), which reflects their lordship of the manor for about four hundred years, is probably post reformation (1534) but would certainly have been present by the late 17th century. Had it been pre-reformation it would have had to have a cover to protect the Holy Water and evidence of this would be clear on the stone rim.

There was also an early fresco design consisting of small scarlet horizontal lines of masonry patterns, one high up on the chancel arch and five others on the upper part of the round south pillar. These were painted over in 1966. It is likely that these were the remaining evidence of extensive early wall paintings in both the nave and the aisles which were typically covered in whitewash at the time of the reformation. They have been estimated to have been painted in the 13th century, when the church was enlarged, and may well have included religious scenes. These were deemed popish at the reformation and once whitewashed may well have had texts of scripture painted on top. On the floor by the Lady Chapel altar in the south aisle was the 14th-century cast iron grave slab covering the grave of Johne Coline (of Socknersh) which was moved to the wall in 1856 and has next to it a 15th century slab to an unknown individual.

In 1714 the four bells were recast with the fifth being added by 1724. In 1725 the steeple was retiled by Thos. Peckham who was paid £4.10s.0d. for "renewing the shingles". The clock curiously chimed every four hours. The routine diocesan survey of 1724 also notes that the outside was in good repair although some of the pews needed repairing. Two hundred families were said to worship at the church. Outside in the churchyard family tombs were the fashion for richer families and many examples can still be seen. One such dates to 1735 when Thomas Hussey obtained a faculty for a vault or burying place in the south west of the churchyard measuring length north to south fifteen feet and breadth east to west ten feet with an additional parcel of land for an entrance. This was to be "exclusively for the use of himself, his family and his friends". This was approved by William Burrell, Rector, George Jordan, Vicar, William Constable and John Coney, Churchwardens, and a list of local inhabitants.

After five hundred years of only minor alterations all was to change in 1856 with the drastic restoration and rebuilding instigated by the Rector, the Rev. Joseph Gould. The areas rebuilt included the chancel, the west porch and both aisles, which were widened by three feet, and all the roofs. It is fortunate that, despite the almost total disappearance of the original historic structure, the new church, including its windows, was a reasonably

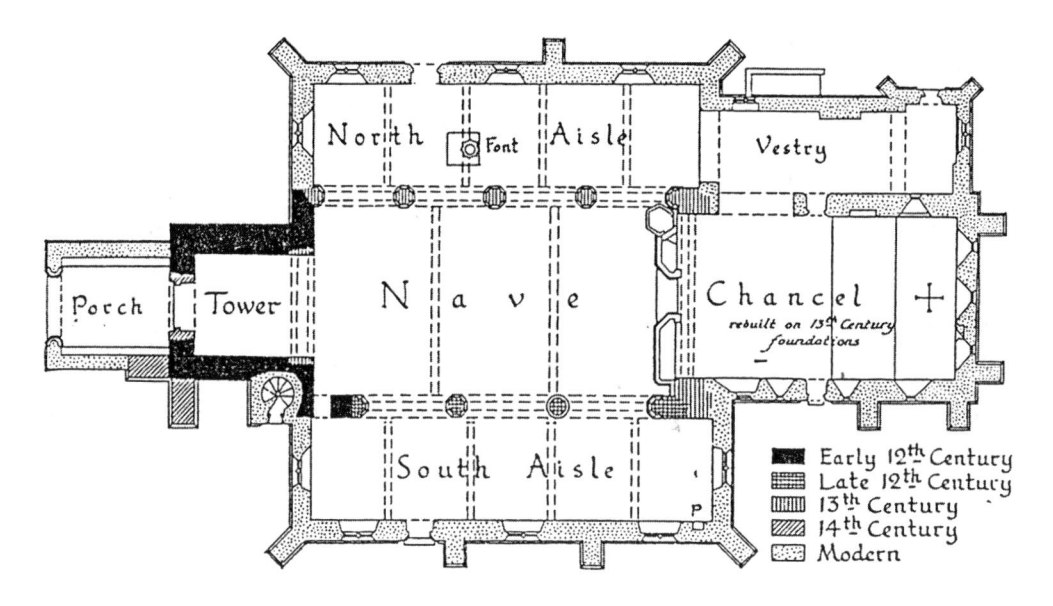

St Bartholomew's architecture

faithful reproduction of the old. In particular the chancel was rebuilt directly on its old foundations in the 13th-century style of architecture. The reasons for this rebuilding are not known but are likely to be a combination of the energy of Joseph Gould, lack of space, the fashionable necessity to install heating and the self-confidence of the Victorians who felt that everything, including churches, should reflect their taste. The porch, also a copy of the original, was embellished by the wrought iron gates given by Mr W J Tilley (of the Franchise) and cast by Master Drew. As part of this restoration the floor level was lowered and this required the ground outside also to be lowered and over three feet of earth had to be carried away from one side of the tower. The churchyard was subsequently levelled and tidied, the sheep removed, and the whole appearance and presentation improved. With the sale of the toll gate in Bell Alley, and the adjacent house, the road was widened and the churchyard extended down the slope below the line of trees.

St Bartholomew's after 1856

As part of this restoration the organ was moved from the singing gallery to the eastern end of what is now the vestry and the gallery was removed. In 1878 a new organ was built and in 1892 was moved into its present position when the vestry was further extended to the north aisle, with a new arch being created for the organ next to the priests door. This organ lasted until 1954 when it was completely rebuilt and modernised at a cost of £2,500; the old pipework was reinstated after restoration. It was again restored in 1996. The new clock was installed in 1889 in memory of Rev. John Coker Egerton and built by

Smith of Derby, who guaranteed the timing to within ten seconds a month and also made the great clock in St Pauls Cathedral. The east window in the Lady Chapel is a memorial to Joseph Gould and the adjoining windows in the south wall to his wife and parents.

In 1893 two of the old bells were recast and rehung at a cost of £245 which was defrayed by subscription and money left by Isobel Hughes (the aunt of James Philcox) who died at Young's Garden in 1882 aged eighty. A sixth bell was given in memory of Sarah Tilley (of Franchise and Garstons). In 1949 one of the 1714 bells was recast in memory of Rev. R L Martyn-Linnington and an extra bell, a new No.l, was given in memory of Fl. Lt. Charles Woodbine Parish DFC. To these was added a new No.2 bell in memory of the men of Burwash killed in the 1939-45 war, thus producing a full peal of eight bells. Just two of the original 1714 bells remain today.

The altar, reredos and pavement of the sanctuary were dedicated in 1911 as a memorial to Rev. Charles Frewin Maude, Rector from 1888 until he died at the altar celebrating Holy Communion in 1909. The work was largely done by local craftsmen to the design of Sir Charles Nicholson who later was also responsible for the war memorial at the top of Bell Alley. He also designed the new choir stalls which were dedicated in 1913 and given by Mrs Angela Louisa Anderson-Morshead (nee Hughes) in memory of her cousin the solicitor James Philcox (of Youngs Garden). These choir stalls replaced the Victorian ones of 1856. The east window, a faithful copy of the old one, commemorates the work of Rev. R L Martyn-Linnington (Curate 1890-1902, Rector 1909 until his death in 1925).

In 1966 the nave roof, consisting of the 1856 tie beams and moulded king post, was boarded below the tie beams and painted white. The panelled chancel roof was also boarded. The church was totally redecorated, including painting over the frieze, and in 1989 the old flooring had to be replaced. In 1997 the church was rewired and new lighting installed at a cost of £25,000. The new chandeliers were made by Dave Hedges at his forge in the High Street. Other recent additions include the Sawyer window (1955), the Bishop Cooper memorial and the war memorial tablet. The modern stained glass window by the south door commemorates Colonel Sawyer's service in the RAMC and with the Scouts, while Bishop Cooper was Bishop of Korea from 1930 (having worked there since 1908) until he was taken prisoner by the Chinese communists in 1950. The war memorial tablet records the names of sixty-three of the men of Burwash who died in the 1914-18 war and fourteen of those who died in the 1939-45 war.

So, the St Bartholomew's of 2000, containing part of the original structure built nine hundred and ten years previously, has been enlarged, restored and altered over the centuries but essentially remains as the single link between the Norman Burwash of

St Bartholomew's in 2000

Domesday and today's 21st century Burwash. The name of St Bartholomew was certainly attached to the church by 1310. He may possibly have been adopted as the patron saint because it was a popular name of the manorial family of Burghersh; it has also been suggested that the original dedication may have been to St. James as evidenced by the even earlier grant of a fair on May 1 each year.

The Millennium has been commemorated by a stained glass window costing £12,500, designed by Meg Lawrence, next to the north door, and given in memory of Colin Spencer Wills who lived at Old Brick Farm. As well as depicting St Bartholomew the window design contains two illustrations of two thousand years of christianity, one being an eclipse (1999), and the other reflecting the parable of sowing and reaping showing agricultural methods through the ages. In addition comprehensive floodlighting was installed at a cost of £10,000 and the footpaths in the churchyard are being relaid at a further cost of £10,000.

38 *Chapter Two*

Meg Lawrence

St Bartholomew *Patronal Saint*
holding flaying knife
formalized background: fig tree
thought to be one and the same as Nathanael.
Called by Christ
John I vv.47-48
"When thou wast under the fig tree I saw thee."

Chapter Three

RESTORATION AND GEORGIAN
1660 - 1837

The restoration of the monarchy in 1660 released a feeling of freedom. The strict and sober way of living that had been the rule for the previous fifteen years was joyfully replaced by fairs, maypoles and dancing. No doubt the mood in Burwash reflected this national celebration and the recently restricted beerhouses re-opened again. It was a time when music and the arts flourished in free expression and scientific research covering mathematics, physics and kindred subjects was encouraged, leading to the foundation of the Royal Society in 1662. The King, ably assisted by his Chancellor (first minister) Edward Hyde, later Earl of Clarendon, set about reconstructing a more constitutional monarchy and establishing a working relationship with Parliament that learnt from and drew on the lessons and traumas of his father's reign, the Civil War and parliamentary rule. Generally a more relaxed and peaceful way of life returned to the country but in religious matters there was still tension and the ever-present seeds of intolerance. The Act of Uniformity (1662) demonstrates these divisions. The Act authorised the updated and improved prayer book for use throughout the country, and also gave legal status and freedom from prosecution for dissenters. But against this it required clergymen to sign up to the liturgy and doctrines set out in the Act. By coincidence it was on St Bartholomew's Day in 1662 that nearly one thousand clergymen felt it necessary to resign their livings rather than sign up to the Act, and this number soon grew to two thousand, one fifth of the total clergy. This split was exacerbated in 1665 by the Five Mile Act which forbade any non-conformist minister from living in or visiting any place where he had been the minister and subsequently resigned.

In Burwash, history virtually repeated itself from one hundred years earlier when the closet Catholic priests had been harried: this time it was the Vicar, the Rev. Thomas Goldham, who was ejected because he would not sign the Articles of the Church of England contained in the 1662 Act. He moved to Brightling and set up a school there to provide an income to support his family. He also gathered together a number of people who wished to worship along non-conformist lines of prayer and study. There was other later evidence of the presence of non-conformists in the village with the licencing of the house of David Nokes in 1693 as a place for Anabaptists to gather and worship. Thomas Goldham was replaced as Vicar by Rev. John Webb (1662) while Wail Attersole gave way to Richard Baskett as Rector in 1663.

Charles II was succeeded in 1685 by his brother the Catholic James II. His reign was to last just three years. His religious beliefs and promotion of Catholics might have continued to have been tolerated but the birth of a son and heir after fifteen years of marriage implied an indefinite continuation of Catholic rule that was unacceptable to most Englishmen. In 1688 his nephew William of Orange and his wife Mary, daughter of James II by his first wife, were invited to take the English throne. The terms on which they accepted completed the process of change from absolute to constitutional monarchy with limited, clearly defined, powers. Mary died in 1695, William in 1702, and they were succeeded by Mary's sister Anne (1702-14) who, being without an heir, was in turn succeeded by the Hanoverian George I whose great-grandfather had been James I. This Hanoverian succession was implemented through the Act of Settlement which also stated that every Sovereign must be a member of the Church of England, as well as removing their power to wage war. Both George I and II preferred their native Hanover to England and this lack of emotional tie to this country allowed Parliament, particularly during Walpole's long ministry (1721-42), to consolidate its control on policy and particularly on the country's finances. Overseas minor Dutch and French wars had been followed by Marlborough's great victories at Blenheim and Ramillies during the War of Spanish Succession which was ended by the Treaty of Utrecht in 1713. In North America, by 1750, after one hundred and fifty years of immigration and colonisation fuelled by the persecution of the non-conformists, most of the eastern seaboard had been settled and the colonists were starting to get a feeling of independence that was to grow strongly in the years ahead. In India the steady expansion of the East India Company was resisted by the French and included some heavy reverses such as the Black Hole of Calcutta (1756), before Clive emerged victorious in 1761 and the East India Company reigned supreme.

Trade increased along with the extension of England's influence round the world. Banks and insurance companies were started, the financial and commercial press began in 1692, and in 1694 the Bank of England was founded as the first joint stock bank with one thousand, three hundred shareholders and the power to issue notes. The financial system that was to back England's expansion of international trade and colonisation over the next two hundred and fifty years had its roots in this period. It was strong enough to stand the financial strains of Marlborough's wars and then of the South Sea Company crisis of 1720 where optimistic forecasts of its future profitability saw its shares rise from 130 to 1000 between January and the beginning of June only to fall to 180 during that month. Panic ensued and the Bank of England led a rescue that restored calm and confidence and led to Walpole, who had provided guidance and sound advice, emerging as the man in whom the public had confidence.

At home almost every aspect of life prospered as the nation moved peacefully from Stuart to Hanoverian rule. It was a period when men of stature emerged in many walks of life. As well as Marlborough and Walpole there was Sir Isaac Newton, with his brilliance in the fields of physics and astronomy, men of letters and poetry such as Milton, Bunyan, Dryden, Pope, Defoe and Swift. In music there were Purcell and Handel, in architecture Wren, Inigo Jones and Adam, with Capability Brown designing gardens and landscapes. Painters Gainsborough, Reynolds and Hogarth, furniture makers Chippendale and Kent, were all part of a long list of distinguished figures who between them gave Georgian England its style and pattern.

As well as Newton there were advances in many aspects of scientific research including medicine, where important progress was made during the late 17th and early 18th centuries. It also featured a battle between the Royal College of Physicians, who wanted exclusive rights over medical practice, and the Society of Apothecaries who offered a cheaper service as well as dispensing medicine and pills. It took a decision of the House of Lords in 1703 to settle the dispute leaving the Apothecaries as a lesser body who could direct remedies rather than carry them out. Thus began the division that led to dispensing chemists. Midwifery was accepted as a specialisation and dentistry started to advance beyond the drawing of teeth.

In Burwash the medical profession was well established with Dr Cruttenden in practice by 1725 and Dr William Parker by 1729 and they were joined by Dr John Jenkins by 1743. They supplied, in 1744, to the Overseers of the Poor, two dozen purgatory pills (2s.0d.), night medicine (3s.0d.), box of pills (1s.6d.) and charged 1s.6d. for bathing spots. By 1768 Dr Cruttenden had been succeeded by his son Dr Henry and his new colleague was Dr Thomas Baldock.

Combined with growing international trade there was price stability at home and increasing interest in improving agricultural methods that had hardly altered over the centuries. Despite disastrous harvests and near famine in 1698 and 1709 these improved methods led to increasing employment in farming but this unfortunately did little to address the general level of poverty in towns and country. It was the appalling conditions in towns that had led in 1665 to the worst of the outbreaks of bubonic plague since the Black Death. Thousands died throughout the country and while there is no direct evidence that it affected Burwash it is likely to have done so and it seems that there was a burial ground at Crowhurst Bridge. It was however the last major epidemic of this plague and it ended in London with the fire of 1666 which lasted four days and destroyed one thousand three hundred houses. Although his grand plan for a magnificently laid out new capital was rejected, Christopher Wren was to leave his mark on London through his fine churches and other buildings.

Thus, despite advances of knowledge and rising employment there were, in every parish, a considerable number of families who fell into poverty. As well as the unemployed these also included the lower paid, as an agricultural labourer earning £18.0s.0d. per annum in 1720 could expect to pay £3.0s.0d. rent, spend £9.0s.0d. on food and have just £6.0s.0d. left for fuel, clothes, tools and repairs. There were two hundred families in Burwash in 1724 and of these some thirty-five fell into the category of poor and received relief from the Overseers of the Poor who still administered the poor rate in accordance with the 1601 Act. Each year between £85 and £130 was collected, according to the need, and given out either as regular cash disbursements, as payments for work, or as food, clothes, fuel or other essentials. In some other areas of the country however there was considerable exploitation of the poor and vulnerable and an example of this was in the practice of abducting girls to be married; there were priests who were said to have solemnised six thousand such marriages a year, earning £75.0s.0d. a month in fees. This led to the 1753 Marriage Act which required banns of marriage to be read in church for three successive Sundays before a wedding could take place: a practice which still continues today.

In the early 18th century there emerged a widespread concern throughout England about the lack of education available to poorer people. The sons and daughters of the aristocracy and wealthy still had private tutors or attended one of the public schools, while tradesmen and merchants sent their children to grammar schools or to small local schools, generally taught by clerics, where five or ten would be taught in the parson's house. The poor had nothing and the concern was both philanthropic and practical: there was wasted talent as "witty" boys and girls would be of much greater use in whatever trade they eventually took up if they could read, write and do arithmetic. There was also a religious aspect which welcomed the teaching of Christian knowledge and virtues. This mood resulted in Charity Schools being founded which were supported by voluntary contributions and managed by local committees of governors. Nationally there were over one thousand such schools by the end of Queen Anne's reign and in Sussex numbers grew to well over one hundred by 1730. Burwash was part of this growth as in 1727 subscriptions were collected for "raising a sum sufficient to maintain a Charity School in Burwash". The sum of £204.5s.6d. was pledged from thirty-six of the wealthier local landowners and inhabitants. The list was led and inspired by £100 from the will of the late Rector, Rev. George Barnsley, with £5.5s.0d. from both the Rector, Rev. Peter Pickering, and the Vicar, the Rev. George Jordan, 20 guineas from the Duke of Newcastle and 10 guineas each from Thomas Hussey, Mary Dyke and John Cruttenden. These were followed by 3 guineas from William Shadwell, 2 guineas from John Butler and then all the other subscribers with either a guinea or half a guinea. There was one defaulter, Samuel Coney, who promised a guinea but having not paid up three years later was crossed through. The deed of appointment of Trustees was drawn up by the lawyer William Shadwell and duly registered on 25th March 1731. The money raised was initially lent to Walter Waters "for which he gave a bond to pay interest at 4%", repaid in 1730, and then used to purchase Palmers Farm (twenty acres) near Wadhurst in April 1731. The farm was let to Mr. Saunders at £9.0s.0d. per annum and for the rest of the century the rent from this farm provided the income which covered the teachers' salaries and all other expenses incurred in running the school. The account book was originally kept personally by Thomas Hussey but on his death in 1735 his executors paid the credit balance of 10s.4d. to the Vicar, George Jordan, and thereafter he and his successors in office acted as guardians of the finances. Hussey's final account was audited by the Churchwardens John Coney and John Tisehurst.

The school had opened as soon as the money was raised in 1727. Initially eighteen children were enrolled and this number quickly rose to twenty-five by 1728 and remained between twenty and thirty for the rest of the century. A list "of the charity children at the several schools in Burwash Sept. 29 1728" shows twenty-five names of both sexes with an age range of six to twelve years. Two of the children are however marked "gone" and "out". The pupils were divided among four teachers and taught in the individual teachers' homes. It was intended that they were taught the basics of reading, writing and arithmetic but as two of the teachers, Margaret Marten and Mary Page, could only sign for their wages with an "X her mark", it must be doubtful as to what standard was achieved. Margaret Marten remained as a teacher until 1752, signing with an X to the end. By the mid 1730s the number of teachers had been reduced to three and this remained constant for seventy years. The teachers were paid between 1s.8d. and 1s.11d. per pupil, depending on the length of the term, giving them an annual income of approximately £1.15s.0d. each, out of which they provided all books, pencils and other requirements. The total teachers bill of about £6.0s.0d. was covered by the rent from the farm even after King's Tax of 15% had been deducted, and most years there was a modest surplus of a pound or two.

In 1710 controversy had again broken out in the church. Throughout Sussex, and particularly locally, there had continued to be considerable sympathy with the non-conformist movement. Edward Polhill (Frenches) was an eminent puritan theologian and author who in 1678 had written "Spectrum Theologiae in Christo", a definitive Christian analysis. Many other local families maintained their links with non-conformist groups, such as Edward Collins who held Presbyterian services in his house (Square Farm) while outwardly attending and conforming with the Church of England. John Webb was still Vicar, although he left most of his work to his Curate, and was described by a contemporary dissenter as being "a dishonest man who gave much offence to the people". In 1710 four gentlemen walked out of his morning service as they "resolved to hear him no longer". They met again that afternoon and the Burwash non-conformist church was founded "to provide a serious and godly ministry". Rev. Edward Dean was appointed Minister. To start with they held services in one of their houses, but in 1713 Edward Polhill, grand-nephew of the theologian author, financed the building of the old independent chapel or meeting house on the site where the village hall now stands. The Polhills remained leading members of the national movement and their kinsman William Polhill became President and Chairman of Dissenting Deputies in London in 1779. Financial backing was assured for the fledgling Burwash chapel when in 1726 Elizabeth Cruttenden, sister of John of Fontridge, left "a messuage and eighteen acres known as Crowhurst Bridge Farm" to the Dissenters: the annual rent of £28.0s.0d. paid for the Minister and his expenses. Edward Dean remained Minister for thirty years, being succeeded by Rev. Thomas Paine (1745-65) and Rev. Daniel Mann (1765-88). It seemed that initially six or seven families joined the new chapel (as was recorded in the 1724 Diocesan survey which also stated that there were "no papists" in the parish) and by 1766 there were twenty adult members plus their children.

At St Bartholomew's John Webb was replaced as Vicar by Rev. George Jordan in 1717. Jordan, born in 1689, was the son of Thomas Jordan, a wealthy merchant, and was to become an influential person in the diocese. He was appointed a Canon in 1717, Prebendary of Chichester (1723-45) and Chancellor of the diocese (1725-50); he also held other vicarages and rectories. Until this time the Vicar and vicarage and Rector and rectory had been separate sinecures, usually with absentee incumbents: Jordan became the first person to be both Rector and Vicar of Burwash when he additionally became Rector in 1737. The two offices have remained together ever since. At his own expense in 1721 he built the Rectory (The Glebe) on the site of the old 17th-century vicarage, part of which building can be found at the back of the Georgian house. He probably laid out the fine gardens and orchard. He married Ann in 1716 and they had fifteen children, some of whom were to marry into local landowning families. Jordan appears to have been a respected caring man who, unusually, had become resident in the parish and devoted a good part of his time to parishioners as well as to his other ecclesiastical duties: this probably helped to heal the rifts and resulted in a more peaceful atmosphere pervading the community.

※

This period saw a development in Burwash which was to cause a significant change in the appearance of the High Street and no doubt was also of benefit to its economics. This was the start of a move by members of local wealthy land-owning families into the village itself. Until now these families had lived on their estates, possibly spending some of their time in London, and probably using the village only to satisfy some of their minor day-to-day requirements and to sell some of the produce from their farms. They had played their part as Churchwardens, Overseers of the Poor, and magistrates, they had owned property in the village for renting but until now they had not lived there. Now they began to move in, and at the same time, and perhaps as a result of this quiet influx, a number of the other better-off inhabitants upgraded or enlarged their houses, or even built new houses, and all of these reflected a Georgian style of architecture. This trend started in 1672 when John Coney, grandson of Mark and Helen (Byne) purchased Mount House

Mount House

from John Stephens. John Coney's son, also John, added the western wing in about 1720, put in the staircase and probably at the same time raised the level of the ceilings downstairs and put in Georgian proportioned bedrooms. He also inherited a further part of his great-great-grandfather Thomas Byne's estate in 1702 and purchased some adjoining farms in 1705, thus assembling a considerable estate round the south of the village from Mount House to Bowmans. Mount House was lived in by successive generations of Coneys, who regarded it as their principle residence, including Bicknell Coney who was a Director of the Bank of England and a druggist of Leadenhall Street; he was also Secretary of the Corporation of the Sons of the Clergy. On Bicknell Coney's death in the early 19th century the estate was inherited by his son, Rev. Thomas Coney, who was vicar of Batcombe, Somerset. Thereafter the house was rented out. During their long residence in Burwash the Coneys contributed much as they rose in wealth and status.

Rampyndene

The next to arrive, in about 1680, was John Butler who immediately started to accumulate property. He was said to have made his money from timber but he gives more the impression of being a property dealer as at various times he was owner or head lessee of twelve different properties including Perrymans, Batemans, Ham Place and Denes. It was however at Rampyndene that he left his mark by largely demolishing the existing building and constructing the current house in 1699. The Dawes family had sold it to Richard Swayne in 1673 and he left it to his kinswoman Elizabeth who married John Cowper: they sold it to Butler for £70.0s.0d. Curiously Butler never lived at Rampyndene (living instead at Ham Place) and renting it from 1699 to 1716 to Thomas Jenkins, a barrister, and then to George Jordan in 1717 when he arrived to take up his duties as Vicar and needed somewhere to live while he rebuilt the vicarage. Butler sold Rampyndene to Thomas Hussey in 1718 for £280 and after Jordan went to his new house in 1721 the Hussey family moved in and were to remain until 1840 when Thomas' great-grandson Edward died.

A little further east the lawyer William Shadwell, who had set up his legal practice in the village on his marriage in 1715, purchased Denes House from Rev. Edward Wilson and The Ivy from William Morphew (or Morpheus) in 1720. He lived at The Ivy until his death in 1749 and rented Denes House out until 1743 when it was rebuilt in its current form at the time of his daughter Mary's marriage to John Constable. The stability of residence and ownership of that age is demonstrated by the fact that the same families were to possess three houses (Rampyndene, Mount and Denes) for a total of five hundred and twenty-eight years between them.

The Ivy

48   Chapter Three

The exact date when Adams Strake (Burghurst) was enlarged and altered is uncertain but it is likely to have been before 1782 when it was advertised for sale as a large house. An earlier date is supported by the fact that some of its alterations are almost identical to those in Denes House and could well have been carried out by the same builder or architect, or one house could have been copied from the other. Both had Georgian style rooms and fittings superimposed onto older buildings which were not

Adams Strake (Burghurst)

demolished but exist today beneath the Georgian work. The staircases and balustrades are also identical as are a variety of other internal details. The ownership of Adams Strake passed from the Polhills through several hands to the schoolmaster William Williams in 1783 and then to the Hyland family by the 1820s.

Another house which received similar treatment of covering up rather than destroying the old, and which also has the same details on its staircase as Denes and Adams Strake, albeit with superior inlay work on the banisters, is Youngs Garden. The date of its alterations is probably 1775 when it was purchased by James Philcox on his marriage to Mary Constable, John and Mary's daughter. Philcox had arrived to succeed to the law practice of his wife's grandfather William Shadwell. The Philcox's lived at Youngs Garden until James' grandson, also James, died in 1896 and it was almost certainly in their time that the western extension and second front entrance was added, perhaps originally to

Youngs Garden

segregate business callers from social ones. The original house at Youngs Garden had been sold in 1713 by John and Joan Bunce's son Thomas in order to pay off his mortgage to Thomas Dyke. The purchaser was John Walker whose granddaughter, Elizabeth, married to Henry Goldsmith (Junior), inherited it in 1742 together with her sister Ann. As both the Goldsmiths and the Walkers had other houses it was sold in 1753 to Thomas Parham whose surviving brother and heir then sold it to James and Mary Philcox.

The Goldsmith property included Brickhouse (Old Brick) and Platts farms and also still included Hoppers Croft (Church House) and all the land between the Square and Ham Lane behind the High Street cottages. Henry (Junior) had died in 1765 and been

Hoppers Croft (Church House)

succeeded by his son Walker whose daughter Ann married the rich lawyer Robert Tourney in 1795. As Walker Goldsmith seems to have been living at Brickhouse it is quite likely that the modern Hoppers Croft (Church House) was built to

Grove Villa (St Anthony's)

replace the original either on his daughter's marriage or soon after. Robert Tourney died in about 1834, Ann a few years later but Tourneys lived here until the 1870s.

Down the High Street, Grove Villa (St Anthony's) was built in 1790 and the White House in 1732. This latter house contains a fine staircase of turned and moulded balusters and was purchased in 1772 by Dr. Thomas Baldock, the newly arrived surgeon, and his wife Jane. Their son John became a solicitor and went into partnership with James Philcox to form Baldock and Philcox; his son John (the younger) was also a solicitor and partner in the firm. John (the younger) inherited the White House and after his death his widow Lavinia remained there until 1864.

White House

At the western end of the village, in 1805, John Flurry purchased the fields from behind the modern Crediton as far as Spring Lane "late Walker formerly Dawes", "lately a messuage erected". This messuage was probably the old building that lies within the modern Dawes House with the name coming from the family of John Dawes who had acquired the property (of St. Giles) in 1639. John Flurry lived there and farmed Dawes Farm (fifty-seven acres) until he died aged ninety-one in 1842; his sisters Ann and Frances lived to be ninety-three and eighty-two respectively and his wife Jane died in 1847 aged ninety-two.

Rampyndene plasterwork

Of these 18th-century buildings Mount House retains most of its original features while Rampyndene is an outstanding example of a William and Mary house, with the central hood above the front door containing fine plaster work, and inside is the original staircase with more fine plaster moulding and contemporary moulded panelling. These Georgianised buildings, with the exception of the newly and probably better built White House and Grove Villa, all incorporated the locally fashionable and practical trend of tile hanging which provided much improved heat retention and protection against the weather. This almost certainly led to many other houses in the High Street gradually adopting this practice and covering up the old timber, wattle and daub. The old facades are often uncovered when alterations take place in modern times. The new building trend was not confined to the village high street, with the splendid new rectory (The Glebe) and the new Fontridge House belonging to the first half of the century and Holt Down (Holton) and Witherhurst to the second half, with many other houses having Georgian extensions or facades added to them.

So by the end of the 18th century the medieval appearance of Burwash had all but disappeared. As well as an altered appearance it is likely that life in the village also changed.

52   Chapter Three

The street would have echoed to the sound of horse and carriage and there would have been greater bustle and prosperity as the shopkeepers and other tradesmen supplied the needs of the larger houses and their growing families. The establishment of a thriving law practice (Shadwell then Baldock and Philcox) would also attract general trade as would the presence of the Doctors.

There had no doubt been hostelries and coaching inns in Burwash for centuries to satisfy the needs of both local inhabitants and passing travellers and the name Rose & Crown often dates back to the War of the Roses when the Crown was linked to the locally favoured rose of either York or Lancaster. However the first recorded mention of a public house is in 1712 when John Walker was tenant of the Bear which was owned by Nathaniel Cruttenden. The Walkers were succeeded by the Carters in 1740 and when Nat Cruttenden died in 1770 he left the Bear to his only daughter Mary. His will refers to the Bear and its land "adjoining the hospital" which implies a hospital of sorts somewhere between Chaunt House and the inn. Edward Foster took over the Rose & Crown from his father in 1748 and stayed until 1770 when it was acquired by William Martin. The Bell

Rose and Crown

was also in business, known then as "The Five Bells", from the number in the church tower opposite from 1724 to 1893. At this time publicans were not the only suppliers of alcohol as Elizabeth Inskip, wife of the carrier John Inskip, supplied five quarts of beer (cost 1s.3d.) to the watchers over the coffin of Thomas Skinner in 1743 and then beer for his funeral costing 2s.0d. She also supplied other services for burials, charging 2s.3d. for "laying Dame Davis's child forth" and supplying the affidavit.

By the 1740s there were over fifty shops, traders and craftsmen in the village, reflecting both the growing importance of Burwash as a trading and shopping centre for a wide surrounding district and also the increased business in the flourishing village. There were five butchers, seven shoemakers, three breeches makers, two tailors, a glover, a hatter as well as five general stores. In addition there were a wide range of carpenters, plumbers, glaziers, coopers and two blacksmiths, one being the Fuller family who plied their trade near Pump Court for over a hundred years. Tobacco and powder or dust (snuff) were supplied by William Polhill. Among the general stores in 1735 John Nepecker included both nails and butter in the range of goods he sold at Guestling (Linden) which was probably built or rebuilt at the start of this century. In 1707 it had been described as a "house and tallow house called Guestling" when it was owned by Edward Austen, junior, before his family went bankrupt in 1732. The Austens had been well-to-do minor property owners and shopkeepers in Burwash since the 16th century and had frequently been churchwardens and overseers. Nepecker died in 1740, and then his widow Ann in 1743, when the business was acquired by Richard Johnson who was to remain there until his death in 1789. Thereafter Guestling and next door Colemans (Barclays Bank) were both variously residences and small shops. Johnson was plainly a sharp businessman as he acquired a variety of properties in and around Burwash and was active in lending money against mortgages. In 1772 he was too quick to seize mortgage land from Robert Carter (also then landlord of the Bear) and the Manorial Court ordered him to return it. There were no local banks at this time and virtually all the money lending and financing was done by individuals, mainly shopkeepers and landowners, who would often take a mortgage on property or assets. The arrangement was sometimes recorded in the Manorial book and the lawyer of the time would draw up the deed (called an indenture because of its wavy outline) which would be witnessed by other responsible citizens. The charity school fifty years earlier had lent its subscription money in this way until it made its long-term investment in the farm. Money was thus recycled through the village society and reputations were carefully protected.

The other main general shopkeeper was Robert Busbridge, descendent of the Haremere Busbridges, who married Ann, daughter of the wealthy Henry Goldsmith (senior) in 1743, having been in business at the Old Granary/Yew Tree since the 1730s.

His wares included salt, silk, soap, sugar, ivory combs and thread and he conducted his business there until his death in 1774. There is no evidence as to who, if anyone, took over his business until John Ellis appears in 1813 to own the house and shop which he kept until 1832.

John Dodswell, clockmaker, was supplying oil for the church clock, and also cleaning it and seeing to the chimes in 1751 and he may well have been carrying out his trade from what was to become Noakes clock and watch shop. Dodswell was still there in 1780 and his widow Elizabeth in 1790. There were also a large number of shopkeepers and tradesmen whose residences cannot be traced with certainty. The Blundens had been residents since the 16th century and their hatters shop (in the Square) remained open until the end of the 18th century during which time they were strong members of the non-conformist chapel. The Mugridges appear in the mid-17th century and their glove shop, also doing occasional breeches mending, continued through Henry and then his son Thomas who in 1742 had married Ann Cross. She taught at the Charity School from 1752 when Thomas died. William Elphick carried on his cordwainers business from the 1750s and in 1772 purchased "a messuage lately erected (about 1750) near Sellars Brook" which house still bears his name.

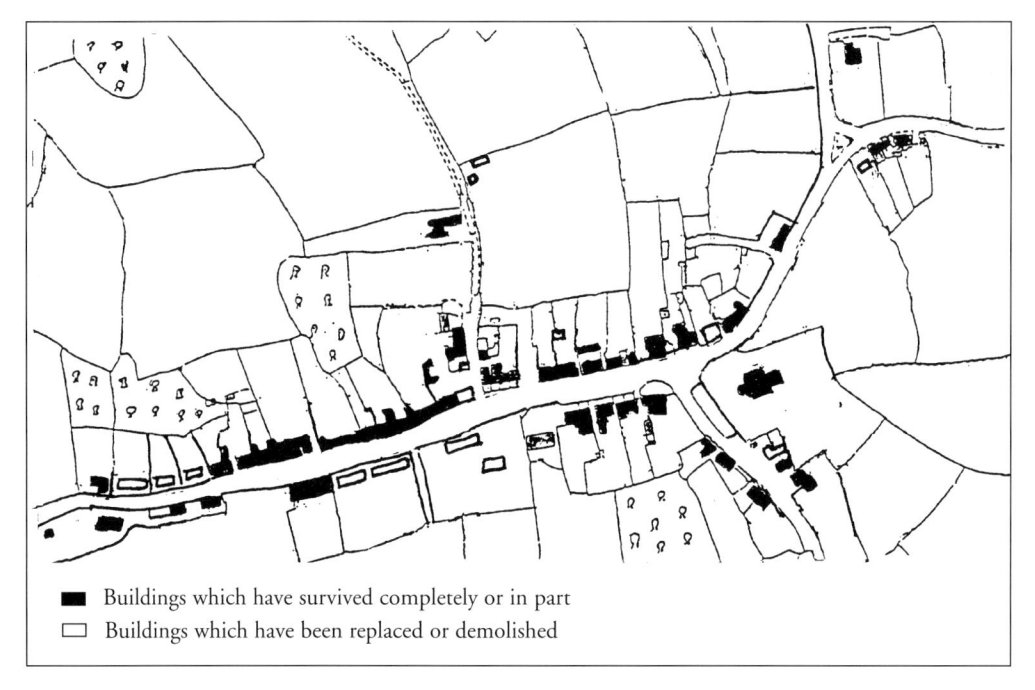

■ Buildings which have survived completely or in part
☐ Buildings which have been replaced or demolished

Burwash in about 1750

Many of the shopkeepers supplied goods to the Overseers of the Poor; these goods were paid for out of the poor rate and supplied free or at nominal cost to the poor who were then often compulsorily contracted to earn a wage by working on local farms. A typical sample of purchases included in 1743:

	s	d
Robert Busbridge - Shopkeeper		
½ a pound of soap		3
a pound of candles		5½
gallon of salt		9
7 lbs of Cheshire cheese	2	0
½ a pound of sugar		2
Mr Paine - Grocer		
A scythe	2	6
1 quart oatmeal		2½
A gimblet		2
Warwickshire cheese 13 lbs	4	1¾
Mrs Nepecker		
1 pint oil		8
1 oz thread		3
1 dozen shirt buttons		2
4 yards Russia cloth	1	8
1½ yards Irish cloth	2	3
Tho. Hicks - Butcher		
Neck of mutton	1	7
Root of a tongue		8
For a cheek	1	0
Sheeps head		5
3 stone + 6 lbs of beef	7	6
Tho. Pope - Weaver		
For weaving 102 yards of ticking at 4d per yard	£1 14	0
63 yards shirting at 3½d. per yard	18	4½
Henry Mugridge's		
A pair of gloves		7
A pair of breeches	4	0
Mending breeches		3
An apron		10
Jno. Breach - Cordwainer		
Soling + nails for Jas Leney's shoes	1	0
Mending one shoe for young Sinden		4
A pair of shoes for Wm.Insell	4	6

James Brook			
Bread for Easter Communion			10
Oil for clock and chimes			2
For looking after clock and chimes for one year	£1	0	0
For looking after the linnon for one year		9	0
Harbart Wood - Carpenter			
For putting up pins in the church		1	6
For a coffin and burial of Mas. Elliot		9	0
For 1 day mending the shingles on the church		1	8
For 87 shingles at 3s. per hundred		2	7½
		14	9½

Harbart Wood was also the Parish Clerk as his family had been for some generations and they were to continue this tradition for many years to come. The Parish Clerk of this time was a general village manager and factotum and was often the Sexton: Harbart Wood charged 2s.0d for digging a grave. The Clerk needed to be literate and was involved in most aspects of village and church life and received either a wage or payment in kind.

The poor rate was also used for a variety of other purposes. In 1742 free schooling was provided for Nick Jenner for the year at a cost of 4s.0d. while both he and his brother Sam had their heads shaved at a charge of 6d. each. Young Thankful Ticehurst was a heavy drain on the parish: after he had committed a petty crime, Robert Busbridge charged £1.19s.11d. to "attend on Thankful Ticehurst and carry him to Battle" to bring him to justice and then "hire of horse to carry double to Lewes". Counsellor's fee was £1.1s.0d., clothes 6s.0d., and widow Blunden was paid 2s.0d. per week to keep him. Robert Noakes, carrier, charged for "expences on the road for a carrying Ed Primmer to Bethlem"; these included tolls or road charges at Frant (3d.) and 7 Oaks (3d.) and 1s. 6d. for "eating and drinking in London" - total bill £1. 7s. 1d. A further charge for enforcing the law was made by Isaac Holman, Constable, who in 1750 was paid £1.12s.0d. for "carrying Thomas Venice and John Venice to Horsham gaol by order of two of His Majesty's Justices, viz. John Nicholl and John Fuller Esq." Abraham Holman senior, carpenter, was paid 7s.0d. for a coffin for John Bowyer and 6s.0d. for a new hog hutch with two holes, while John Cruttenden supplied a forty-four stone hog for £5.3s.6½d. As well as the poor rate the parish received an income from the Worshipful Company of Girdlers, where a charity had been established by Thomas Nevitt in 1633 in memory of his wife Obedience, daughter of Robert Cruttenden. He directed that each year £1 be paid to the vicar for preaching two sermons and £1 10s. 8d. to be distributed in money and bread to the poor. Unfortunately it seems the Girdlers paid neither promptly nor in full as in 1744 when five years in arrears they paid only £8.1s.2d., leaving a shortfall of £4.12s.2d.

Towards the end of the 18th century other traders arrived. The first Waterhouse, William, carpenter and coffin maker, is mentioned in 1768 having married in 1750, and by 1780 John Fleming, hairdresser, is in business in Rover Cottage. He was joined by his son John who succeeded him by 1799: John junior married Ann Geer in 1780 and raised twelve children, including James, born in 1804, who would contribute much to the village in the 19th century. A few doors away Thomas Shadwell was to set up his fruiterer's shop in the 1820s at the end of the row that, having been known as "The Row" for two hundred years or more, now took on his name. Richard Manktelow arrived about 1800 as a young man to begin his cabinet making business in what is now the newsagents and where he was to remain for fifty years. At about the same time a little further along on the other side of the road, just beyond Novar, Henry Heathfield purchased from John Matthews a "messuage formerly a smithy now a wheelwrights". Heathfield was joined in the business by Samuel Venness and when they died Heathfield's son, also Henry, carried on the business.

In the early part of the 18th century land and farms around the village were still concentrated in the ownership of a few long established families, but from the middle of the century the pattern started slowly to break up. This was partly due to the severe economic troughs suffered regularly by agriculture, partly due to the estates being rather too small to be financially viable, and partly due to the demand for small estates from those who had made money out of business or commerce. Although the last Cruttenden did not finally leave Tott until 1867 the main estate in and around Fontridge Lane was sold following the death of Nathaniel in 1770, he being the son of Anthony and Mary (both buried in the tomb in the middle aisle of St Bartholomew's) and described as "the last male heir of an ancient family". Nathaniel left all his land and other property to his only daughter Mary, married to Rev. John Bishop, Rector of Sedlescombe. She steadily disposed of the property, including the Bear Inn, until only her distant cousin was left at Tott.

To the north of the village the Polhills had lived at Frenches since 1639 and had owned the surrounding land since before 1600, and although they retained ownership of some land and some houses in the village the last Polhill at Frenches died in about 1715. The properties then descended through the female line to a cousin Thomas Dyke, grandson of a Sarah Polhill and Sir Thomas Dyke. He succeeded to the land including Frenches in 1715 and added to his fortune by marrying Mary Still, daughter of Robert Still of Cowden. Their only son and heir, Richard Still Dyke, married Anne, eldest daughter of the Rev. George Jordan, and she inherited the Polhill/Dyke estates on his death in 1761. They do not seem to have had any surviving children and shortly after her husband's death Anne married Henry Hone Haviland, of a landowning and clerical family. Although Anne did not die until 1794 the land was gradually sold throughout the century, some of it to the Ellis's who were distant cousins through the sisters Mercy and Mary Gillam marrying respectively Robert Ellis (in 1692) and Edward Polhill (1687). John Ellis (son of Mercy and Robert) was farming Southover and Winters by 1740 and this family was to stay there well into the next century. They were to be joined at Frenches in 1780 by Thomas Blundell who married John Ellis's granddaughter Frances in 1785. All these families were strong non-conformists, carrying on the tradition of their Polhill ancestors.

Planning regulations in the 18th century were enforced by the local manorial court. In 1779 "John Shorter erected a cottage without licence and the manor gave notice to John Shorter to take down the said cottage before the next court under the penalty of 40 shillings". Large landowners were also affected as in 1793 Anne Dyke (Haviland) pulled down a barn on her land without licence. The court ruled that if she did not re-erect it, the site would be forfeited.

When George III had succeeded his grandfather at the age of twenty-one in 1760 he was the first of the Hanoverians to regard England as his natural home. This led to a more general popularity for the monarchy that survived his lunacy and the resulting Regency periods (1788-89 and 1811-14) and extended into the shorter reigns of George IV (1815-30) and William IV (1830-37). These seventy-seven years witnessed developments that were to start a reshaping of the world in a series of events that are still continuing at the millennium in 2000. Of these changes the most far reaching were the advances of all forms of science and the inventions which led to the industrial revolution. In the cotton industry the 1780s saw Hargreave's spinning jenny, Arkwright's water frame and Crompton's mule; the iron bridge over the river Severn opened in 1776 and was followed by Rennie's iron wheels and the development of steel in the 1790s. Watt's steam engine also dates from the 1790s as does Maudsley's carriage lathe and by 1800 there were eighty-four steam engine machines in Lancashire. In transport Mr Pickford started a fleet of barges running day and night on the canal between London and the Midlands. Collectively this all led to a steady migration of population from the rural South to the fast growing towns of the North: Manchester grew from a population of fifty thousand in 1790 to one hundred thousand in 1815 and Oldham grew from four hundred in 1760 to twelve thousand in 1800.

For Sussex the increasing use of coal then coke in the iron smelting industry had led to the steady closure of the local iron works as the industry moved to the rich coal fields and iron ore seams of the North. This led to unemployment in Burwash, like other villages, although this was partly offset by rising employment in agriculture as forest clearance, combined with improved methods, increased the intensity of agricultural methods and thus the productivity of the land. Mechanisation had not yet arrived and all farming activities used large numbers of workers. Crops were now rotated on a planned basis and selective breeding improved the livestock and the quality of the meat. Burwash by now also had a series of brickworks all using the very suitable Wadhurst clay. There was one (near Oakdown) at Burwash Common by 1791, but the most central was immediately behind the Bear which remained until 1839, when it was discontinued and levelled to form a bowling green. Others were to appear near the top of Spring Lane, at Claws farm, just north of Southover and down Bell Alley on the western side where a deep ravine can now be seen.

The Burwash unemployed still had the safety net of the 1601 Poor Law Act and they were also given employment, paid and unpaid, to repair roads, bridges and public facilities. Some seemed to exploit the system such as John and Philadelphia Blunden, both described as being on the "poor" list, who had fourteen children between 1779 and 1800 while receiving local cash benefit. From about 1815 Bough Farm with its ninety-six acres was owned by the Parish and provided productive employment for some of the local poor until the passing of the Poor Law Reform Act (1834) abolished the workhouse system, which resulted in its sale. Bough Farm seems to have been run on humanitarian methods but there is no doubt that some other workhouses abused the rights of their inmates. The local workhouse was sited at Burwash Common (at the back of what is now Pooks Hill View and Church House) and there is evidence of its existence from 1791 to 1823, but by 1839 this building was referred to as the old workhouse, which implies that it went out of use at the same time as Bough Farm. When set up in 1791 it was fully furnished at a total cost of £9.1s.3d., including pots and pans and a dresser with drawers for 7s.3d, and a table and stool for 1s.6d. The governor's wages were £15.0s.0d. a year. The 1601 Act had made each parish responsible, through the Overseers, for their own poor but this was changed by the new 1834 Act. The single parish system was replaced in favour of groups of parishes and Burwash joined with eight others to establish the Poor Law Union of Ticehurst with an elected board of guardians supervising paid officials. From then on payments were not made to "able bodied male workers and their families".

There was an ethos throughout this time of collective parish responsibility that not only assisted the poor but also led to the local justices ensuring that there was reasonable law and order. This local conscience generally meant that rural village life was fairly self-contained without interference from central government. Only in matters of taxation was the power of government felt whether it was the hated window tax, income tax or land tax. A more accepted form of taxation was the National Lottery; this had started in 1694 and continued intermittently until 1826 with one hundred and seventy lotteries being run in that period. Pitt saw its use in raising taxes by exploiting the gambling instincts of the population and in 1768 the prize money was doubled from £10,000 to £20,000 and the price of tickets was halved from £20 to £10 each. Tickets were then sub-divided and there are records of Sussex villagers and shopkeepers purchasing one sixteenth of a ticket for 16s.0d. There was thus considerable excitement in Burwash when the regular draw took place with great ceremony in London's Guildhall with the media of the time reporting the results. There is no record of a local winner but a publican in Abingdon spent a large part of his unexpected wealth entertaining friends and hangers on. The popularity of the lottery also increased markedly when prizes were paid in cash from 1767 rather than in government bonds as hitherto.

Events overseas were shaping the world of the future as well as increasingly having an influence on local English life. In 1789 the French Revolution saw the effective end of their monarchy. Louis XVI and his queen, Marie Antoinette, were ultimately executed in 1793 and the scene was set for the long and bitter struggle between France and most of the rest of Europe. The Napoleonic war lasted until the English victories at the Battles of Trafalgar (1805) and Waterloo (1815), which led to peace through the Treaty of Vienna (1815). This long war played havoc with the economy as the huge cost of keeping a large army and navy meant increased taxes and rising prices. As always this had the most effect on the poor, with the price of bread reflecting the rise in wheat price from 43s.0d. per quarter in 1792 to 126s.0d. a quarter in 1812. When the end of the war seemed likely to reduce wheat prices the government protected the farmers by passing the 1815 Corn Law, which imposed heavy taxes on foreign grain thus preventing the importing of grain then being produced much more cheaply in the North American prairies. The United States of America had already won its freedom from England through the War of Independence (1772-83).

The perennial and intractable problem of England's relationship with Ireland surfaced again during this period after years of increasing unrest. Irish radicals in Ulster formed a "United Irishmen" society and the possible emancipation of Catholics was widely debated. American and French support for the Catholics put pressure on England and rebellion and civil war followed. The troubles were ended by the Act of Union in 1801 whereby Ireland's parliament disappeared and the country was governed directly from Westminster in return for an increased number of seats in the House of Commons. This temporarily brought an uneasy peace as the Catholics believed they had achieved a deal that was in their interest.

The cultural side of England changed its mood in sympathy with the economic and social changes taking place. Sir Walter Scott, Blake, Jane Austen, Byron, Wordsworth and Coleridge were influenced by urban poverty, revolution and a desire to be seen to have vision or an ideal. Furniture was becoming more ornate and Nash was to influence the style of buildings, Turner and Constable painting.

In medicine the death rate was starting to fall as treatments were improving as a result of teaching and research at the medical schools in Edinburgh and the London hospitals. Cod liver oil was taken internally rather than externally, the value of fruit, vegetables and a balanced diet was recognised and following Jenner's experiment with vaccination from cowpox in 1796 the National Vaccination Establishment was set up in 1808. Some of these new methods took a little while to reach country villages but by 1800 Burwash's Dr Thomas Baldock also became the official vaccinator. He wrote that he "begs leave to inform the public that he attends on people desirous of having the smallpox by inoculation, either at their own homes, or accommodates them with all necessaries in houses he has provided for that purpose for three weeks after inoculation, at one and a half, two or three guineas per person. He engages to attend them in the distemper with the utmost care and fidelity, pursuing the new and most approved methods now practised". He was succeeded as village doctor by Dr Thomas Abel Evans who initially set up in Chaunt, before renting Mount House from Rev. Thomas Coney.

The roads of England were, if anything, deteriorating as increasing traffic and lack of upkeep combined to make many of them impassable. Since Saxon times it had been the responsibility of parishes to maintain all their roads using the poor or forced labour or levying taxes on the rich. Most parishes did little and in 1726 Defoe had written of an ancient lady of good quality in Sussex who was "drawn to church in her coach with six oxen; nor was it done in frolick or humour, but mere necessity, the way being so stiff and deep that no horses could go in it". A little earlier, in 1694, an agreement had been drawn up by the respective surveyors of Brightling and Burwash "to repair highway between Burwash and Brightling": "to be mended and repaired by the surveyor of Pish of Burwash until the east end of the cottage of John Cundit" (Bell Alley). It was signed first by the surveyors John Baker and Edward French and then by some inhabitants including John Busbridge, Laurence Noakes, Tho. Cruttenden and John French - presumably because they would be paying the bill.

In order to improve at least the main roads the turnpike system came into being at the start of the 18th century. A separate turnpike trust with its own Act of Parliament was created for each stretch of road; the trustees were local residents who then took

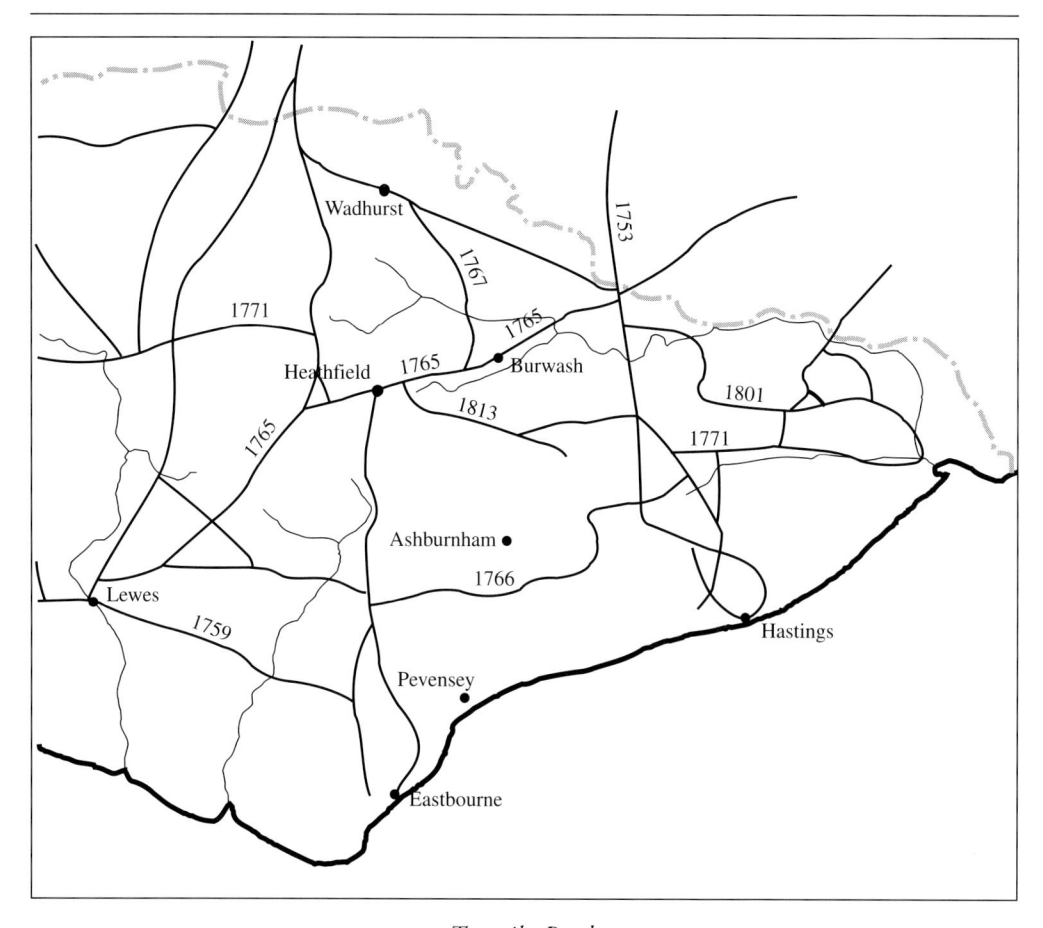

Turnpike Roads

responsibility for the upkeep and repair of the road and recouped the costs by charging tolls to travellers. In the middle of the century there was a sharp increase in the number of such trusts, rising from one hundred and eighty in 1748 to five hundred and thirty in 1770. In 1765 the Sussex Turnpike Act was passed which was "an act for repairing widening and keeping in repair, the road leading from the turnpike road at Hurst Green through Etchingham and Burwash to the extent of the said parish of Burwash". The Board of Trustees met regularly and their decisions were implemented by three officials, the surveyor, the clerk and the treasurer. The toll for anyone using the road was assessed on the basis of a standard unit which was a coach, a score of cattle or sheep or a single horse. All charges related to this unit, the value of which might vary from time to time. Local traffic and farmers in the parish were exempted from paying the toll. Capital sums for road repairs or improvements were financed either by the Trustees or by raising a mortgage on the tolls. In

1767 an additional stretch was added to the Trust, being the road from Burwash Common to Stonegate and Wadhurst. The Burwash Trust seems to have provided a satisfactory service and the routine inspection in 1840 reported that the Trust consisted of twenty-three miles, nine tollgates and two sidebars. It said that "the main part of the road is in good condition but largely repaired with sandy gravel, the tolls not producing sufficient to purchase hard stone or cinders" and "the whole of the road is repaired by the Trustees". The Stonegate spur of four and a half miles with one gate "the greater part of the road is in good condition having been repaired with hard material" but "100 yards either side of Witherden Bridge" was not the responsibility of the Trustees. It may have been that the revenue shortage was due to the charges being too modest as the neighbouring trusts charged "for every landau, coach, berlin, chariot, chaise, calash, chair, caravan or hearse drawn by six horses one shilling; if drawn by two horses 6 pence and if by one horse 3d.". The Trust continued until in 1830 it was added to the Ringmer and Heathfield Trust, which managed the road to Lewes, and effectively swallowed by it. Road surfaces gradually improved and were given a significant boost by the process invented by Macadam which led, by 1840, to many miles of comparatively smooth turnpike roads throughout the country.

※

When the Rev. George Jordan had died in 1755 after forty years in the parish he was succeeded as Rector and Vicar by Rev. John Courtail who served fifty years, and was also Archdeacon, until his death in 1806, when Rev. Whitfield Curteis took over the parish until 1821. These long periods of continuity brought calm to St Bartholomew's and with the churchwardens being drawn from the leading shopkeepers or farmers there emerges a picture of orderliness with the books being tidily kept, monies collected to maintain the church and look after the poor, full congregations and balanced finances. It was Curteis who in 1816 sold the old Rectory building in the lane off the High Street "it being dilapidated and beyond repair". He used the proceeds to help finance the building of the new school the following year and "to reimburse himself for the redemption of land tax"; the o ld Rectory was described as "now a cottage".

Perhaps because of this stability and the general lack of religious controversy, the non-conformist chapel was having a more difficult time. It too had had only three ministers in sixty-five years but after Rev. Daniel Mann's death in 1788 they were without a minister for three years and then had eight in thirty-five years. During Mann's ministry membership had remained steady with new recruits being balanced by deaths: in 1778 it was recorded that "Widow Smith was left in much sorrow and trouble with six children, her husband died in the midst of his days, cut off by a bad fever". Widow Smith was given 2s.0d. They were, however, fortunate in receiving substantial financial backing from a number of reasonably wealthy residents including Thomas Blundell now the farmer of

Frenches. In 1800 a new gallery was built in the old chapel and the pulpit moved. The bill was £25.18s.7½d.: this was made up of John Bowles, carpenter, £18.12s.5½d; Edward Pilbeam, glazier, 16s.9½d; Richard Ellis, blacksmith, 6s.8d; Wm. Thompson, mason, £6.2s.8½d. The bill was met by Thomas Blundell £10.0s.0d, Wm. Thompson £3.3s.0d, the sale of timber at Crowhurst Bridge £2.14s.0d., and some smaller subscriptions. In 1811 the porch was removed from the front to the west end, with the door to face the road and the gate opposite and the "square pews to be taken down and replaced with forms with back rail". In 1812 numbers were up to sixtyfive "May the Lord add many more of such shall be saved", and in 1814 a new gallery was added along the front of the church. In 1813 Thomas Blundell had died aged seventy-five years, with one of his last acts being to secure the future of the chapel having "purchased this place for the use of dissenters of Independent denomination herein assembling" according to the old tablet found in the vault of the chapel.

But problems were looming. In 1815 twenty-four persons calling themselves Baptists were dismissed from the chapel and formed a church at Shovers Green. The dismissal was "signed on behalf of the church by William Thompson, William Waghorn, William Mepham, Deacons 26th November 1815" and said "These presents from the Church of Christ at Burwash sendeth greetings, to show we most cordially comply with the request of those members that they should be dismissed from the Church for the purpose of forming themselves into a Baptist church in the hamlet of Shovers Green…". Then in 1816 the minister John Green resigned after one year "in lack of having vision". In 1818 six members left after a dispute about doctrine and in 1822 Rev. Robert Biggars excommunicated Richard Siggs, Sarah Cottingdon and Mrs Woodsell, and Wm. and Ann Waghorn were dismissed for disorderly conduct. In 1824 a further twentyone people left or were dismissed and the final blow came in 1828 when, led by William Buss, those with Calvinist views left and built their own meeting house at what is now Chant Meadow. Mr Weller was initially appointed minister there to be succeeded later by William Buss. In 1829 Rev. John Press arrived at the old non-conformist chapel and lived at Brickhouse Farm where John Lade, the church treasurer, "gave him his bed and board and use of his carriage to convey him to and fro. This prevented the chapel from being shut up or falling into the hands of unreasonable or wicked men". Press stayed until 1849 and new life was soon to be breathed into the chapel community by the shopkeeper John Buss Noakes. Throughout this time non-conformists continued to be buried at St Bartholomew's as evidenced by their record that "Wm. Cornford a servant of the church who died 28th December 1799 and was the last corpse buried in the Burwash churchyard in the 18th century as vulgarly supposed".

The Charity School had continued with little change over the second half of the 18th century with approximately twenty-five children being taught by three teachers in their homes. Strict account was kept of numbers with Ann Mugridge (widow of Thomas Mugridge, Hatter) having 4d. deducted in 1762 "because one of the scholars was not put to school till about the third week of the quarter" and in 1797 four shillings was taken from each teacher's wages "on account of the school being shut for a month" (due to illness). However wages had crept upwards and by 1795 a teacher's annual income was £2.10s.0d. or 7s.0d. per pupil compared with 5s.6d. fifty years before. This slow rate of inflation was reflected in the rent of Palmers Farm (still owned by the school), which rose from £9.0s.0d. per annum in 1731 to £10.0s.0d. in 1765 on a change of tenant, £11.0s.0d. in 1790, again on a tenancy change to John Collins. However, in 1808, Collins agreed to pay a rent of £18.0s.0d. fixed for eleven years and "to do all the repairs and find all materials for the same except rough timber". At the end of the eleven years that rent was raised to £25.0s.0d. per annum in 1819 and then, reflecting the problems of agriculture, lowered to £15.0s.0d. in 1823. Throughout this period the finances of the Charity School quietly prospered. By 1791 nearly £100 had accumulated and the churchwardens, John Vigor and William Baker, instructed Archdeacon Courtail to purchase £100 capital stock in 4% annuities and "as the balance will not be sufficient" to charge his own account with the balance and recoup the money later. In 1800 they switched from 4% annuities to 5%, incurring a capital loss of £15 in the process, and instructed Hoare & Co., Bankers of Fleet Street, to receive future dividends on their behalf. By now Mr Courtail's writing was deteriorating and in 1804, two years before his death, Edward Hilder and John Noakes (churchwardens) signed the minutes of a meeting at which William Constable was elected trustee and treasurer of the charity.

Other schooling had become available in Burwash at intervals during the 18th century. In addition to a number of private schools where educated spinsters taught small numbers of pupils, the Rev. Richard Swinfer Edwards (Vicar) at the age of twenty-nine opened Edwards School in 1761. This lasted until 1772 and he taught Latin, Greek, writing and arithmetic. Edwards advertised that "conveniency of boarding may be had in a sober family not far distant". In 1783 William Williams purchased Adams Strake (Burghurst) and advertised a boarding school for boys "in a large and commodious house for this purpose with ¾ acre for playground" and "tea, if required, at 1 guinea extra". Williams' school closed in 1793.

Around the turn of the century the Charity School was to enter a period of expansion with the numbers increasing sharply so that by July 1808 Richard Barnard was paid £8.0s.0d. for half a year's salary to teach thirty-four boys and Lucy Reeves £10.0s.0d. for forty girls, whereas a few years earlier the salaries were for seven or eight children each. The finances were also improved as timber was sold from Palmers Farm to raise £188.1s.6d.

(£195.15s.5d. gross less 2½% for cash, 17s.0d. for grubbing out the trees, £1.10s.0d. for measuring the timber and £2.10s.0d. auction fees), which was invested in a further £200 of 5% stock. The income from £300 stock plus the farm rent just about covered the salaries, helped by legacies (£45 from William Constable) and occasional subsidies from wealthy local residents. Local philanthropy was then stirred by the increased numbers and in 1817 there was "a meeting of the principal inhabitants of Burwash" who agreed:

> "1. That there are many children entirely without education.
> 2. The school funds cannot educate more than 70 children.
> 3. The morals of the lower class would be improved by education.
> 4. A subscription be raised for the above purposes.
> 5. Two committees be established to supervise the boys and girls schools."

Immediately following this meeting Rev. Whitfield Curteis personally purchased from Walker Goldsmith an orchard measuring approximately two hundred feet by forty feet which ran along the road from just below Hoppers Croft (Church House), where Goldsmith's daughter Ann Tourney lived, to the top of Shrub Lane. Curteis purchased a one thousand year lease for £9.2s.6d. at an annual peppercorn rent with permission to "erect any messuage, dwelling houses, cottages, schoolhouse or schoolhouses". He immediately built the school and in 1819 the diocesan visitation commented on the "recently established National School which was built at the expense of the then Rector". The school built consisted of two rooms of equal size, each twenty-nine feet by thirty feet for eighty-nine boys and ninety-one girls respectively. Pilbeam was paid 13s.0d. for painting the school, Benjamin Wood £25.6s.2d. for "fitting up", the blacksmith Thompson 13s.5d. for fireirons and bellows, and the printing of "School Regulations" cost £2.0s.6d. In 1832 Whitfield Curteis passed on the lease, the land and the school to his successor Rev. William Mackenzie and the churchwardens Richard Button and Francis Russell for the nominal sum of 10s.0d. He had been a truly great benefactor.

From 1817 annual school subscriptions totalling £35 to £40 were received from about twenty-five people and by 1823 a total annual income of about £60 from all sources covered the two teachers' salaries which now amounted to £40.0s.0d. and all other expenses of running the school. In a typical year these included: a mop 1s.3d., broom 2d., half a pound of soap 4d., repair of school clock (Noakes) 2s.0d., black lead pencils 6d., and making trousers for prizes 8s.6d. In 1827 the school became known as the National School and by 1831 there were one hundred and forty-five pupils consisting of ninety-five boys and fifty girls. James Fleming, the hairdresser, was now paid a salary of £40 per annum plus 2s.0d. a quarter for every boy above sixty. In 1826 Miss Ann Tournay, daughter of Robert and Ann, took over the girls part of the school.

At about this time smuggling became a major occupation in Sussex and Kent. Sussex had a long history of this trade beginning with the smuggling of wool in Saxon times. In 1272 Edward I imposed a tax on foreign trade in wool and hides, to pay for his wars, so that by 1356 wool was making the outward journey and illegal gold foreign coinage the return. During the Civil War bullion and arms had been sent abroad for the Royalist cause and later, during the Napoleonic Wars, emigrees were traded for escaping French prisoners. In the middle of the 18th century a broad range of taxes were imposed on spirits, tea, salt, lace, jewellery and other goods. In 1770 a pound of tea costing 5s.0d. in France sold for £1.0s.0d. in England. So the profits were large and so was the pay: a casual labour smuggler could earn 3s.6d. a week, a carrier £1.1s.0d. a week and an armed minder could double this. Even though the death penalty had been introduced in 1662 and other penalties including flogging and deportation, these meant little to poor, unemployed and often starving people and there was no shortage of recruits to become "owlers". Many of the men were known only by colourful nicknames such as "Poison", "Pouncer", "Butcher Tom", "Nasty Face" and "Slippery Sam", which each told its tale.

Most of the smuggling was run by well organised gangs who covered, and fought to protect, a particular stretch of coast and the inland hinterland containing the distributors' network. Despite the inter-gang warfare and the many bloody battles with the Revenue men, smuggling acquired a degree of social respectability and many otherwise law abiding citizens were happy to provide finance or purchase the products:

> "Five and twenty ponies
> Trotting through the dark
> Brandy for the Parson
> 'Baccy for the Clerk
> Laces for a lady, letters for a spy
> and watch the wall, my darling, while the Gentlemen go by"
>
> Rudyard Kipling

There is no firm evidence that Burwash was involved in this trade but there are a number of reasons why it is probable. Two of the most notorious gangs in the south-east were the Mayfield and Hawkhurst gangs and it is highly unlikely that Burwash did not come under the influence of one of them. This is supported by the fact that the village lay on the crossroads of fairly minor roads directly inland and a safe distance from the easily accessible beaches of Pevensey and Eastbourne. Then there are the gravestones in the churchyard with the skull and crossbones, and the entry in the church records of the death of Thomas Waterhouse in 1803 describing him as "smuggler". Finally, the Admiral Vernon pub, named after the leading Revenue man of the time, could either have been sarcasm or bluff. The many colourful tales of escapes through High Street attics, underground passages and cellars full of contraband are possible but unproven. Perhaps the best evidence is social. In 1784 a troop of Light Dragoons was moved into the area to combat the smuggling threat and they were followed by the 11th Light Dragoons and the Norfolk Militia. Shortly afterwards Mary Muggeridge married Joseph Dann, a soldier in Captain Money's troop and there were, in the same year, three baptisms where the father was referred to as a private in Money's troop, or a private in the Militia.

Smuggling declined in the 19th century as the ending of the Napoleonic Wars allowed taxes and duties to be lowered and also released a large supply of trained sailors who joined the Revenue services. Reduced profits and fast ex-naval cutters made life less attractive and on shore the improved turnpike roads assisted the customs officers more than their quarry. As a sign of the more law abiding mood one of the leaders of the Hawkhurst gang, Neri Potten, married Margaret Carly and became a well-to-do tenant farmer near Burwash.

An incident that put Burwash into the national news, and may well have been connected with the smuggling of spirits, was the trial of Hannah Russell and Daniel Leaney at Lewes Assizes in 1826. Hannah, the illegitimate daughter of Mary Wickham, was born in 1794 and married in 1818 to Benjamin Russell, son of William and Sarah Russell. They then had three children and ran the Wheel public house. During her husband's temporary absence in America, Hannah commenced an affair with Daniel Leaney (aged eighteen) who then moved into the pub with them. On 15 May 1826 Benjamin was found dead in Glyddish Wood and Dr Thomas Abel Evans, on opening the body, found evidence of arsenic. Hannah and Daniel were charged with murder. The trial took place on 31 July and lasted from nine in the morning until seven in the evening, the Court being crowded until the last moment. In evidence Robert Crowhurst, shopkeeper (at what is now Abbots Antiques) said he had sold arsenic to Mrs Russell "for the mice" and Joseph Oliver said he saw her in the house putting arsenic on bread and butter which she said was for "mice". Robert Bowles the blacksmith said Hannah Russell told him "she and her husband went out between four and five in the morning somewhere towards Gleddish Wood, to meet a man with a tub of spirit (contraband), and that he (her husband) ordered Leaney to go up there to convey him home". Other witnesses also saw Leaney in or near the wood. Leaney himself was reported as saying that he and Russell were stealing a sack of corn when Russell had a fit and died but he also gave other conflicting stories. The Jury took just fifteen minutes to reach their verdict of guilty and the Judge put on his black cap and passed the death sentence on them both, saying that their bodies should be dissected and anatomised. The newspaper reports over the next few days said that Leaney "admitted many offences against the laws, particularly smuggling and poaching" and they both "had long been known to be connected with the gangs of daring smugglers that infest the coast". Daniel Leaney was duly hanged at

Horsham the following Thursday but by then the Judge was having doubts about the verdict on Hannah. After months of legal debate she received "the King's most gracious pardon" on 24 February 1827 and was released from prison. This encouraged a lengthy debate by letters to the Sussex Advertiser in which many aspects of the trial, including Dr Evans' evidence, were questioned. Hannah herself returned to Burwash and moved in with Thomas Chandler who was a local shoemaker: this relationship caused Chandler to lose his arrangement to supply shoes to the poor through the Overseers. They were married in 1828 and had three children, but after his death in 1834 she produced an illegitimate child in 1838 at the age of forty-four. Hannah finally died in 1871 in Burwash and was described as "a tough old woman".

One of the principal problems of rural areas in the 18th and 19th centuries were the interwoven issues of the state of the economy, the health of agriculture, unemployment and the provision of poor relief. The general pattern was of inflation and boom in war years followed by slump and unemployment afterwards. The numbers employed in agriculture had risen from one and a half million in 1725 to two million in 1775 and then again to two million, nine hundred thousand by 1831. At the same time there had been a trend away from permanent employment to weekly or even daily hiring. The Poor Law had put the provision of relief onto the parish and the operation of the Poor Rate through the overseers had operated reasonably satisfactorily in Burwash for many years. Winter layoffs were the norm but to minimise calls on the Rate there was an unofficial agreement with farmers to offer employment first to men with children. In the 1830s a number of factors now stirred up feelings to breaking point. There was general political unrest which was to lead to the Reform Act of 1832; there was massive unemployment and poverty in the slump following the Napoleonic wars and the accelerating introduction of machinery on farms offered an enormous threat to the now very large agricultural workforce. This collectively led to the countrywide Swing riots (named after the mythical Captain Swing) of 1830 which started in Brede. Burwash was the third parish to rise because of the "harassing manner in which they (agricultural labourers) were treated": machinery was broken, arson was rife and overseers were dumped in the next parish. Troops were quickly deployed and the 5th Dragoons were sent to the Weald, with deportation following for those responsible who were caught. The rising fizzled out but attention had been drawn to the problem. Wages were raised by local farmers but the discontent rumbled on, exacerbated by the 1834 Poor Law Amendment Act which was seen as repressive and had led to Burwash becoming part of the Poor Law Union of Ticehurst. This general discontent was the start of organised protests by labourers about their conditions which was to lead to the formation of Unions and other collective bodies in Victorian times.

Chapter Four

DENES HOUSE AND ITS INHABITANTS

The origins of Denes House are not known but it is likely that there has been a house on the site for some four centuries. Its proximity to the church, frontage onto the High Street, the surviving earlier houses below in Bell Alley and the known presence of houses to the west (on the sites of Ivy, Rampyndene and Mount House) make it probable that it formed one of a row of medieval houses on the south side of the road stretching at least as far as the old rectory (old Rectory Court). Within the existing Denes House is an older house, that survives in the front half of the building. This part is of heavy timber construction, with oak beams and wattle and plaster walls; it has lower ceilings and the smaller room proportions of an earlier age. There is an L-shaped extension at the western end and an old barn behind which was later used for horses and carriage. Internally the house looks as if it could have been either three cottages or a single long low house which probably dates from the 16th or 17th century. The name Denes, or Dene, is a mystery although there is a very slight possibility that there was at one time a Dean of Burwash as the records show in 1224 a certain Gualteris Delanus de Burghershe (Walter, Dean of Burwash). If there was such a Deanery it could have been connected to this house.

In the early part of the 17th century it was owned by the Waterer family and in 1630 Thomas Waterer and his bride Elizabeth Purchin (of Brightling) moved in. In 1675 Thomas Waterer died and left it to his widow who passed it on to their daughter Elizabeth who was married to Nicholas Manser of Mottynsden. Elizabeth ultimately left it to her cousin Ann (nee Purchin) who was married to Edward Wilson, clerk, younger son of Sir William Wilson Bt. of Eastbourne. Edward was Rector of East Blatchington, Vicar of Framfield and Vicar of Rye.

In 1714 the young lawyer William Shadwell married Susanna, daughter of John Wood, the elder, of Burwash and moved to the village to set up his legal practice. He was the son of Thomas Shadwell and his wife Mary (nee Dabson of Ringmer); William's older brother Thomas had married Susannah Gunn of Middleham, also in Ringmer. William and Susanna Shadwell were to have five children but only one, Mary, born in 1719, was to survive childhood. At first the Shadwells lived in rented accommodation until in 1720 he purchased two houses, Denes House from Edward Wilson, and The Ivy next door, from William Morphew (Morpheus or Morfey). He lived in the latter all his life, probably improving it and giving it its current appearance.

William Shadwell established a thriving practice, his name appearing on a vast number of contemporary documents, and this business on his death in 1749 passed to Thos. Parham and later to James Philcox whose son, also James, formed the long lasting partnership of Baldock and Philcox.

Shadwell rented out Denes House until 1743 when he gave it to Mary in anticipation of her forthcoming marriage to John Constable of Shoyswell, Turzes and Court Lodge farms. Either William Shadwell or his future son-in-law John Constable carried out extensive work to Denes House in 1743 and the result was the structure that can be seen today. The original house, or row of cottages, was covered by a Georgian veneer, merely disguising the structure without altering its older, smaller proportions. The back part of the house was added on and had rooms of Georgian height and proportions, with mouldings and fireplaces to match. The result of the alterations was a medium sized but fairly plain Georgian village house which has hardly changed its appearance or internal layout to this day.

Denes House

Denes House and Its Inhabitants **73**

The Constables were duly married in 1744 and had twelve children between 1745 and 1761. Of these, three died in infancy, and six, although living to middle or old age, did not marry. Martha married John Fry (of Frys, Spring Lane) at the late age of thirty-eight and it was only the eldest son, William, and daughter, Mary, born in 1745 and 1748 respectively who continued the family story. John Constable seems to have led an uneventful life as a wealthy landowner and he hardly features in local affairs. He died in 1776, his wife Mary dying seven years later in 1783. They did, however, live to see the double wedding on 21 February 1775 of William to Barbara Strother, daughter of Rev.George Strother of Penton Mewsey, Hampshire, and Mary to the newly arrived lawyer James Philcox. James and Mary Philcox purchased Youngs Garden and were the first of three generations of Philcox to live there and practice law in Burwash, while William and Barbara soon moved into Denes House. Here they had four sons but young William died at birth, William Philip at five, and George Strother at nine. Only the second son, John, survived. William was a Justice of the Peace, churchwarden and played a considerable part in village and church life also becoming a trustee and treasurer of the Charity School in 1804. The house itself hardly changed from his parents' time but when Barbara died in 1801 William married again. He and his second wife Mary lived at Denes House until William's death in 1810, and on Mary's death it passed to their surviving son John with their extensive other property. John Constable was married to Frances Dodson and was now Vicar of Ringmer, living at Middleham which had come to him indirectly from his great-great-uncle Thomas Shadwell. Denes House then entered a sad period when it was either unoccupied or let, often to the Curate of St Bartholomew's, for nearly forty years.

In 1856, a Doctor James Weston Combs, who qualified in 1850, was appointed surgeon of the Burwash medical division of the Ticehurst Union at a salary of £36.10s.0d. per annum, and married Louisa Philcox, granddaughter of James and Mary. She was the daughter of the second James Philcox and sister of the third, both of whom were by then partners in Baldock and Philcox. The Combs initially rented Denes House from Louisa's cousin the Rev. John, but when he died in 1864, followed by his wife in 1866, they purchased the property from John's executors. Combs made himself locally unpopular by also purchasing The Ivy over the head of the popular tenant John Barrow. The Combs at first entered fully into village life and as well as his work at Ticehurst James had a thriving practice in the village. But then all three of their children successively died, the two boys under the age of six and Anna Louisa aged seventeen, and James turned to drink. In September 1879 he was admitted to Matlock, a home for alcoholics. He spent the next few years in and out of Matlock and on one of his spells at home in 1884 he was shouting so loudly in the road outside the house that morning service was interrupted in St Bartholomew's. He was sacked from his post at Ticehurst and struck off the medical register, dying in 1890. His widow lived on at Denes House, which was by now known as

Combs House, until her death in 1902. As Louisa had no surviving children Combs House and The Ivy passed to her cousin Angela Louisa Hughes who was the daughter of the Rev. Albert Hughes. Louisa Combs died a rich woman for among her numerous cash bequests totalling £6,000, she left £500 each to the Clifford sisters of Church House, and to Helen Egerton, and £100 to her goddaughter Katherine Egerton.

Denes House and the High Street around 1900

Angela Hughes had also inherited Youngs Garden on the death of Louisa Combs' batchelor brother James Philcox in 1896 but she never lived in Burwash. She married Raymond Yonge Anderson-Morshead in 1912 but by then had sold The Ivy to Henry Wemyss Feilden in 1907, abruptly terminating Charles Brooks' lease. She initially rented Denes House to Mrs Bostock but after she left in 1912, Angela sold it in 1919 to Helen Egerton for £1,500. Finally she sold Youngs Garden to Mr and Mrs Bowen in 1922. Angela Anderson-Morshead acknowledged her good fortune by giving new choir stalls to St Bartholomew's church and putting a plaque in the chancel which traces her ancestry (slightly inaccurately) back to the Constables; when she died in 1931 she established the Louisa Combs memorial fund to provide and pay for a nurse in the parish and gave £1,000 to endow a bed in a hospital for the poor in further memory of James Philcox. In the churchyard the main Constable family tomb is flanked by the graves of their relatives, the Philcox and Combs families.

Helen Egerton was the widow of the Rev. John Coker Egerton, and moved in with her three unmarried daughters Katherine, Helen Mary and Caroline Augusta. Her fourth daughter Sybil had married Austin Charles Longland QC and her son John had emigrated to South Africa where he died in 1929. Helen Egerton, on her husband's death in 1888 had first lived at Ashlands with her husband's cousin Ellen Gould and had then moved to Hurst Green, so this was a happy homecoming to the village where she had lived as a young wife. Helen Egerton lived at Denes House until her death in 1942 at the age of ninety-one and her surviving daughters stayed there until 1967 by which time Helen and Caroline had died and Katherine and Sybil Longland decided to sell. The Egerton ladies were gifted artistically and musically and ran a small music school in the western, or servants, end of the house which was also used as a flat for a short time by some of those made homeless by the bombs in Shrub Lane in 1944. Helen Egerton had also inherited the Advowson of Burwash Rectory (the gift of the living) from her husband and in 1927 she decided it was in the long-term interest of the parish for the living not to be owned by a single individual and she therefore gave it to her husband's college Brasenose, Oxford. She stipulated that "the best man is appointed regardless of Diocesan or other pressure" and "the Rector should not be an extremist in either direction" and the living should "never be sold or fall into the hands of a Bishop or patronage board".

Mrs Waite owned the house briefly from 1967-70 and then Mr and Mrs Clifford Lavers lived there for thirteen years: sadly their son Mark was killed in the Hither Green rail accident of 1967 and they made gifts to the church in his memory. The Lavers were followed by the Hulbert Powells (1983-85) and Chips and Sally Bishop (1985-93) who sold it to John and Audrey Barkshire.

In many ways, much as Burwash is a microcosm of English or Sussex rural life, so Denes House is a typical village house and its story is mirrored in many others. It had been the home of one family for almost two hundred years, another for nearly fifty years and then had five owners in twenty-six years in the last quarter of the twentieth century. The old stability of village life and families has been replaced in modern times by a constantly changing population.

Chapter Five

VICTORIA TO WORLD WAR
1837-1918

Queen Victoria came to the throne in 1837 on the death of her uncle just after the start of an era which was to enjoy one of the longest periods this country has ever known without a major conflict or threat from the outside. This lasted from 1815 to 1914 but it was to end with one of the bloodiest wars of all time which was also to become an historical watershed that saw a dramatic change in the structure of life in England. This long peace, only interspersed with short or minor wars, combined with the growing economic importance of the Empire, allowed the people and the government to turn their thoughts and energies inwards to domestic matters and the serious business of industrialisation and wealth creation.

There were continuous and progressive changes in science, medicine, industry and commerce as well as in education and social reform. Trade Unions grew in influence after the 1825 Act legalised them and the 1871 and 1875 Acts increased their power. The Amalgamated Society of Engineers grew from twelve thousand members in 1851 to twenty-four thousand in 1860. The co-operative movement was founded in 1844 by the Rochdale Pioneer Society. In 1870 Dr T J Barnardo opened his first home and in 1878 Rev. William Booth founded the Salvation Army. The Boys Brigade came into being in 1883 and in 1884 Arnold Toynbee opened "Toynbee Hall". In 1863 Charles Kingsley published "The Water Babies" depicting the life of Grimes and little Tim, and the 1864 Chimney Sweep Act restricting the use of child labour quickly followed. Other reforms included the Sale of Food and Drugs Act 1875, which lasted until 1928, setting a comprehensive list of standards but unfortunately missing practices such as putting salt in beer to create more thirst. The 1850 Factory Act followed the 1842 Report on Children's Employment by the committee under Lord Shaftesbury who was later to form the Shaftesbury Homes as model dwelling houses. The 1848 and 1866 Public Health Acts compelled local authorities to provide sanitary inspectors and led to the subjugation of the rights of individuals to the interests of the population to enable comprehensive sewerage to be introduced. Further Acts in 1888 and 1894 created more representative and accountable local government.

In the political arena a succession of great statesmen and politicians dominated the scene including Wellington, Gladstone, Disraeli, Salisbury, Rosebury, Balfour and Asquith, and in 1908 a young Winston Churchill was appointed President of the Board of Trade. For the first time newspapers brought news of politics and politicians to the population and both pubs and clubs witnessed fierce debates on the issues of the day. In 1842 Barry's new Houses of Parliament were opened but when, in 1884, the House of Lords held up the Franchise Bill designed to make the franchise more equal, newspaper headlines said "Peers against the People" and, referring to the hereditary peerage, "mend them or end them".

The Great Exhibition, designed to show off the nation's industrial prowess, opened in Hyde Park in 1851 and sport flourished through the popularity of figures such as Dr W G Grace (cricketer) between 1870 and 1886; the Football Association was founded in 1863 and the first Rugby Union club, Blackheath, in 1860. The National Trust was formed in 1895 and in the arts this was the age of Dickens, Thackeray, Trollope and Bronte, of theatre and pantomime, Sadlers Wells and St James Hall. Only in music did few great Englishmen emerge, the performances being dominated by European composers. `In medicine ether was replaced by chloroform and the British Medical Association was founded in 1854.

Transport was revolutionised by the introduction of networks of railways covering most of the country. In 1825 the first steam train ran from Stockton to Darlington, by 1837 there were five hundred miles of track, by 1843 two thousand miles and 1848 five thousand miles. In 1841 the London to Brighton line opened. The only obstacle to progress was the reluctance of landowners to allow railways to be built on their property and this was overcome by the compulsory purchase powers included in the individual Railway Acts that gave the authority for each line to be developed.

The South Eastern Railway Company, motto "Onwards", laid their line first from London to Tonbridge, extended it to Tunbridge Wells in 1845, and were then authorised to further extend it to Hastings in September 1845. This part opened in three phases, Tunbridge Wells to Robertsbridge, via Stonegate (then known as Ticehurst Road station) and Etchingham in September 1851, to Battle by January 1852 and Hastings a month later. This local development was repeated all over the country and was a great national achievement. However an immediate side effect was the bankruptcy and closure of the network of toll roads as the faster, more comfortable and cheaper railway travel, with connections all over the country, quickly supplanted the comparatively uncomfortable coach rides. The one thousand one hundred turnpikes of 1850 had shrunk to eight

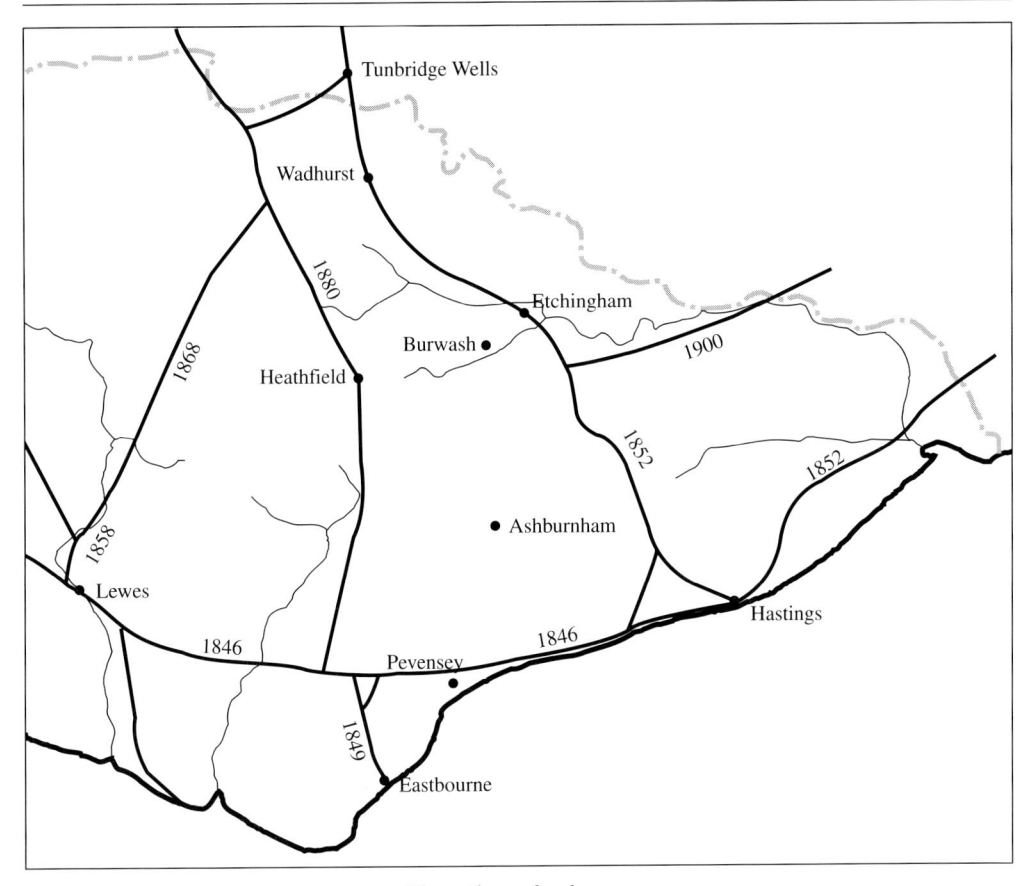

The railway development

hundred and fifty-four by 1871 and two by 1890. Tollhouses were sold and the responsibility for the upkeep of the roads passed back to the local authority. In Burwash the main turnpike through the village and the four mile spur from Burwash Common to Stonegate were closed and the Trust liquidated in 1866, just fifteen years after the railway opened. Its revenues had declined steadily from their peak of £2,409.6s.8d. in 1834 to £1,877.11s.0d. in 1850, at which time its debts stood at over £5,000. Of the four tollgates, the one between Denes House wall and the churchyard (Churchgate) was removed in 1855 and the tollhouse, standing where the churchyard is now extended, was purchased by the Rev. Joseph Gould for £9.0s.0d and pulled down. In 1866 James Philcox purchased the tollhouse on the Stonegate road (Swinggate), which abutted his property at Goodsole, for £10.0s.0d. and the tollhouse (Towngate) next to his own house Youngs Garden for £35.0s.0d. The fourth gate at the top of Spring Lane (Wheelgate) was purchased by the neighbouring blacksmith John Crossingham the elder for £25.0s.0d. Sadly the tollgate keeper at Wheelgate, Joseph Morris, committed suicide on losing his job.

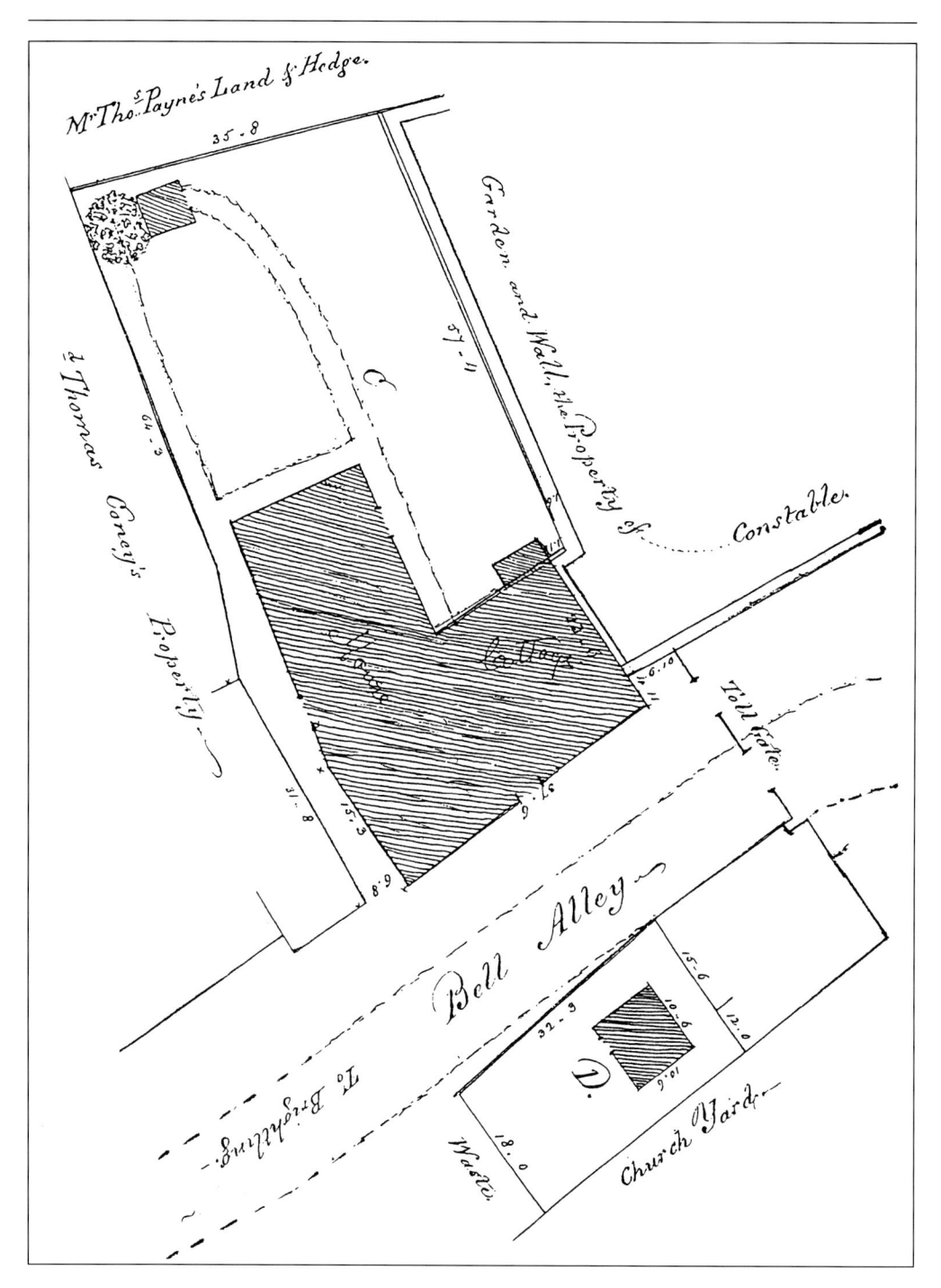

Bell Alley tollgate (Churchgate)

The other effect of the railway development was on employment. In Burwash, by the year the railway opened in 1851, there were twelve railway workers living in the village, and a few years later Philip Knowles, a platelayer, was living in a small cottage at the Crowhurst Bridge crossing and his wife Hester was the gatekeeper, opening and shutting the gate for road users. By 1870 the duties of gatekeeper had been taken over by their son Charles, aged fourteen who, when his parents died, succeeded his father as platelayer and his wife Caroline took over as gatekeeper; this family arrangement continued into the 20th century.

By 1860 daily transport was provided to Etchingham Station by William Mainwaring, the publican at the Admiral Vernon, while Amos Jenner of the White Hart offered a weekly service to Lewes on Mondays. By 1887 Albert Hawkins had taken over the Admiral Vernon and, as well as the daily transport service, had been appointed the official agent for the South Eastern Railway and the London Chatham and Dover Railway. James Hicks of Lime Cottage also offered a daily service to Etchingham as well as a Friday journey to Hastings. By 1914 the service to Etchingham had increased to four times daily but it was not until the 1930s that a regular bus service arrived, going to Tunbridge Wells several times daily as well as to the station.

The energy of the Victorians was remarkable, as was their self-confidence and self-belief, but their often very necessary reforms and legislation were also the start of the state beginning to take responsibility for the way people lived their lives. There was emerging a centrally set framework which initially had most impact on London and other fast growing cities but also began to effect villages such as Burwash.

In 1829 Sir Robert Peel (when Home Secretary) had founded the Metropolitan Constabulary (the Met., staffed by Bobbies or Peelers as they were known). He also paved the way for police forces outside London through the passing of the permissive County Police Act (1839) which allowed Justices in counties to establish police on the lines proposed by the Royal Commission of 1838. Before this in Sussex only Brighton had had an organised force and the rest of the county had only two types of officers: High Constables appointed by the Hundred, and Petty Constables appointed by the parish. This early form of neighbourhood watch led to individuals being required to serve as constables for twelve months, unpaid. Such was the unpopularity and indeed accompanying physical danger, that appointees often actually paid substitutes to act for them. The Sussex Constabulary was founded in 1840 with Captain Mackay as its first Chief Constable. Its use was soon proved by the 1847 Lewes Bonfire Night riot when burning tar barrels were rolled through the streets and fifty men from the Met. were drafted in to assist the one hundred and thirty local officers.

The Police House 1859

Police houses and lockups gradually spread, but only slowly until 1857 when Mackay ordered a vigorous building programme of fifteen new police stations which included Burwash. The Police House was built in 1859 providing accommodation for a sergeant and a constable and their families as well as cells and offices. It was built on the western part of the old site of Olivers Garden replacing the cottage built by Richard Reeves in 1831. The land and that dwelling were purchased in 1859 for £225 by William Vidler Langridge, Clerk to the Peace, for the new police station. The cost of £585.16s.0d. included the destruction of the old cottages, re-using their bricks, and building two cells with walls 14" thick, each containing "a deal bench 3" thick with a 1½" deal board for a pillow".

Sergeant John Peerless and Constable Henry Maynard were duly installed and soon in action. Late in 1859 a special train of thirty-six carriages from London brought people down to attend a prize fight. The train stopped four hundred yards short of Etchingham Station at 10.45 pm, dropped the people and waited the other side of the station until 2.30 am, when the second fight was over, and then returned to pick them up. The policemen heard of the fight and tried to reach the ring to stop it, but were surrounded. They summoned help but by the time it arrived the crowd had left. The sergeant and constable were personally commended for their action while the railway company was criticised for bringing a large number of people to commit a breach of the peace and for the dangerous expedient of leaving a train on the track between stations for nearly four hours.

Another incident occurred in 1865 when Maynard's successor John Ditton had arrested a certain Henry Weston, aged sixty-two, who had been sentenced by the Hurst Green Bench to four months imprisonment for assaulting his wife. He put him in the cells but when he next came to observe him Weston had hanged himself using two handkerchiefs tied to a water pipe. The Coroner's Court was held in the Police House and found that he was not "of unsound mind memory and understanding but lunatic and distracted". The foreman of the jury was Edwin Honeysett and the rest of the jury were all upstanding local citizens such as Fleming, Vigor and Rochester.

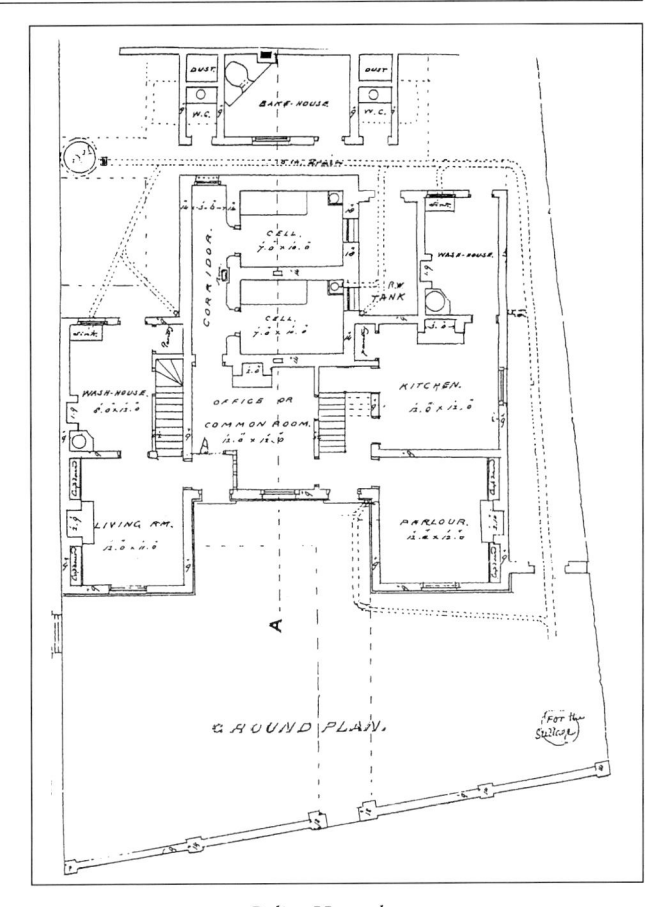

Police House layout

Bicycles were introduced to the Force in 1895 "only for the rapid pursuit and following up of suspected criminals". The instructions forbade racing and said "no constable over thirteen stone may ride a bicycle". A little later instructions were issued that "all P.C's will have their hair properly cut once a month".

Many forms of communication were being developed with the most important being the introduction of the postal system and the telegraph network. From about 1850 an increasing number of private companies offered competing telegraph services and concern was expressed at the number of unsightly telegraph poles that were appearing not only along the new railway lines but also along roads. In 1868 the companies were effectively nationalised when the Post Office took them over while two years earlier in 1866 the Great Eastern Steamship had laid the first telegraph line to America. In 1875

Graham Bell invented the telephone and by 1878 the first telephone in Burwash was installed by Bentham Fuller at the village stores.

Of at least equal importance was the introduction of a national system of postage. There had been a postal system of sorts for some hundreds of years and back in the 17th century a single sheet, folded and sealed (as envelopes had not been invented) cost 2d. to be sent from Burwash to London. By the 19th century there was a regular flow of letters but as every individual item was weighed and then franked before being carried by a private carrier this means of correspondence was largely the preserve of the better off. In 1840 Rowland Hill came to the conclusion that to charge a single rate for all normal letters, regardless of distance, would average out and that the ease and speed of fixing a single prepaid stamp would encourage a far greater use of the system. Thus the Penny Post was introduced, the Post Office was formed, and within three years the number of letters nationally had grown to four million a week and in twenty-five years had reached twelve million. In Burwash John Blunden had opened his shop in Villiers and was appointed Postmaster and Post Office Keeper in 1841. By 1860 letters arrived from Hurst Green by mail cart at 2.30 am. and were delivered by 7.30 am. The collecting box closed daily at 10 pm. (Sundays 9 pm.) and the letters were despatched by 11 pm. Money orders were also cashed and issued by this office and a Savings Bank facility was added. By 1878 John Woodall had taken over as Postmaster and there were two deliveries a day at 7 am. and 2.30 pm. but by 1895 it had been relegated to being a sub-Post Office, at which time letters were also required to have Sussex S.O. added to their address. Parcel post started in 1883.

༻༺

Heating and lighting were due to be transformed by the use of gas. By the early 1800s gas lighting was introduced to streets and homes in London and this led to the formation of the Gas Light & Coke Company in 1812. The Burwash Gas Company was formed towards the end of the century with its works next to the brickworks at Claws. Here it made gas from coke and supplied the village with gas for heating, lighting and cooking. The Ticehurst & District Water & Gas Co. pumping station, which was at Crowhurst Bridge railway crossing, provided the means of supplying the gas to the village.

༻༺

Education was another subject close to Victorian hearts and they gradually moved towards a system of universal schooling. From 1833 national schools had been given small grants to assist in the education of the poor to replace the rather proscriptive voluntary grants given by the "National Society for Educating the Poor in the Principles of the Established Church" since its formation in 1811. The 1833 Factories Act had established the principle of public inspection and this spread to other fields such as mines and then to schools. By 1858 schools inspectors were examining progress in reading, writing and arithmetic and grants were paid according to the results. The 1870 Education Act was to formally adopt this principle. There was also an advance in women's education led by two evangelists, Miss Beale (first Headmistress of Cheltenham Ladies College) and Miss Buss (North London Collegiate School). They set standards for boarding and day schools for girls that were to survive well into the next century. Girls in Burwash had however been receiving education in equal numbers to boys since the start of the Charity School in 1727. The Charity School, now called the National School, had, despite the alterations and improvements, outgrown its old premises on the Square and in 1843 moved to a new site in Bell Alley. Before it moved an inspection stated that the old school building was in bad repair. At the new site there was provision for nearly three hundred and fifty boys, girls and infants and a new young Headmaster, Alfred Cox, took over the new school at the age of twenty-three and at a salary of £40 per annum "and two shillings and sixpence for every scholar per quarter beyond sixty". It was also recorded that in consideration of Mr Cox's good conduct the agreement was to take effect from 1st January 1843, although Cox did not start until March that year. In 1844 he married Matilda Thompson, a neighbour in Bell Alley. Sadly he succumbed to alcohol by 1867 and was replaced by George Ansett in 1870 who was to be Headmaster for seventeen years before he in turn handed over to

The National School

Hugh Thornton and then James Self in 1895. The old school premises on the Square were let out unaltered as accommodation and garden until three new pairs of cottages (now Broads Cottages) were erected in 1863. They collectively generated an annual rent of £5.10s.0d. In 1853 the school farm in Wadhurst was sold and the proceeds plus £200 realised from the sale of government stock were used to purchase Bines Farm at Witherenden. This too produced an increased rent. The school estate was further improved by the purchase in 1867 of two cottages next door to the school, for £305, to house staff and provide an office.

Then came the Education Act of 1870 which stated that education should be available to every child and that schools were to be paid for out of local rates and governed by locally elected boards. It also made the provision of elementary education by the local council compulsory where the existing facilities provided by Anglican or dissenting churches was inadequate. The test applied meant there had to be school places available for one-sixth of the population. Burwash had two thousand, two hundred and thirty-two inhabitants, requiring three hundred and seventy-two places, which were well covered by a combination of the National School (343) and the new St Philips School (111) at the Common. Thereafter the government grant was based on a mixture of attendance percentage and quality of results as measured by the annual government inspector's visit. The 1870 Act was followed by the 1902 Act which was one of the most far reaching pieces of legislation of the time. It brought all schools, public elementary, and voluntary or private, into a single system whereby responsibility for the provision of education passed to County Councils. Local school boards were abolished and replaced by managers who, in return for providing the buildings, were allowed to retain the appointment of teachers. They also received a much larger subsidy, from local rates, to enable them to maintain buildings and employ and pay a reasonable number of teachers. Burwash received its share of the increased grant although the 1872 inspector's report graded the school as poor and required it to improve accommodation, attendance, and create a proper separate infants class. This was done but for some years the school continued to receive critical reports and in 1880 was fined for twenty-five per cent absenteeism and employing two unqualified teachers. In 1885 the grant was reduced from £145 to £110 for similar reasons. Matters improved after the arrival of Mr Self and the inspections and reports steadily got better.

School life very much revolved round the village calendar, with summer holidays being fixed by the hop picking season and varying in length from six to eight weeks depending on the speed of the harvest. Holidays were also given on Fair days and the days of the horticultural show. The school itself had an annual feast which in 1867, as well as providing food such as beef and plum pudding included games of football, trapbat, cricket, races, catching halfpence on the back of a chair, scrambling, sack races and three legged races.

Another preoccupation of the school was constant disease. Measles, mumps, influenza, whooping cough, chicken pox, ringworm and scarlet fever all had the school closed regularly for several weeks by the Medical Officer but the worst threat, accompanied by deaths, came from diptheria. In 1901 and 1902 the school was closed for five weeks, reopened for two weeks and was then closed again four times for periods varying from one to four weeks as the disease reappeared again. In 1898 Alfred Akehurst and his two brothers were sent to Dr Hines who diagnosed "the itch" and in 1913 the Pennells family of six were sent home "because of their unclean state". When brought back after being washed by their mother they were inspected and rejected because "the two boys' clothes were still verminous" and the family was put under the supervision of the NSPCC.

In 1910 the school building was first used as an election polling station. Empire Day (May 24) was another holiday and typically in 1911 "the children were assembled in the playground around the Flag, Empire songs were sung and an address given by Colonel Fielden CB. The Drum and Fife Band played the National Anthem, all boys standing at the salute. A procession was then formed and headed by the band paraded through the village with banners flying. On returning to the school buns and oranges and ginger beer were distributed." These annual parades continued until 1918 when war rationing made it impossible to get refreshments and the parade was abandoned, never to be reinstated.

During this time there were still a number of private teaching establishments with Mrs Pilbeam running a Dame School for trades people's children and Miss Shavell a school for the "better class of farmer". A Roman Catholic school was opened in Spring Lane when the new church was built towards the end of the century. But by far the longest lasting was Mrs Emma Pagden who combined her dressmaking with running a school in her home from 1837 to 1884. Henry Pagden had come to Burwash and lived with his young local bride Emma throughout their married life in part of the old Rectory. Here Henry carried out his tailors business and their children including Henry Junior (1845) and Thomas(1847) were born. Emma also had her day school in the house and this no doubt kept the family going after Henry's early death in 1865, at which time her two sons started their own tailors business at the ages of seventeen and nineteen. Emma Pagden accused the National School of enticing her pupils away in 1876 but moved to Gideon House at about that time, when she had sufficient numbers to employ Fanny Flack, living next door in Popes Cottage. Emma finally gave up her school in 1884 at the age of seventy after fifty-seven years of teaching, having been a monitor at the Charity School in the Square, then starting her own school at the age of thirteen in her mother's house before she married Henry. She now joined her sons in business, calling herself a draper until she died in 1892.

The long period of peace was punctuated only by a few relatively short, if historically memorable, wars but the army was totally reformed by Edward Cardwell's Army Regulation Bill (1871). These reforms stemmed from the inadequacies shown up by the Crimean War (1854-6) in incidents like the Battle of Balaclava and the heroic but ill conceived Charge of the Light Brigade. This war was also notable for Florence Nightingale's achievements in bringing nursing skills and care to the battlefield which led to a new standard of nursing in hospitals at home and abroad. This campaign was the first where newspaper commentators were at the front line, reporting the successes and mistakes of the Generals and bringing the flavour of the battles and conditions of the soldiers to the notice of the public. Reform was thus both necessary and inevitable and Cardwell's fundamental changes covered equipment, training, and organisation and also introduced the County Regiment system, with local recruiting and pride; this system still lies at the heart of the Army. Curiously the 35th Foot, raised in 1701, had been named Sussex Regiment in 1805 and received its Royal title in 1832. Cardwell's action led to the new Regiment being firmly rooted in the County until its absorption into the large Queens Regiment in 1966. The Boer War of 1899-1902 featured the new County Regiment who have South Africa on their battle honours. The Royal Sussex were later to have twenty-three Battalions in the 1914-18 war with six thousand eight hundred casualties. This local emphasis was also endorsed by Lord Haldane in 1907 when the Territorial and Reserve Forces Act founded the Territorial Army based on the same geographical links.

Serving with the Royal Sussex from the start of the Boer War were William Watts, Edward Farley and John Mewett and they were joined in 1901 by five more volunteers, Privates F Brook, C A Brooke, J Woodall, Funnell and Maskell. Also serving in South Africa were Corporal (later Sergeant) Albert Jarvis (with the local C Company 1st Cinque Ports Regiment), Stephen Isted (19th Hussars at Ladysmith), Edward Pennells (Rifle Brigade), Horton Aitkens (South African Light Horse) under General Buller, and William Watson (Royal Lancashire). Pennells was killed in December 1900 but the rest returned safely. At home Burwash had twenty-eight men in the volunteer 4th Bn. Royal Sussex and Second Lieutenant Jefferson (Laurelhurst) was gazetted into C Company.

Before this Burwash had had its share of men serving in the forces earlier in the century and in 1858, just after the end of the Crimean war, there were three in the cavalry, four marines, four sailors and four infantry, serving in various parts of the world. Of the cavalrymen Sergeant Major Bond had served nineteen years with the 11th Hussars in the Crimea and France, collecting four campaign medal clasps. Sergeant Russell had been with the 16th Lancers and in 1859 John Pankhurst, son of William and Martha of Pump Court, came home after seventeen years with the 9th Lancers in India. Alfred Cornwall, son of

Aaron of Southside, was serving with the Marines in China, Private Booth with the Artillery in Corfu, and John Collier's brother George was killed at Lucknow while serving in India as a Corporal in the Rifle Brigade. But not all had successful careers: William Pope, who joined the 24th Foot in 1871 with Ed Jenner, overstayed his leave a year later and was arrested. John Sawyer, however, joined the Royal Sussex Regiment and made his way steadily up the ladder to become a Sergeant by 1885 and to receive a request from the Adjutant, Captain Pierson, to sign on for another six years with the Colours in 1886. Burwash wives also travelled, with Ellen Fleming, sister of James, marrying Sergeant Parkins of the Royal Artillery and spending ten years in India, returning in 1876, while in 1871 Henrietta Price of Tott Cottage married Sergeant William Eaton of the Grenadier Guards. Others serving included Sergeant Brown (Transport), Private Dann, (90th Foot), Charles Lester (Signalman HMS Ready in the Persian Gulf), Stephen Pope (Marines), James Gorringe (Navy), and Stephen Mainwaring, who started as a waiter on RMSS Nizan (P & O Line) in 1882 before being promoted to saloon steward on the India and China route.

✤

The growth of industry effected much of England but in Sussex it was the health of agriculture which decided the level of employment and the state of the local economy. This varied between different villages, depending on their crops and soil and the proficiency of the farmers. The price of wheat, and thus bread, had been kept high by the Corn Law, which was repealed in 1846. The protection given to farmers by this Law had also led to steady employment and with the greater intensity of farming the numbers working on the land slightly increased even with the introduction of more machinery: this was contrary to the expected unemployment which had earlier led to the Swing riots. The anticipated ruination did not follow the repeal as the 1850s and 1860s were years of good weather and harvests, with a lot of land under the plough, and prosperity reached its peak by 1870. A series of bad harvests then opened the floodgates for foreign grain. Cheap Russian grain was followed by more from the great American prairies where a combination of economies of scale, growth of railways, new machinery, cheap land and fast economical ships led to large volumes being exported at low prices which drastically undercut English prices even though these halved between 1877 and 1885. The result was that imported grain grew from 2% of consumption in 1840, to 24% in 1870 and to 65% in 1890. As a result between 1871 and 1881 ninety-two thousand workers left the land and rural unemployment hit a new peak. The agricultural depression of 1875-84 which caused this was followed by a deeper one in 1891-99; more land went out of production or was returned to pasture for sheep and milk. The meat trade was also hit by the start of frozen meat imports from Australia, New Zealand and South Africa. In Burwash this cheaper meat was sold by Noakes Butchers (Chateaubriand) in 1870 and was enthusiastically purchased by the poor. The decline of British agriculture continued, as did the steady drift of the population to the new towns or to the hope offered by emigration.

One of the effects of rising rural unemployment was the embracing of the union concept by agricultural workers. Kent had been militant for some time and in 1873 its annual labourers union rally attracted eleven thousand, with five hundred from Sussex. In 1874 the Burwash branch of the Agricultural Labour Union was formed with seventy-four members and Mr Shearman as chairman. The branch was immediately torn apart by dissension especially on the issue of union sickness benefit. There were rallies during the summer of 1874 culminating in a procession on August 1st attended by four hundred and fifty people who finished the march in church where the Rector preached a sermon on the subject "Let brotherly love continue". The branch prospered but Shearman succumbed to pressure and resigned.

There had been emigration for some centuries for a variety of reasons. Early emigrants to America went to avoid religious persecution, and whenever an economic crisis hit England there were those who went abroad to seek employment, a better life and perhaps a hoped-for fortune. Burwash, like other villages, had seen some emigration, often from those who wished to escape the law, but the colonisation of Australia had encouraged a steady stream since 1819 when labourers could receive public assistance to make the journey. The concessionary fare was £2 but to qualify for free transport a couple had to be an agricultural labourer and domestic servant with two children or less. Thus George Blackford and his young bride Hannah Relf left his parents at the Blacksmiths Arms and emigrated to Australia in 1859. Then Charles Maynard, son of John and Sarah, at this time publicans at The Bear, who had been a Queen's scholar, musician and an apprentice schoolmaster under Alfred Cox in 1851 when aged 15, went on to become a successful schoolmaster in Hobart, Tasmania by 1860. Thomas and Nancy Twort had also left for Australia in 1858, and in addition there were a number of villagers who went to North America. They were followed by the disillusioned ex-Union chairman Shearman in 1875 with the Union contributing 4s. 0d. towards his fare. Thomas Eastwood went to Brisbane in 1885 and Harry Isted, son of William and Eliza of Lime Tree Cottage, and John Burgess sailed on the ORIANO in 1886 from Plymouth to settle in the Swan River Valley in Western Australia.

Religion flourished during the Victorian era and Burwash probably reached its religious peak as measured by the number of churches and size of the congregations. The national survey of the Diocese in 1851 showed St Bartholomew's with a total average

Sunday congregation at all services of five hundred (hence the enlargement of 1856), the Independent chapel two to three hundred (hence the new larger chapel of 1864), the Wesleyan chapel sixty, and the Calvinist chapel one hundred and forty-five. In addition they had nearly as many again in Sunday schools. This growth in other churches as well as the Church of England had been given a boost by the 1836 Marriages Act which allowed marriage ceremonies in Roman Catholic and Dissenting churches provided they were registered with the newly formed Registrar of Births, Deaths and Marriages.

In Burwash the Calvinist splinter group was led by William Buss who, after his expulsion from the Independent chapel, had built the new chapel in 1829 at Chant Meadow. Buss was a remarkable man: an agricultural labourer who signed the wedding registry with an X in 1837 when he married Harriot King, he then taught himself to read and write and became Minister at the chapel, after Mr. Weller, from 1843 until his death in 1872.

The main Independent chapel (now called the Congregational chapel) had been weakened by the repeated defections to other sects in the early years of the century. However the chapel was gradually revitalised by the return to the village of John Buss Noakes in 1839 after serving his grocer's apprenticeship in Uckfield. He and his wife Frances, and later his son John Simmons Noakes and his wife Sarah, were to be at the centre of the chapel for over seventy-five years. When John Buss Noakes arrived he found open dissension and the Minister, Rev. John Press, spent most of his time in his Heathfield chapel with Burwash getting only evening prayer once a month. Press said "there was no hope", "he could not be in two places at once" and he only "kept Burwash because of the dowry". Press left in 1849, replaced by Mr Watson until, in 1860, William Mather arrived. Mather provided stability and leadership and remained until his death in 1892. By 1864 the congregation had increased and a new chapel had been built, largely due to John Buss Noakes' efforts. The new chapel, next to Mount House, was described as a "neat and substantial building". It was certainly impressive and could seat a congregation of one hundred and fifty. Noakes became Senior Deacon and one of his final acts in 1887, the year before he died, was to launch an appeal to pay off their debt of £200. £203 was raised.

The old chapel was now unused and for some years was locked up but in 1886 a proposal was put forward that it be used as a library and as a home for the "Working Men's Institute and Reading Room" which had been founded in 1882 and had seventy-five members. A committee was formed of the Rev. Coker Egerton, John and George Fuller and William Ellis and an agreement was drawn up for its use at a peppercorn rent "provided it was kept in good repair". This proposal was given further encouragement by the Public Library Acts of 1892 and 1894 (Local Government Act) which allowed rural communities to have an official library. John Simmons Noakes, by then a Deacon, was not impressed as he felt the building was being "used for improper purposes". But greater trouble lay ahead.

92   Chapter Five

It was felt that a new, larger and better facility should be built to house the institute and library and that if the old chapel was demolished its site would be ideal for this purpose. Whereupon William Ellis, the only surviving old committee member, claimed the building for himself saying it was worth £60 - £100 and £6 p.a. rent. His case was helped by the fact that in 1896 it had been found that not only the other committee members but also all the trustees were dead, and the new appointees - the Pastor H. Suffolk and the Deacons, Thomas Dray and J S Noakes - had not been party to the original agreement. Led by J S Noakes a legal battle ensued and eventually Ellis lost when in 1898 Judge Emdon gave his verdict. A cottage in the village was hired as temporary premises in 1901 and on 10th August 1903 the Reading Room Committee met with Lt. Col. Arthur Sutherland Harris (of Burwash Place) as Chairman and "a scheme for a new and more commodious building for the village" was discussed. It was decided to ask Mr Cayle, architect of Tunbridge Wells, to inspect the old chapel and to advise as to it being in a suitable position for the new village institute and also to draw out plans and give an estimate of the cost. It was thought advisable to have some definite proposal to submit when calling a public meeting and before making an appeal. In June 1904 the appeal for the estimated cost of £700 was launched and fund raising began. Sutherland Harris held a ball in

Congregational Chapel

London which raised £120, there were bazaars and other events and eventually the money was raised. In 1905 Cayle was replaced as architect by H Chatfeild Clarke FRIBA from London who drew up the final plans, which were approved by the Committee. In 1906 Lusted and Sons quote was accepted for a large hall with dividing folding doors, a games room, billiard room, reading room, lavatory and entrance lobby. In 1907 the new Institute, eventually known as the Village Hall, was opened.

St Bartholomew's shared in the general religious revival largely due to the immense energy and enthusiasm of Reverend Joseph Gould who was Curate from 1824-40 and

The Village Institute 1907

Rector from 1840-67, purchasing the Advowson in 1835. Gould was responsible for the substantial restoration and rebuilding of the church and also for the idea of building a new church at Burwash Common. One of his last acts before he died was to lay its foundation stone. Gould was succeeded by his nephew Reverend John Coker Egerton, the diarist, who had been Curate. Egerton was followed in 1888 by Reverend Charles Frewin Maude, a distant relation of the Maude-Roxby's, who died at the altar steps in 1909 while giving communion. He was succeeded by Reverend R L Martyn-Linnington (1909-25). One of the features of St Bartholomew's at this time was its choir which numbered twenty-eight with eleven trebles, five altos, five tenors and seven basses. The choir also took part in local singing

1880 Burwash Singing Class Concert.

Expences.

	£	s	d
Music for Concert – postage & carriage –	1	4	0
Performers Fees –	6	6	0
Piano, with carriage to Burwash & back to J. Wells –	2	9	0
Programmes.		11	6
H. Blackford – 4 journeys –		10	0
Mr Chatfield's bill for platform &c.	1	10	0
Do. For help in moving & loading piano		2	0
Lighting –		3	6
Candles. paraffin & lighting for practices. as per bills –	1	11	3
Lamp broken after Concert –		3	0
Notices of Concert & postage		10	0
Paid by Revd J.C. Egerton to Church singers body since last concert. Decr 1878 £1"2"0 – Mar 1879 £1"4"0. June 1879 £1"0"0 Oct 1879. 1"6"0. Decr 1879. 1"4"0 Mar 1880 1"5"0	7	1	0
	22	**1**	**3**

Receipts.

	£	s	d
Morning – Tickets & programmes 10"19"0			
Evening Do Do 5"1"0	16	0	0
Deficiency	**£6**	**1**	**3**

1880 Concert

concerts which, although well supported, were not always a financial success.

At Burwash Common St Philips was completed in 1867 and consecrated by the Bishop of Chichester. The sermon was preached by the Bishop of Gibraltar who was the brother of Georgina, Emily and Sophia Trower who had been the moving force behind getting the church built. The sisters had purchased Buckles in 1864, renamed it Hollyhurst, and then considerably enlarged it from its original "little farm with 20 acres". They moved from Redhill as Sophia wrote "it threatened to become almost a suburb of London". In November 1864 they took possession of Hollyhurst with Georgina and Emily moving from their temporary lodgings in the White House. Sophia came down from Fulham on "23 November, a cold ungenial day, with pouring rain and a gale from the south west. The road was deep in mud, our fly was creaky and slow and piled up inside and out with baggage. As the sitting rooms were not yet in order, and building still going on for the new rooms, we dined upstairs in Emily's bedroom, drank our toasts and ate our oysters in primitive style". The sisters soon felt that this rather rough area would benefit from a church "the Common was the description of all that was reckless, rough and rude and its inhabitants bore the character of smugglers and poachers". They therefore gave an acre of land, engaged an architect and helped fund the cost of £2,465 for the church, churchyard and furniture. The following year a school was added at a cost of £426.15.0d and within three months had a roll of one hundred and nineteen children. This replaced the borrowed facility that they had used since they opened their first weekday school in 1866. "Miss Thompson was our schoolmistress and little Thomas Russell our monitor. We began with thirty children and Mary and Harriett Pope were among the first, tiny little twins who never missed plodding through the deep muddy lanes from Forge Farm." In 1877 the new Parish of Burwash Common was formed from parts of Burwash, Mayfield and Heathfield and with St Philips at its centre. A further eight acres were given by the Trowers on the high ground of the common to build a parsonage at a cost of £2,127. The Trowers' connection lasted until 1923 when Sir Walter Trower, a nephew of the sisters, died and all their property was sold. The house has now reverted to its original name of Buckles with the name Hollyhurst being carried on by one of the row of houses next door. On the other side of St Philips another substantial house, Oakdown, was built between 1871 and 1874 by the Hon. Mrs.Holland.

In addition to the various Protestant churches, a Roman Catholic church was to return to Burwash after over three hundred years. In the 1870s the rich Spanish family of de Murrietta and de los Heros bought Southover and in 1887 built the church of St Joseph's in its grounds. The architect was Bernard Wheeler, the cost £20,000 and the Bath stone and Italian marble building could accommodate a congregation of two hundred and fifty. Madame de los Heros ensured part of the congregation by sacking all the Protestants working on the Southover estate and only hiring practising Catholics - or those who converted. The church was followed by a Catholic school which appears to have started in 1890 in an iron structure that seems to have been opposite Holton House, in which it is thought that Mass had occasionally been said before the church was built. The school moved to the Southover site and could then accommodate two hundred and ninety-nine children but the average attendance under the first mistress Miss Sullivan was about thirty, which by 1899 had declined to twenty. The numbers remained very low until the school was revitalised after the 1914-18 war. The church itself was not viable as a parochial unit and after the de Murriettas left in 1893, due to financial difficulties at home in Spain, the church and presbytery were let to the Salesians. They ran a novitiate and looked after the spiritual needs of Catholics in the parish.

The Victorian era saw the first substantial changes to the buildings in the village for centuries. During this long period there had been only a few new buildings, and the general change in appearance from timber frame to tile hanging in the 18th century, but the majority of the houses were substantially unaltered and many totally without any form of improved facilities. The 19th century witnessed a number of the older buildings being replaced, infilling occurring and improved domestic facilities gradually being installed. It also saw the start of the expansion of the village, with houses being built on all the roads and lanes leading into it.

Burwash in 1839

At the east end of the village, down Shrub Lane, in 1850 only Old Shrub Farm (Nos 52 and 53 - The Shrub), Crowhurst Bridge Farm and a few simple cottages existed. The first new building took the name of Shrub Farm (Woodrising) and

Shrub Farm (Woodrising)

was built in 1857 by John Relf who farmed eighty acres by 1881. It was next owned by Miles Simpson, a retired silk merchant, who named it Shrub House and after him came Joseph Sheild, a farmer, before it was purchased by the Blaikleys. In addition to the crossing keeper's cottage other developments included the first six houses of Greenfield Road towards the end of the century and Kildare and Nos. 37 and 38 (Shamrock) in the same period.

At the top of Shrub Lane the sixteen houses comprising Bankside were built in the later part of the century, taking as their gardens an additional part of the orchard of Hoppers Croft (Church House). Next to them were the three pairs of 1863 cottages (Broads Cottages) and above them stood Irelands Cottages, taking their name from

Bankside

Irelands and Broads Cottages

Robert Ireland, master builder, and Soanes Cottages, owned by George Soane (or Sone), grocer and shopkeeper. These three lots of cottages together housed up to eighteen families. Included among them were the Blundens who carried on their hatters business until the 1850s when William Blunden died and his two sons, also in the trade, left the village. With their departure went the last hatters business in Burwash. Soane moved briefly to Farleys Corn Stores to become a sub-distributor of stamps but after his death in about 1855 his widow Susan, who was his second wife and twenty years younger, moved back to the cottage and became the local agent for the Norwich Union. Hoppers Croft was still occupied by the Tournays: Thomas had inherited the property on the death of his mother Ann (nee Goldsmith) and lived there with his sisters Ann (who had taken over as the girls' teacher at the National School) and Eleanor and uncle Joseph Goldsmith. By 1870 Ann had inherited the property and she then sold it in about 1873 to Mrs Ellen Clifford (widow of Isaac, bookseller of Tunbridge Wells) who lived there with her two young daughters Edith and Mabel. Mrs Clifford changed the name to Church House and after she died in 1900 her daughters continued to live there until the 1950s.

Adams Strake (Burghurst) had been acquired earlier in the century by David Hyland whose family by now owned or farmed Court Lodge Farm, part of Tott, Ham and Bowmans. When he died in 1855 his widow Charlotte stayed there with her son George, who was an officer in the GPO in London, and his wife Caroline. When George died the property was bought by F W Aitken, solicitor, in 1897. He took in J C Andrews as a partner and the firm of Aitkens and Andrews moved their offices here from Brickhouse Farm (Old Brick). They also acquired the goodwill of Baldock and Philcox and when their clerk Charles Brook lost his lease of Ivy House in 1907 he moved into the house which became both home and business premises, as was often the custom of local solicitors. Guestling (Linden Cottage) was purchased in 1866 by Edwin and Mary Honeysett from

Henry Piper and they continued the business of grocer and draper that had started there with Austen, Nepecker and Johnson over one hundred and fifty years earlier. The Honeysetts also acquired Colemans next door (Rose Cottage then Barclays Bank) which they let out while using the garden as a store for the shop. Colemans was variously described as "yards, garden, land together with a bakehouse since used as a woodhouse and office and the appurtenances thereto belonging". Pump Court was one or two residences with the Blackmiths yard next door and together with Dudwell, Bower and Oakbeam and Swan, Cygnet and Lime, provided accommodation for labourers, cordwainers, pattern-makers, dressmakers and other craftsmen operating one man businesses from their homes throughout the period.

The Noakes family purchased Yew Tree and Old Granary in 1842. They had originally rented them from Joseph Sawyer who had acquired the premises from John Ellis in 1832. Sawyer had also owned Oakbeam, Bower and Dudwell, and Chilston House, but was forced to sell them all when his business failed. Noakes & Son were grocers and general shopkeepers run by the leading non-conformists John Noakes senior and his son John, who was known as John Buss Noakes after his mother Elizabeth Buss. When John senior died in the 1850s John Buss Noakes took over the business, to be joined by his son John Simmons Noakes. When John Buss Noakes himself died in 1888 his widow Frances moved next door to Grove Villa (St Anthony's) where her daughter, a school teacher, had lived since 1865. The business now became Noakes Brothers with Walter joining his brother John, and remained in the family until after the 1914-18 war.

Burwash in 1910

Everton Cottages and the dwellings behind were divided into between four and eight units at various times with the front and back often being in different occupancy. Thomas Leadbetter lived in No.1 for over fifty years being a gingerbread baker and was still working there, aged eighty-five, in 1880. Another long-term resident was Harry Spears, cordwainer, who lived at No.3 until he died in the 1880s after which his widow Ellen remained in residence. In Ham Lane there were still a number of very poor, near hovel, dwellings, now gone although the sites can still be identified from the unploughable patches. The main dwelling was Ham Place, on the site of the Oast, which was farmed with sixty acres including Brooksmarle. On the south western corner of Ham Lane the premises seem to have been butchers for many years as John Park and John Vigor were running butchers shops next to each other by 1840. Vigor left in the 1850s and in 1870 Henry Park sold out after his father John Park hanged himself in the kitchen because of pain from a fractured skull. The buyer was James Jarvis who arrived in Burwash in the 1840s from Warbleton and had already purchased the corn stores (Farleys) and rented Ham Place farmland. He next bought the Blacksmiths Arms (Post Office and Foreman Freeman) before buying the butchers and houses to the corner of Ham Lane. These last he rebuilt in 1875 as they stand today. James' son Thomas had trained as a butcher elsewhere but came home in 1870 to marry Fanny Vigor and run the shop. Thomas' brother Albert farmed Court Barn Farm while another brother Henry was regarded as the National School's brightest pupil and in 1872 qualified as a veterinary practitioner. He was taken into partnership by Charles Taylor and following Taylor's death was in sole practice from 1883. Thomas and Fanny had five children. The eldest James built a shop in Burwash Common (where the nursing home Ashwood is now), the second, Albert, fought in the Boer War and on coming home was set up in the new shop in Etchingham. The third son Robert farmed Court Barn Farm with his uncle Albert, and the youngest Fred (F J Jarvis) fought in the 1914-18 war with the Northumberland Fusiliers before coming home to take over the Burwash butchers from his father. The only daughter Alma married Frank Daunt.

Beyond the Corn Stores was a draper and grocers (Chilston) owned first by Thomas Stone in 1840, then James James and then in 1857 by Traiton Rochester until he retired in 1873, by which time the business was close to collapse. However it was taken over by William Ellis who expanded the business and in 1897 was also appointed agent for Barclays Bank and various insurances. Ellis soon took his son William junior into partnership and by 1915 they were grocers, drapers and milliners. It was William Ellis junior who became Secretary of the Working Men's Club and Reading Room at the Old Chapel in 1887 and was involved in the later dispute there. Next door (Chateaubriand) was the other Vigor butchers shop run by John's brother Thomas. Thomas continued until about 1876 when the business was acquired first by George Lavender and then by another

Ellis Grocers, Corn Stores and Blacksmiths Arms (and Pig)

Noakes, Edward, who kept it until about 1915. Villiers was John Blunden's Post Office from 1840 to 1878 when he became a plumber and glazier, leaving the property to his wife in 1908 until she died in 1920. Their three daughters then sold it for £700. The two dwellings in between Villiers and the butchers were variously used as private residence or shops with Martha Fleming running a toy repository, stationers and book shop in what is now Broadview Kitchens from 1875 until after the turn of the century.

Another branch of the huge Noakes family owned the long standing clock and watch makers in Noakes Cottage. John Noakes started the business in the 1830s when he married Elizabeth and it was continued by his son Henry after his death in 1875 until about 1900. In Rover Cottage was the hairdresser and schoolmaster James Fleming (brother of Martha, Ellen and Fanny) and his wife Ann (nee Ellis). He had taken over the business from his father John who died aged eighty in 1839. James was also choirmaster and organist at St Bartholomew's. From his appointment in 1837 to his death in 1872 he missed only three Sundays and he also kept the church organ tuned and in repair but when he died it had to be replaced (in 1878) as nobody else understood it. He composed the Burwash Christmas Carol "Hail Happy Morn". His son took over the hairdressing and

Rover, Noakes and Villiers opposite Gideon and Chaunt, looking east

wigmaking business but soon gave up and the premises were then used by James' brother-in-law John Woodall who assumed the Post Office business in 1878 and who had married his sister Fanny. Woodall remained Postmaster there for over thirty years and by the end of the century had become a Roman Catholic thus starting the long line of Woodalls who have been staunch supporters of that church in Burwash ever since.

The old collection of cottages by now called Shadwell Row had Thomas Shadwell carrying on his fruiterers business in Revenue Cottage from the 1820s until he died in about 1875, whereupon his widow Mary carried it on for a further ten years. At Smugglers Cottage lived William Twort, rat catcher, and his wife Mary, until he died and his son Thomas inherited the business. Thomas and his wife Nancy both wanted to emigrate to Australia, having no children, and raised part of the £2 needed for the fare by selling their dog and ferret for £1 to their next door neighbour James Copper in 1858; he carried on that business for another twenty years.

Richard Manktelow was still running his cabinet making business (at O'Neil's Newsagents) and he continued for a short time after his wife Ann died in 1845. He was then followed there in 1850 by William Coppard, variously stationer, solicitor's clerk, tax collector and stamp distributor.

The houses next door (Village Stores) were mainly private residences until Bentham Fuller arrived in 1870 and after setting up as grocer and draper was soon having work done to improve and enlarge his premises. By 1878 he had become agent for W A Gilbey wine and spirit merchants. He appears to have taken Richard Paine (vet and journalist) into partnership for a short time around 1885 but by 1890 his son Fred seems to have been in sole charge and so he remained until around 1920. In 1871 living upstairs was Elizabeth Tarrow, widow of Colonel Tarrow, with her two daughters who were both born while they were living and serving in Perth, Western Australia.

The lawyer Baldocks were succeeded at the White House in 1864 by John Fuller, surveyor and house agent. The Fullers (no apparent relation to Bentham)supplemented their income by taking in lodgers, including the Trower sisters, and lived there for some forty years until 1910 when Dr Arthur Wm. Statter Curteis became the village Medical Officer and public vaccinator and set up his surgery here. Further along (at Abbots Antiques) John and Ann Hilder had their bakery from about 1870 assisted by their son William, a miller, and three other children aged sixteen to nineteen, described as assistant bakers. This business was continued by their daughter-in-law Sarah well into the 20th century. Next door was the old coopers business (Lime Tree).

Lime Tree, Hilders and Tudor House

West End in 1890

Around 1900 the old road level in the western part of the High Street was raised beyond Autumn, Spring and Peartony and the row of 17th century cottages were replaced by the four houses comprising Nos. 1-4 Merrivale. As a result of this the shops beyond (BHI, now empty, Chaplins) had their new entrances at what had been first floor levels rather than at what had become their basements. Wren Cottage, however, retains the old level. The three old shops were owned by William Thompson, builder, in the 1840s and 1850s. His widow Elizabeth sold them to Henry Dann who was in business as a tea dealer in Everton Cottages before starting his grocer and drapers business here in his new premises in the late 1860s. He and his wife Sarah stayed there until about 1884 when they sold the property to Herbert and Carrie Wrenn who had arrived in the village in 1871. Mrs Wrenn had soon become a teacher at the Congregational Independent Sunday School. Beyond Wren Cottage was the White Hart Inn (Cheriton).

West End with Victorian and 20th century changes

The White Hart (Cheriton), Wren and shops (at the old street level)

Opposite was the old chapel which, after years of being unused, was to become the Village Institute. Behind was Ashlands, originally just land owned by the Rev Gould, where his daughter Ellen built the house of that name in 1871. She lived there until her death and adopted as her daughter Emily Shackleton whose brother Charles was to die of fever in Matebeleland in 1893 aged twenty-five. Between Ashlands and the road was Highfields, the village cricket ground. The first mention of cricket had been in 1750 when Burwash just lost to Mayfield. Matches took place regularly after that with the village and other organisations fielding sides. In 1877 Burwash lost to the Common scoring 160 runs to 196 in their two innings, and in 1880 Browns, Pagdens and Blundens Shops XI beat the village club by 5 runs. In 1886 young Pilbeam (of Bell Alley) wanted to join the village cricket club but was told there was a rule against swearing; he responded by asking if he could pay a higher subscription and swear when he liked. In 1893 Mr H Russell's XII scoring 126 and 14-0 beat Mr Barlow's XII who managed only 63 and 76.

In between the old chapel and Novar, Henry Heathfield Junior now ran the wheelwrights which then became John Browns coachbuilders. John Brown's son Joseph and his wife Miriam (nee Hicks) emigrated to the United States in 1909 on the LUSITANIA, joining Miriam's two brothers who had established themselves in New York. Joseph was an

Novar and Browns Coachbuilders

accomplished carriage painter in his father's business and also designed and made the board in St Bartholomew's that shows the past Vicars and Rectors. They made their home in New York and their second son, Joseph junior, obtained a masters degree at Colombia University and taught history in Floral Park School, Long Island from 1933-69. He died aged ninety-three in 1995.

The old buildings on the site of Avon and Garymore were a row of six cottages and they, together with the row now comprising Cobblers and Wrenn's cottages, were all also owned by the builder William Thompson; he and his wife Elizabeth lived in Cobblers and let out the rest. By 1879 William had died and his widow sold four of the five cottages to Herbert Wrenn. She remained living in Cobblers, retaining the right to use the well (on payment) and share the passage (also the costs).

The Bear was one of the six public houses in Burwash during Victorian times, the others being the Admiral Vernon, the Bell, the Rose & Crown, the Blacksmiths Arms and the White Hart. These were in addition to other official and unofficial beer and drinking houses in and near the village, and contemporary accounts show quite a high level of drinking and alcoholism. There was a steady turnover of landlords in the six pubs and also changes of jobs, as well as of hostelries. Katherine Weller ran the Bell for fifteen years after previous joint landlords Benjamin Wood had left to become Parish Clerk and John Parsons to run the Blacksmiths Arms. In 1871 Mr Smith succeeded Katherine Weller, having previously been a gardener and freelance musician. He lasted only seven years before returning to private life in 1878 and being succeeded by William Farley who began the long occupancy of the Farleys with Louisa succeeding her husband and then handing over to their daughter Nellie. Farley had previously briefly run the Blacksmiths Arms following William Russell who had succeeded John Parsons. Russell then moved to the Admiral Vernon before returning to farming at Holtons. Henry Blackford took over the Blacksmiths Arms and his wife Alice and then his son George ran it until it ceased to be a pub in the 1920s. The confusing changeovers were completed by the Mainwaring family, who were involved in so many village enterprises, and had John running the Blacksmiths Arms in the 1840s and William the Admiral Vernon from 1856-73. Albert Hawkins became the landlord there in 1884 and he and his wife Emily ran an efficient and friendly pub, being succeeded by their daughter Gertrude and her husband Ernest Lusted. During their time you could buy bacon and eggs at the next door grocers (in one of the cottages) and she would fry them over their open fire for your breakfast; she also allowed the police from next door to come in for a quick pint after hours. The Rose & Crown and the White Hart existed quietly but the Bear was always expanding and by 1895 Robert Vigor was advertising "The Bear Commercial Hotel with good stabling and lock up for coaches; pleasure parties catered for." Behind the Bear, in the car park, were some of the village

The Bear

allotments and in 1869 there was a dispute over their size, as to whether they should be ¼ or ⅛ acre. It was said that the employers, mostly farmers, favoured the smaller size so that their labourers did not spend too much time on them. The allotments seemed to get moved from time to time as their land was needed for building or other purposes and by 1885 they were next to the cricket ground at Highfields. Prior to this the Bear car park had been the village bowling green and now it reverted to fairground and the site of village markets and by 1887 there were cattle sales on alternate Wednesdays.

Cattle going to market about 1900

Next door to the Bear, Kimberley, which was largely rebuilt earlier in the century, became the home of John and Sarah Maynard who were farming after leaving the Bear. It then became a bakery before Charles Brook, solicitor's clerk, moved there in 1875 prior to renting The Ivy in 1893 from Mrs Combs. In The Cottage was young Thomas Pagden and his wife Hester who moved from Victoria Terrace in about 1885 to be next door to his mother, Emma, in Gideon House. Thomas was in partnership with his brother Henry who lived with his wife Annie next to his parents' old home in part of the old Rectory. The brothers continued together in the tailors business until 1898 when they were each joined by their own sons and two separate firms were formed as H W Pagden and Sons and

Gideon

Thomas Pagden and Son. Both these businesses continued until the 1930s. Further along, in Sadlers, Stephen Brown established his sadlers and harness makers business in about 1845 in the premises previously used as a coopers by William Mancer. Stephen was succeeded by his son William thirty years later and when he died in about 1885 his widow Sarah continued the business until handing over to her sons Stephen and John. They continued until the early part of the 20th century when the Burwash Gas Company took over the premises as its office and showroom to complement its works down Shrub Lane. Southside was rebuilt in the 1870s as two cottages on the site of the older buildings, of which the cellars remain.

Chaunt House had began its long connection with medicine with the arrival there around 1820 of Thomas Abel Evans, surgeon, who was to carry out the post mortem on Benjamin Russell. He later moved his surgery to Mount House. He was followed as village doctor in 1856 by James Combs at Denes House until his disgrace in 1880, and then the equally ignominious departure of his successor the Australian Algernon Cohen. Cohen had only three months experience when he was appointed and he was called to treat Charlotte Maskell following the miscarriage of her seventeenth pregnancy. As her condition deteriorated he gave her the "usual" remedies of ergot, digitalis, opium and

Chaunt House

brandy but she died after taking permanganate of potash which Cohen had failed to label 'not for internal consumption'. Cohen ordered "immediate burial as decomposition would soon set in and the body would swell". Following official enquiries Cohen was ordered to resign. His replacement was William Barton MB who took the surgery back to Chaunt House in 1882 and was described as surgeon, medical officer and public vaccinator. His successor in 1889 was Arthur Green and by 1899 Joseph Cox Hines had taken over and rented Mount House for his home and surgery. Shortly afterwards Thomas Conley opened his chemists shop at Chaunt House which was to remain a chemist until 1979. As well as their duties as public medical officers the doctors had a considerable private practice and there were a range of residential or corrective institutions to which private patients could be sent. One of these was the Ticehurst Lunatic Asylum which in 1851 out of sixty patients housed eight clergymen, two baronets, fourteen gentlemen, seventeen gentlewomen, one banker, one surgeon and an Earl's son.

Behind Chaunt House was the Calvinist chapel and across the alleyway were the five cottages of Victoria Terrace built in the latter part of the century for £500. On the High Street there was then a row of cottages (Portland Terrace) that had recently been built to replace the old delapidated row and behind them was the old Rectory. These three sets of buildings housed up to sixteen different families of labourers, shopkeepers and craftsmen. It was a constantly changing and overcrowded population but there were some noteworthy residents. The Westons, father and sons, carried on their blacksmiths business for fifty years, presumably roughly where the forge/garage currently now stands. The Brooks, again father and sons, were well regarded carpenters for seventy years. Henry Pagden senior had set up his tailor's business there as a young man and by 1860, next door to the Pagdens, in half of the old Rectory lived Thomas Nash who ran his boarding school in this small house together with two governesses and four scholars. As well as being a schoolmaster Nash was also a Wesleyan preacher and he had as his lodger William Mather, the Minister of the newly built Congregational chapel next door.

When the Coneys had ceased to use Mount House as their residence after Bicknell Coney's death, it was rented out, first to Dr. Evans, then to a succession of Curates, and then in 1854 to Charles Taylor the vetinary practitioner when he got married. He and his wife Charlotte took in lodgers, including John Coker Egerton both when he was a Curate (1857 to 1860 and 1863 onwards) and subsequently Rector. It is likely that he rented Mount House cottage. In 1885 the Coneys sold the whole of their remaining Burwash estate and Mount House was bought for £3,050 by John Schroeter of Laurelhurst after a fierce bidding battle, at the auction in Tunbridge Wells, with John Leyland Fielden, the owner of next door Rampyndene. The bidding started at £1,200 and Fielden made his final bid at £3,000. Bowmans, Biggs Farm and other land and cottages were also sold. Taylor's daughter Fanny continued to live at Mount House after his early death at the age of fifty-two in 1883 and the house was continuously rented out until Wilfred Maude-Roxby and his bride Dulcie Schroeter moved there in 1914.

The Husseys had left Rampyndene for their main residence at Scotney Castle, Kent in 1840 and although they continued to own some land and property this was effectively the end of this family's association with Burwash. The house was bought by Commander Alfred Royer, RN Reserve List, and his wife Hannah; after Alfred's death his widow sold it to John Leyland Fielden for £725 in 1875. Fielden had been a soldier and arctic explorer and he soon managed to have a bitter row with the Rector. It started with a disagreement on whether or not the decalogue (ten commandments) should be displayed in the church. Fielden was strongly in favour while Egerton felt there was no place in the church where it could be legible. In 1878 Egerton then accused Fielden of enticing Dissolving View Men (Indian rope trick artists) into his home and making them drunk on spirits. The final confrontation was in 1885 when Fielden erected a fence in front of his house enclosing a portion of the footpath and sward that from time immemorial had been used by the village. Fielden believed he was within the law, having acquired the land, but Egerton was determined to defend ancient rights. As a result, when Fielden's wife Eliza died he refused to have her buried in the churchyard and instead erected a mausoleum in Rampyndene's garden, endowed with £700 of 3% India Bonds for its upkeep. It was endorsed with the instruction that "if Palestine or the Holy Land come under the sovereignty of the British Empire to transport the remains to the portion of the Holy Land which shall be assigned to the tribe of Reuben". It was only on Egerton's death that she was re-buried and the mausoleum eventually dismantled. The Fielden's stayed until 1945 when John Leyland Fielden's great nephew Wemys Fielden's executors sold the house after his death. John Leyland Fielden's father had been MP for Blackburn from 1832-46, supporting Robert Peel, and was created a Baronet on Peel's resignation: his great-great-grandson, Sir Henry Fielden, the 6th Baronet, still lives in Burwash.

The Ivy was two residences throughout this period, with Ivy House occupied by James Philcox's sister Mary and a niece Esther, to be followed later by John Barrow, a farmer, and his wife Eliza. When the whole property was sold in 1867 by the Constable's executors the Barrows, who had wished to purchase their half, were gazumped by Dr Combs of Denes House who purchased the property from his wife's cousin's executors. In Ivy Cottage John Payne had run his shoemaking business for many years but it became a residence when he died in about 1865.

Bell Alley seems to have started its name-change (to School Hill) with the building of the school (1843) but the confusion continues to this day with some title deeds showing both the two different names. The three old cottages on the west side, below Denes House wall, continued in multiple occupancy with up to four families living in each throughout the 19th century. On the east of Bell Alley the cottages dating back to about the 18th century now known as Brightling View and Vines Cottage were first re-named School Hill Cottages and again housed four families. By the 19th century they were owned by the Wood family, who so often supplied the Parish Clerk. Above these cottages, towards the churchyard, was another row of three cottages which were demolished in the 20th century and the remains of which can be seen in the garden walls. Down towards the school, Bellcroft and Fairview probably date back to the 17th century although their shape and layout has altered several times; in the 19th century Fairview was owned by the Pilbeams, another old village family. After the tollgate (Churchgate) was removed, the tollhouse and a hovel below were also both taken away to allow the churchyard to be extended from the line of trees and for the road to be widened.

Next to St Bartholomew's is Garstons, the origins of which are a mystery. It is said to have been built, as an hotel, on the site of an earlier house that may have had religious

Garstons

connections. It was certainly built by 1839 when it was described a "a new house" which means constructed within the last twenty-five years. It could possibly have been used as a hotel in Regency times by people taking the waters at Tunbridge Wells Spa, and by the middle of the 19th century it seems to have become a guest house. In 1871 "an old parish chest was brought in from the Hotel where it had been laid up when the Ch. was restored in 1855": referring to Garstons. It was owned by the Havilands until their bankruptcy, and may well have been one of their speculative ventures. In 1873 it was acquired by Sarah Tilley, daughter of W J Tilley, who had owned the Franchise, and she altered and improved it to give it the shape that is seen today. She lived there until her death at the age of seventy-five in 1892 when the property passed first to Charles Locock and then by 1898 to Mrs Hayley from Brightling who was followed by her daughter.

Behind Garstons was Olivers Garden containing the Admiral Vernon, the row of cottages and shops and the new Police House. The two western cottages (now Glebe and Jasmine) were the first dwellings and date back to the 17th century. By 1691 the Admiral Vernon was built and by 1725 had become a separate property. The eastern cottage (Northview) was added around or after this date and in 1796 the western property was divided again with the Old Police House site being separated from the rest and two cottages

114   Chapter Five

Mainwaring's and the Cottages at The Square

being built on it. By 1831 these had been demolished and a new cottage built by Richard Reeves that itself shortly gave way to the new police house. Opposite these stood two rows of dwellings: one, since demolished, stood where the public car park is now and the other comprises Prospect Cottages. The latter had been built around 1800 by Edward Hilder and the former about 1850 by Edward Bates: these two sets of cottages also varied between being homes, shops or the site of local craftsmen. Square Farm was still occupied by the farming branch of the Noakes family until the early part of the 20th century when it was taken over by Harry and William Morris, sons of Walter Morris, milk dealer and the farmer of Mottynsden.

As well as the constant changes in the High Street this period also saw the gradual start of development around the village. On the Etchingham road Dudwell House was built in 1862 by Andrew Gibbs on land he had acquired from Tott Farm in 1854. He seems to have lived at Tott during this time and he was soon to be appointed a Justice of the Peace. He sat on the Burwash division of the Petty Session which convened on the last Friday of every month at 11.00 in the George Inn at Hurst Green. The

Admiral Vernon and the two rows of cottages opposite

Clerk was always supplied by the solicitors Baldock and Philcox, and then by Aitkens and Andrews, and Andrews & Bennett. In 1892 a new Court House was built on the junction of the present A21 and the road from Burwash and the now twice monthly court moved there from the George. It stayed in this building until the Burwash Petty Sessional Division closed in 1974. Gibbs died in 1888 and Dudwell House eventually became a convent as the Sisters of the Love of God Dudwell St Mary before becoming a residential home in 1993. The only road to Etchingham remained along Borders Lane until about 1860 when the straight mile was formed.

Square Farm and barn

Tott Farm was kept by the Cruttendens until 1867 when John, aged seventy-four and farming the original one hundred and eighteen acres for forty-two years, went bankrupt. This was a sad ending for this long standing local family. Tott Cottages had been built in two phases: No. 1 (now Little Tott Farmhouse) and No. 2 in about 1735-40 and No. 3 added about fifty years later. They had at times been as many as five residences and

Burwash Court House (at Hurst Green)

Tott Cottages

Tottenhurst was built behind them in about 1880. Little Tott had been farmed by Thomas Gillham with ninety-three acres stretching down to Shrub Lane until it was purchased by Thomas Harden, auctioneer and land agent, in 1890 and re-named Meadowbank; it subsequently became Meadowlands. Opposite the then Little Tott were some old cottages which were demolished in the 19th century and replaced further to the west by Capstone and the new Little Tott in the 20th century.

The Glebe was normally the home of the Rector but when Joseph Gould died in 1867 his wife Lydia and daughter declined to move out. Lydia died and Ellen then built Ashlands and moved there in 1871. Egerton moved in and, following his marriage to Helen Breach in 1875, followed the fashion of the time by having a grass tennis court laid. After Egerton's death in 1688, successive rectors lived there until about 1910 when it was sold.

The earlier breaking up of the Cruttenden estate down Fontridge Lane had led to a number of their tenanted farms being purchased and the houses improved. Thus Fishers, Grandtwizzle and Old Brick (Brickhouse) became more important residences. Nearer to Burwash at Magpies Hall lived John Coppard, the local rate and tax collector who both collected and kept the accounts. The accounts were not kept up to date and he was criticised in 1865, 1866, 1868 and 1869. In 1870 the Coppards were apparently burgled and the thief was said to have stolen the account books and exactly £55 which happened to be the deficiency in the accounts. His son Martin confessed to a Vestry meeting that the story was untrue and he, his uncle William, the solicitors' clerk, and others rallied round to replace the money and provide sureties for John to continue his office. His contract was perhaps surprisingly renewed by the Parish.

At the bottom of the Dudwell Valley was Batemans, which house and estate had declined in importance and size over the years. Its history from the 17th century is largely unknown but John Brittan, who lived there in the early 18th century, made some changes and in 1770 a double oasthouse was erected. It was bought in 1892 by John Macmeikan, an architect, who called it "The Manor House" and set about its restoration. He sold it in 1897 to Alexander Scrimgeour who in turn sold it to Rudyard Kipling, the author, for £9,300 in 1902. Kipling lived there until his death in 1936 and when his widow Caroline died three years later she left the house, its contents and the estate to The National Trust as a memorial to her husband. Kipling finished the restoration of the house, installed electricity by harnessing the River Dudwell at the old mill and obtained the advice of Sir William Willcocks, who built the Aswan dam on the Nile, in constructing the canals, sluices and gates that provide the mill with water power for both electricity and milling. He redesigned and restored the gardens and also tried to reconstruct the old estate. He successively purchased Rye Green, Mill Park Farm and Dudwell Mill, a total of three hundred acres, and built the two sets of cottages and the manager's house on the site of the old brickworks in Bell Alley lane. At about this time, Forge Farm, on the site of the old bloomery, was demolished. Kipling wrote many of his works at Batemans and switched his attention from India and the east to Sussex and Kent, with his most local book "Puck of Pook's Hill" (1906) being based on the hill immediately to the south-west of his house.

It was the road to Burwash Common which saw most building activity. Laurelhurst, at first called St Clements, was built about 1860 by John Bateman, next door to the much earlier Judins, and he sold it to Benjamin Breach who lived there for only a few years before moving to Surrey in 1874. His daughter Helen married the Rector John Coker Egerton. Laurelhurst was bought by John and Mary Schroeter and the large house and its magnificent gardens became one of the major establishments of the district. John Conrad Schroeter was a wealthy retired merchant who had made his money in South Africa and he built up a large estate acquiring most of the land between Rye Green Lane and Willingford as well as Bough and Green Hill (The Green or Green Farm) to the north. John and Mary had four children, all girls, one of whom, Dulcie, was to marry Wilfred Maude-Roxby. John died in 1891 but Mary stayed there until her death in 1907; her brother Joseph Jefferson came from Cumberland to help her run the estate, living first at Green Hill and then at Laurelhurst. Green Hill has been farmed for many years by the Newingtons until it was purchased by Schroeter.

At the top of the lane down to Rye Green stood Porchester Cottages, one of which was occupied by William Coppard, solicitor's clerk at Baldock and Philcox and distributor of stamps. These cottages were demolished around the turn of the century and later Coppards was built on the corner. This corner was originally called Coppers Hill and may well have got this name from the fact that some of the Coppards were known by the alternative name of Copper. Orchards was built on the site of Porchester Cottages in 1907 by Rudyard Kipling as part of the improvements to the Batemans estate. Opposite this land there were older cottages on the site of Meadow and Hillcrest and in 1901 Rotherhurst (later Coppers Hill) was built with Martlets as its stables. An old pair of cottages called Windmill Cottages were on the site of modern Windmill with a curious shaped long piece of land attached, running up to the top of the hill, which could have contained a windmill although no traces remain. Witherhurst, which had been altered and tile hung in Georgian times, was farmed by George Fagg Gilbert until his death in about 1871 and then by his wife Eliza. Barn Cottage was built in the 18th century when it was lived in by basketmakers, and Bempton and Park View in 1903. Rocksmead is slightly older, being constructed in 1899 as a gentleman's villa with a carriage house and stabling. By 1915 it was owned by Mrs Louise Bourner, wife of Charles Bourner whose fruit shop was at Novar, and who advertised "apartments with every convenience". Little Meeching was built about the same time and is said to have started off as a laundry. The Rocks were originally five dwellings with their frontage right on the road, but they were rebuilt in the middle of the 19th century as three cottages, extended in the 20th century to four. Likewise Rocks Cottages (previously Stone Cottages) were two small cottages in the 18th century which were demolished and rebuilt on the present site in 1868 again as three, later becoming four. Just round the corner in Batemans Lane stood Little Batemans Farm which was an earlier small farmhouse, buildings, orchard and garden some two hundred yards west of the lane and which disappeared in the 20th century.

On the corner of Batemans Lane, Pippins was built in 1903 as the Red House by Henry Noakes the clockmaker, on the site of the "messuage and garden near the site of Town turnpike gate but which turnpike gate was sometime since removed". He had purchased it in 1886 from Thomas Whitehead. Noakes demolished the old house and presumably built the new one as an investment as he immediately leased it to Miss Towers, the daughter of Rev G C Towers who had been Curate to the Rev Joseph Gould. Kims Cottage was built in the 19th century, just in front of the site of the old forge and smithy, and may well have been known as Cherry Tree House or Cottage when John Mepham and his wife Charity lived there for about thirty years in the middle of the century. One of John's many brothers, Joseph, a groom, lived at the other end of the village in Prospect Cottages and altogether there were thirty-six cousins living in the parish or the surrounding areas. The Mephams were a typical village family, tracing themselves back to the 17th century and having links by marriage to virtually every other long-standing family such as the Pennells, Daws, Funnells, Woodsell, Russell, Morris and Pilbeam. In particular they inter-married with the Jenners and Akehursts (Akhurst or Acres) and it was this part of the family which was to continue in Burwash for another hundred years.

East of the old Yeomans and St Nicholas was the row of cottages at right angles to the road that had been constructed in the 18th century but which has been much altered in appearance during both the 19th and 20th centuries. The Laurels was built around 1900 near the site where the old tollhouse had been, virtually in the middle of the road, with gates across both the main turnpike and Spring Lane. This had been demolished when the turnpike ceased to function and the road widened. Opposite, the 16th-century Paygate Cottage had an additional piece added to the front in about 1880 when Hillside was attached to it. Hillside Cottages were built a little later.

Down Spring Lane, just below the old brickworks, Elphicks was now two residences, while Sellars Brook, which was originally a small cottage and garden on the opposite side of the road, was built on its present site in about 1840 and was variously one or two dwellings. The Blackford family lived there between 1840 and 1870 before moving to the Blacksmiths Arms. Holton had variously been Holt Down and Halt Down over the centuries and had been attached to and detached from the surrounding farm at intervals, and was thought at one time to have been a pub. The medieval barn next door is all that remains of the earlier complex although there are other traces of old stonework. The current house was built in the late 18th century and in about 1880 was purchased by William Summerhayes, a retired physician who had returned from service in India. He occasionally gave talks on India wearing the dress of a native of Afgan. He was followed by John Watson, a solicitor. At Southover, Winters, Brownings and Frenches the Ellis' and Blundells had gone and the last survivors of these families were the Havilands, descended from Henry who had married Anne Dyke (nee Jordan). The Havilands were rich landowners and farmers who unfortunately overstretched themselves and went bankrupt in 1849. Their estates were broken up and these long standing non-conformist intermarried families finally left the district. A G Pooley bought Southover and rebuilt it in a much grander style and he sold to the Catholic de Murriettas, who came and went within twenty years but during that time further enlarged the house and moved the entrance drive to its modern route. They were followed by Cornelius Warmington QC MP JP and then William de Winter JP. Frenches (now called the Franchise) was purchased in about 1855 by W J Tilley. He reconstructed and enlarged the building into roughly the structure which currently exists. He was also responsible for presenting the iron porch gates to St Bartholomew's in the restoration of 1856. Henry Newton, a retired firebrick merchant, purchased the Franchise from him in 1860 and his widow then sold it to Henry Lucas in 1878 for £12,000. Lucas, a bachelor, was the restaurant keeper at the House of Commons and had inherited Mottynsden from his uncle Henry in 1854. He quickly added further land to the Franchise estate and when he died in 1912 he left it all to his sister Anne.

Frys (Burwash Place) had been farmed for many years by John Henty until about 1845. It then passed through several owners and was renamed The Firs by the time Lt. Colonel Arthur Sutherland Harris purchased it in 1898. He spent thousands of pounds rebuilding the house and adding stables and a coachhouse, reflecting his keen interest in horses. The remains of the old 17th-century house can be found as part of the main Victorian building that exists today and which was re-named Burwash Place in 1900 by Sutherland Harris. A keen territorial soldier, he commanded the 13th (Princess Louise's Kensington) Battalion and was a member of the Sussex TA Association. As a churchwarden, JP, Chairman of the Institute Committee, President of both Burwash Cricket and Football Clubs, he played a leading role in village affairs before he sold the estate to James Lacy in 1925 and left the village.

The cottages now known as Holton Cottages and Half Mile Cottage had generally provided accommodation for agricultural labourers working the neighbouring farms but in 1840 Half Mile was the home of Hannah Isted, aged sixty, the first officially appointed village midwife of modern times. Over half a century later, in 1902, a village nurse was also established to provide free care to all parishioners on parish relief.

❧

It is noticeable that during Queen Victoria's reign there had been a steady change in occupation for those who lived in the parish, of which the most important was the drop in the number employed on the land from sixty per cent in 1841 to forty per cent by 1901. This was largely due to increased mechanisation which had started earlier in the century and now gathered pace. The period also saw a steady decrease in the hop acreage which was to almost totally disappear by the middle of the next century as land went under the plough or was laid down to pasture for sheep or cattle as the economics of farming shifted over the years. Those who had worked on the farms became general labourers, sometimes on the roads or railway and sometimes doing any work that was available. By contrast the range and mixture of shops and trades in the village changed little during this time and there were still a large number of different crafts being practised. It is perhaps understandable that there were five dressmakers and three tailors as most people's clothes were made locally or by themselves. Four blacksmiths were needed for the large number of horses which still provided most people's transport and heavy labour and four wheelwrights were needed for farm carts and family carriages as well as other machinery. Two bakers, four butchers, five grocers were essential to supply the local needs in those largely transportless times, but nine shoemakers must surely have found it difficult to earn a living.

Perhaps as a result of slightly greater prosperity, and an increase in people's personal possessions, insurance and assurance had become increasingly popular during the 19th century and local agents were appointed for a variety of companies, most of which have by now been absorbed or disappeared. Almost anyone seems to have been able to become an agent and by 1860 Traiton Rochester (grocer at Chilston House) was agent for Kent Mutual Fire and Life, William Coppard (solicitor) for Liverpool and London Fire and Life, the schoolmaster Alfred Cox represented both the Norwich Union Fire and Life and the Norfolk and London Accident, while Samuel Daw represented Imperial Fire and also Norfolk Farmers (cattle). By 1867 farmer Thomas Gillham of Little Tott had added British Empire Mutual Fire and Life to the range, and others appeared later.

An increase in Parliamentary democracy was another advance during the 19th century which was eventually to lead to universal suffrage. The 1832 Reform Bill had been the first step, abolishing the Rotten Boroughs which for centuries had elected members to Westminster with only a tiny handful of voters, who were often bribed. In Sussex the boroughs of Bramber, Steyning, Seaford and Winchelsea, which had two seats each, disappeared, Midhurst, Horsham, Rye and Arundel each lost one of their two seats and Brighton received two seats for the first time. More importantly for the inhabitants of Burwash the number of county seats doubled from two to four and the local MP was elected from the Rapes of Hastings, Lewes and Pevensey, with Burwash being in the Mayfield polling district. The 1832 Bill went some way towards achieving electoral reform but the population was shifting fast and the vast majority were still excluded from voting by the old rateable franchise system which set a qualifying property level far above most people's means. The Reform Act of 1867 doubled the size of the electorate, moving a long way towards universal male suffrage, especially in towns, as well as further redistributing seats. The process was followed by the Franchise Bill of 1885 which put the male country voters on the same basis as those in towns, thereby increasing the voters in Burwash from one hundred and thirty to five hundred, and the process was finally completed in the next century by the Act of 1928 which included women in its principle of one man one vote on a totally equal basis.

After the Jubilees of 1887 and 1897 the old Queen died in 1901, to be succeeded by the Prince of Wales, Edward VII (1901-10) and then George V. It was thus in George V's reign that this long, eventful but largely peaceful era was brought to a close by the 1914-18 war, the war to end all wars. It caused mass slaughter on a scale never before witnessed. Three quarters of a million men and women from Britain and two hundred thousand from the Empire were to die before the Armistice was declared at 11 a.m. on the 11th November 1918. The system of County Regiments and 'Buddy' Battalions recruited from the same region meant that a particularly bloody battle could inflict large numbers of casualties on a single town or village.

The origins of the war lay in the Balkans when Archduke Francis Ferdinand was murdered by Serbs in the Bosnian capital of Sarajevo. This produced indecision and disagreement among the great powers, Russia, Germany, France and Britain, as to what form intervention should take to re-establish stability. In the confusion that followed Germany invaded Belgium and Britain felt obliged to declare war to defend that country's neutrality.In August 1914 mobilisation began and the British Expeditionary Force (BEF) was sent to France as "incomparably the best trained, best organised and best equipped British army that ever went forth to war". Unfortunately it was trained and equipped for war on the South African Veldt, not for seige and trench warfare. This early force was followed by Territorials and Kitchener's volunteers.

Burwash men were involved as both regulars and volunteers. The first casualties from the village were Marine William Woodruffe and Leading Stoker Thomas Funnell of Hutchings Farm who were both lost in the sinking of the cruiser HMS ABOUKIR by a submarine on the 22nd September 1914. On land the first battle of Ypres saw the loss of Corporal Albert Oliver and Walter Mepham but on the 9th May 1915 in the Battle of Aubers Ridge there were six Burwash men dead before breakfast and eight more were lost in the Battle of Loos in September. In 1916 the first Battle of the Somme cost seventeen Burwash lives and in 1917 sixteen died at Passchendale, with another thirty dying in the last year of the war when first the Germans were reinforced by their armies from the Russian front and then the Allies attempted a costly advance just before the Armistice in November. The names of the dead read like a list of Burwash history, with six families losing three or more relations. They won five medals for gallantry. In total Burwash lost one hundred and thirty-four men in this war which, with an average death rate of about twenty-five per cent, implies that about five hundred took part out of the population of two thousand one hundred and fifty. In Burwash, as in villages and towns all over the country, this toll had a traumatic effect on village life, representing such a high proportion of the young, working marriageable male population; it left an unfillable gap for a generation.

Chapter Six

MODERN BURWASH
1919-2000

When the guns fell silent in Northern France in November 1918 the world to which the soldiers returned had changed for ever. Before 1914 the ordinary citizen, particularly in a rural village like Burwash, could still live his or her life largely without interference or regulation by the state. The previous one hundred and fifty years had seen the growing influence of industry and technology that was increasingly affecting people's daily life and bringing them into contact with the world outside their parish, but many people had still lived, married and died without stirring beyond their parish boundaries or caring what went on in the rest of England. An Englishman could have travelled the world without a passport and apart from minor laws on safety in factories, and against food adulteration, he could generally do as he pleased in a law-abiding manner. By 1918 food rationing had been introduced, news was fettered, and licensing hours for drinking had been imposed. In 1916 even the clocks had been changed with the introduction of summertime. The State was now involving itself with the citizens' daily way of life as never before and this trend was set to continue.

Peace was celebrated positively in a variety of visible ways. First the Cenotaph (designed by Sir Edwin Lutyens) was unveiled by King George V on the 11th November 1920 and on the same day the unknown warrior, selected anonymously, was brought home from France and buried with State honours at Westminster Abbey. He might have been any one of those whose identity was never discovered, including several from Burwash. War memorials were also erected in towns and villages throughout the country to honour the dead and never to forget the sacrifice they gave for peace. A year later, in 1921, the British Legion was formed as a result of Earl Haig successfully arranging the amalgamation of several ex-service organisations that had come into existence at the end of the war, some with a distinctly political bias. The Legion was to provide welfare for ex-servicemen and their families when they fell on hard times.

Chapter Six

Burwash built its memorial opposite the church with the names of fifty-six men inscribed on its six sides. There is another memorial in St. Philip's at Burwash Common for forty-two men and two names are repeated in St. Joseph's Catholic church. The Commonwealth War Graves Commission records forty-four more. The Burwash memorial was designed by Sir Charles Nicholson, Bart, who was consulting architect to seven cathedrals as well as the designer of Government House in Kingston, Jamaica. His

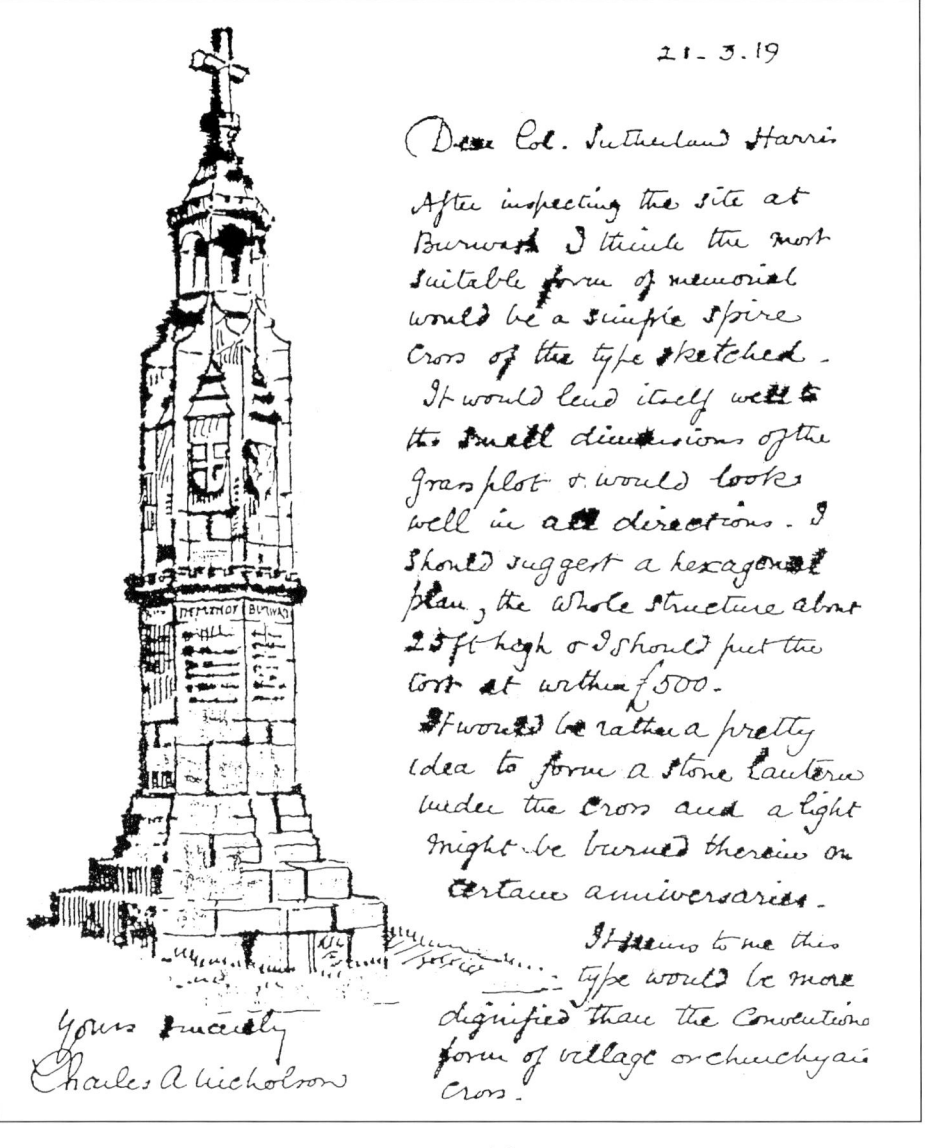

War Memorial design

sketch of 1919 for "a simple spire cross with a stone lantern" was followed, and the total cost of £700 included his fee of £63 and W J Ellis' building charges of £590.2.6d: these costs were met by a wide variety of donations and collections. The memorial was unveiled on 24th October 1920 by General Lord Horne before a crowd of two thousand including seventy ex-servicemen under the command of Major Joseph Jefferson and his niece's husband Lt. Wilfred Maude-Roxby, late of the Shropshire Light Infantry. The Burwash Brass Band under Mr Edward Jenner played "Abide with me", then "O valiant hearts" with a solo by Mr Henry Pagden. Finally after prayers the chairman of the committee Lt. Col. Arthur Sutherland Harris JP, requested Lord Horne to carry out the unveiling. The inclusion of the lantern, still lit on the anniversary of the death of each serviceman, is an unusual feature

Unveiling of War Memorial in 1920

in England, where there are only a handful of others, and is similar to the Lanternes des Morts found in central and southern France. The glowing light, originally an oil lamp lit and then raised by a pulley, stands as a poignant reminder of the lives given in both the 1914-18 and the later 1939-45 wars.

❧

But the men who had fought for freedom in the trenches found factory life constricting and there were disputes over wages, conditions and hours of work. These legitimate grievances, fuelled by rising Bolshevism in Europe, were exacerbated by rising unemployment in northern and midland towns which doubled between December 1920 and March 1921. It reached two million by June of that year, with over half the workforce being unemployed in some coal, cotton and engineering towns. This was the result of chaos in world markets following the war when over-production of primary commodities, fuelled by the glut of shipping, led to tumbling prices. This unemployment, poverty and hunger led almost inevitably to the general strike of 1926 called by the big three unions: railways, mines and transport. The strike largely failed but was followed by the Wall Street crash in October 1929 and the great depression, with unemployment rising from two million to three million in twelve months by 1931. Hardly had recovery started when Europe was drifting towards war again. Hitler came to power in Germany in 1933, the year after the disarmament conference at Geneva, and the same year that the Oxford Union passed the motion that "this House will not fight for King and Country". Nazism in Germany and pacifism in England made the chances of war increasingly likely.

In these troubled inter-war years there were other significant developments taking place. Silent black and white films, personified by Charlie Chaplin, entertained many in the 1920s before sound arrived in 1927. In Liverpool it was estimated that forty per cent of the population went to the cinema once a week and twenty-five per cent twice. Wireless sets arrived in many homes and by 1935 there were nine million sets and it was thought that ninety per cent of the population listened. Dress was changing for men from frock coats and top hats to the universally worn suit and women's fashions had abandoned the old formality. Football matches became a regular Saturday pastime for many and popular newspapers were available to all. Regular holidays were enjoyed by increasing numbers although by 1931 still less than half the population had ever left home for a night.

But perhaps the biggest long-term influence on people's lives was the growth in popularity of the motor car. After Daimler's first petrol-powered car of 1885, progress had been slow at first with a maximum speed limit of four mph until 1896, when the requirement to be preceded by a man with a red flag was also removed. The 1914-18 war had, as one of the few benefits of such a conflict, accelerated the improvement and reliability of engines and in 1922 the first popular car was produced, the seven horsepower Baby Austin. In 1920 there were under two hundred thousand cars, by 1930 one million and by 1940 two million were on the road. After an interruption during the 1939-45 war, caused by petrol rationing and the diverting of production-lines to military purposes, the growth in the number of private cars has continued inexorably. The driving test was introduced in 1934 and the speed limit, after being thirty mph up to 1930 was totally abolished for four years before being re-introduced in 1934 at thirty mph in built-up areas only. The first motor engineer in Burwash was Fred Brook who operated in Ham Lane in the barn next to the Rose & Crown. By 1915 he was advertising cars for hire, petrol, tyres and accessories, and repairs at short notice: no doubt very necessary in those early days of motoring. Fred Brook closed down soon afterwards but was to be followed by Charlie Farley (son of William, landlord of the Bell) in 1918 and Albert Oakley in 1922.

❦

Between the wars the National School continued under James Self until 1929 when he retired after thirty-four years and was succeeded by H G Verrall who was headmaster until 1941. Self's long term of office had given the school stability and continuity but it is clear that Verrall felt the need for change and the introduction of modern methods, and he re-organised the classes and teaching methods, introducing specialisation for the first time. The 1918 Education Act raised school leaving age to fourteen where it remained until the 1944 Act. One of the successes of the school was in gardening and in 1919 they won the Froy Challenge Spade "as best gardening class in the County of East Sussex". They repeated this success in later years. Numbers were a recurring problem and by 1925 had dropped to one hundred and sixty-six which resulted in a member of staff having to be dismissed; under Verrall numbers crept up but were still only one hundred and eightyfive in 1939. Main drains arrived at the school in 1923 but although the building was re-roofed and the playground repaired in 1926, by 1936 part of the playground fell into the road and the infants classroom roof fell in, narrowly avoiding injuring the children: money was tight. The other noticeable development was the introduction of regular medical checks for all the children. Head inspections were carried out each term by the district nurse, annual dentist checks were introduced in 1926 and eye tests in 1929.

❦

In January 1936 George V died and the Prince of Wales became Edward VIII, only to abdicate in favour of his brother the Duke of York in May 1937 because of his own determination to marry Mrs Wallis Simpson. There can be few villages which have as permanent a memorial of that short reign as Burwash, with the small development known as Coronation Cottages which commemorated Edward VIII. George VI had become King by the time Chamberlain concluded his agreement with Hitler at Munich in 1938 which he said brought "peace in our time". Again the spark that ignited the war lay in German ambitions which started around the Balkans, with Hitler proposing the annexation of Sudetenland, part of Czechoslovakia, where ethnic Germans were in the majority. England and France gave in, leaving the Czechs in the lurch and giving the impression that England's other guarantee, of Poland's independence, was also worthless. However, when in August 1939 Germany did invade Poland, England and France felt they had no option but to declare war on Germany when their ultimatum expired on the 3rd September. One of the immediate effects in England was that the evacuation of the cities and the coast began: it was planned that four million would be relocated to the country but only one and a half million went and one million returned home within months. By May 1940 Winston Churchill was Prime Minister, recognised by all as the most capable war leader, and following the retreat of British forces from France through Dunkirk in June 1940 he made his famous rallying speeches including "it has come to us to stand alone in the breach", "we will fight them on the beaches…" and offering the country "blood, toil, tears and sweat". It is necessary to go back some hundreds of years to find someone rallying the English in this manner.

The Battle of Britain, fought in the skies of southern England, started on 10th July 1940 and continued until Hitler suddenly called a halt on 17th September, probably due to the huge losses of Luftwaffe pilots and planes. This was followed by the Blitz, the indiscriminate bombing of towns and cities in an attempt to break the spirit of the British people. This in turn largely ended in May 1941 when Germany turned its attention east against Russia. That particular campaign faltered, as so many before it, in the grip of the Russian winter in December. Singapore fell to Japan in the same month and allied forces were retreating in North Africa. Then came one of the decisive moments of the war when, on 7th December 1941, Japan brought the USA into the conflict by bombing Pearl Harbour. The tide gradually turned and Montgomery's victory at El Alamein in November 1942 was followed by the invasion of Italy and the allies landings in France on D-Day, 6th June 1944. Victory over Germany was achieved on 8th May 1945 and over Japan on 15th August, following the dropping of atomic bombs on the cities of Hiroshima and Nagasaki that month.

The civilian inhabitants of South East England, including Burwash, were more directly involved in this war than any previous conflict since the Norman conquest. They watched the Battle of Britain take place in the skies above them; they were hosts to some of the D-Day forces before the invasion of France and every day the local activities of the Home Guard made their presence felt. Rationing affected everyone, restricting food, clothes, sweets and petrol, and the blackout was imposed in every house. A large number of bombs fell in the area with civilian casualties resulting. Burwash received twenty-two flying bombs and eight hundred and eighty other bombs including seven hundred and eighty-three incendiary bombs and eighty-three high explosives: two civilians were killed and thirty-nine injured.

As soon as war was declared Air Raid Wardens had been appointed, the village shelter was built below the Bear car park and rationing and the other constraints stoically accepted. Gas masks had been issued to the National School in August 1939, followed by

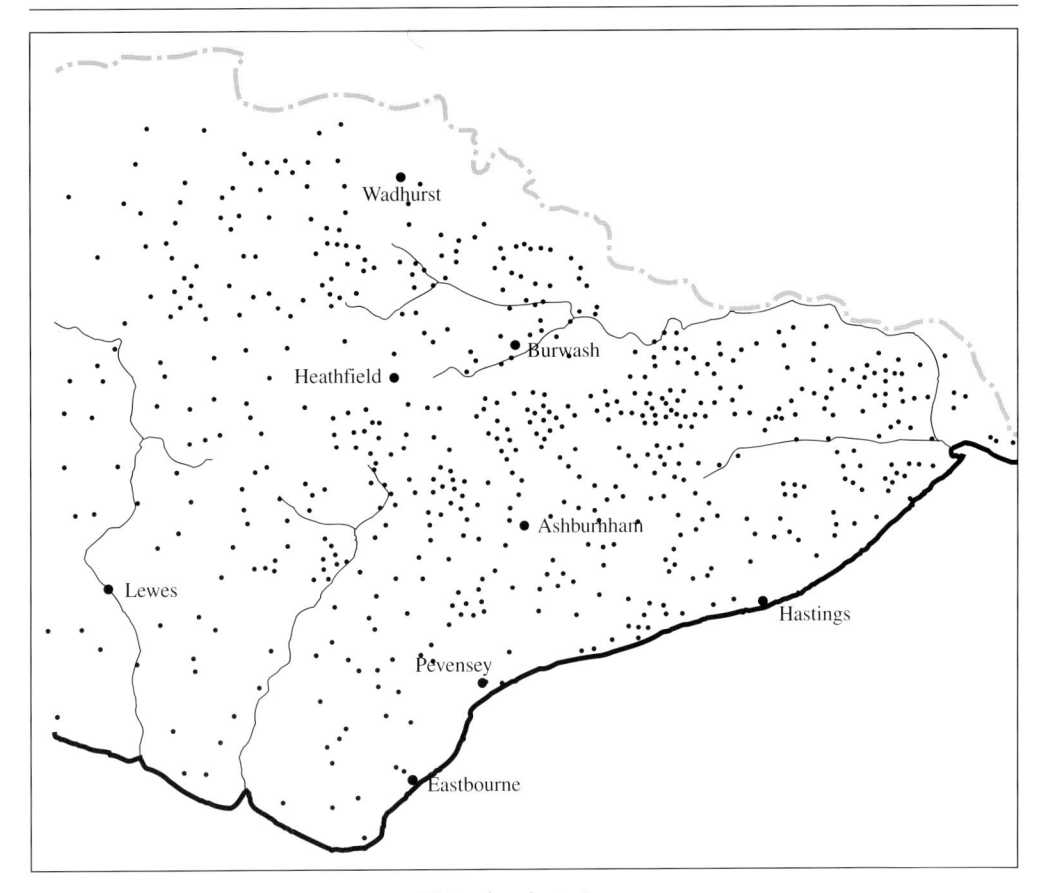

Flying bombs in Sussex

an adjusting schedule to ensure that they fitted tightly. Then in September eighty girls from Morden Terrace Senior Girls School were evacuated to Burwash by the London County Council. The girls were largely housed at Southover, accompanied by four teachers, and the School in Bell Alley worked double shifts each day to cope with the additional numbers. By November the Institute (Village Hall) was being used as extra classrooms until it was requisitioned in May 1940 by 5 Platoon, 19 Battalion Home Guard as their headquarters. The village was allowed to hire it back on Saturday evenings for entertainment at a cost of ten shillings. By that time most of the evacuated children were being taught separately first at Southover and then at Hollyhurst at Burwash Common, except for those living with village families who joined the village school.

In June 1940 the army dug trenches in the field by the school for use during air raids. These raids started on the 5th August and the disruption can be seen from this schedule of raids on three typical days during that autumn:

130   Chapter Six

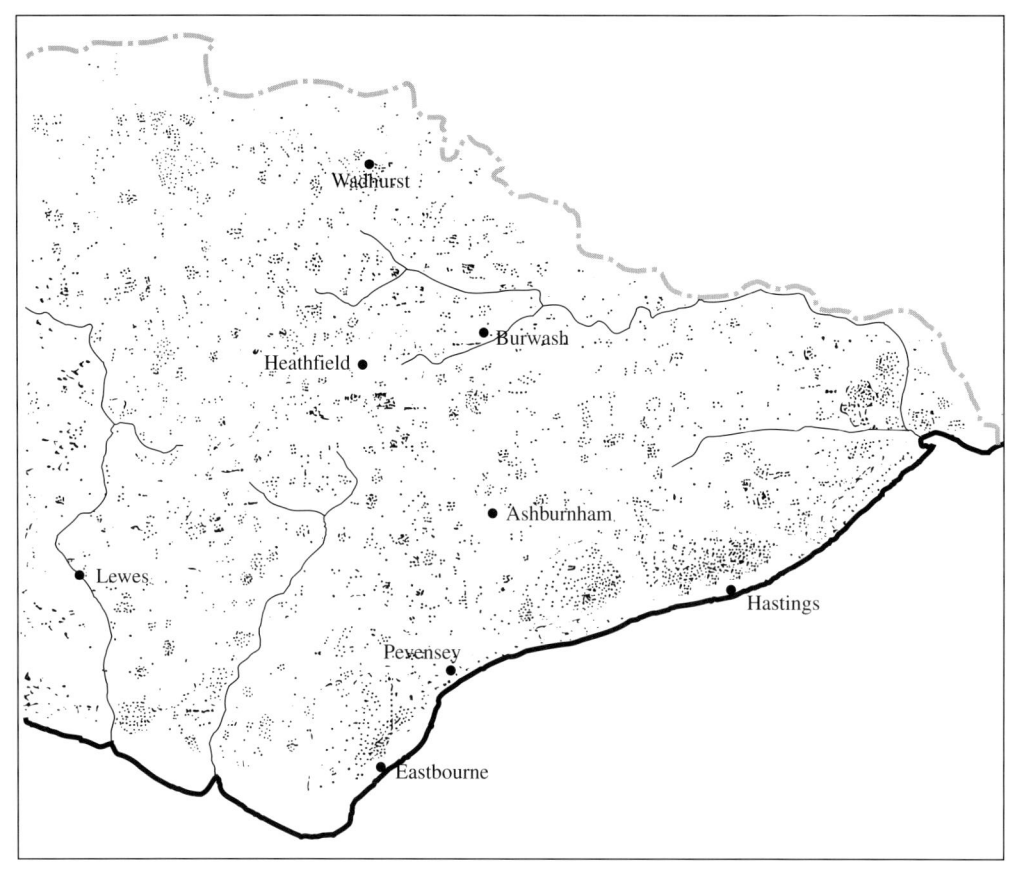

High explosive bombs in Sussex

	Sept 27	Oct 2	Oct 7
First warning	08.50	09.00	09.45
All clear	10.18	12.55	11.30
Second warning	11.45	14.00	12.55
All clear	13.15	14.30	14.30
Third warning	15.10	14.56	15.40
All clear	16.15	15.45	17.20
Total time in trenches	4hr 3min	5hr 14min	5 hours

By 12th October everyone had had enough of this disruption and the parents of fifty-two out of the seventy-two families at the school met and "unanimously agreed not to go to the trenches in future but carry on in school during raids". "School goes on, raid or no raid".

A Burwash wartime working party was set up, raising £62 in 1940 and making over five hundred garments so that a knitted gift could be sent to every Burwash man serving in the forces. The village, like others, settled to a wartime routine, with Canadian soldiers in Dawes House and later in Southover. There were a few lighter moments such as the August Fete in 1940 held in the Rectory garden where the Maude-Roxbys ran the Fancy Stall and Mrs Pagden the Produce. A treasure hunt had one hundred entries and teas were followed by a whist drive.

When the war in Europe came to an end in May 1945 there was an interdenominational service at St Bartholomew's and the village band led a parade consisting of members of the Royal Navy, the Army, the Royal Air Force, Women's Land Army, Womens Voluntary Service, Girls Club, Police, Munition workers, Home Guard, War Saving workers, School canteen and the Working Party. This was followed in August by a service of Thanksgiving after the Japanese surrender and the war thus ended. Another twenty-nine names had to be added to the war memorial, eleven from the Royal Air Force, five Royal Navy and thirteen Army. These losses reflected many of the campaigns with Ernest Bruce and Ernest Titmus dying at Dunkirk, George Clark at El Alamein, Henry Rix in the fall of Singapore, Patrick Ryand in Hong Kong, Roger Evans and Bertram Jenner Akehurst at Casino, and Austin Daw in Normandy. There were of course, as in the 1914-18 war, many more who were wounded or taken prisoner and many who suffered great hardship: there is no memorial to them except the freedom that they won again for this country.

The peace that had been achieved had once more been at a high cost in the loss of human life and the long-term financial effects on the country. The architect of that victory, Winston Churchill, had called a general election in July 1945 and had been rejected by the people, particularly the returning soldiers who wanted a new Britain, the Britain of equality and opportunity that seemed to be offered by Clement Attlee's Labour Party. Changes had already begun. Beveridge had transformed and improved social security benefits in 1943 and now the government offered a programme of housing, health, employment and further social security. Coal mining and the railways were nationalised, as was iron, steel, gas, electricity, BOAC and other industries, including the Bank of England. Perhaps the greatest and longest lasting achievement was the introduction of the National Health Service in 1948 to provide free medicine for all. Although this ideal concept proved unaffordable its spirit remains strongly today.

National Service, introduced in 1947, continued until about 1961, with many national servicemen fighting in the wars of the time including that of Korea, the first that was waged by the United Nations, which had replaced the discredited League of Nations. NATO had been formed in 1949 and the concept of a European state was born with the formation of the Western European Union in 1948. This range of events in the post-war period led to intellectual questions being posed by many, including John Galbraith in his "The Affluent Society" (1958) which queried the direction in which society was going, and what should be its priorities, with the same challenge having been made by works such as John Osborne's "Look Back in Anger" (1956).

The pre-war, experienced politicians gradually retired and were replaced by the new generation of Heath and Wilson. The old order finally disappeared with the end of the tired Conservative government of Macmillan and Home and its misleading catchphrase "You never had it so good". The next period from 1964-79 was a discontented time for the country, lacking leadership and direction, with high taxation (up to 98%), high inflation, a depreciating currency, appalling labour relations and indecision on the relationship with Europe. It also saw the troubles in Ireland return with some of the worst sectarian violence ever known. For better or worse Margaret Thatcher (1979-90) gave the country a positive direction. Under her, industry was privatised again, taxation lowered and the stranglehold of the trades unions removed. However, the ethos of the country was also changed from a caring society regardless of the cost, to one which encouraged the survival of the fittest. The Labour government that followed in 1997 has not significantly altered this philosophical direction.

❧

One of the most far reaching and longest lasting pieces of legislation was the 1944 Education Act, masterminded by R A Butler. This determined the pattern of education in post-war Britain and largely survived the tinkerings of successive governments for over forty years. It reduced the influence of the Church, and the number of Church of England schools and set out the structure within which Local Authorities must provide education following the Eleven Plus examination. All children had the right to stay at school until fifteen, subsequently raised to sixteen.

The National School in Burwash, or the village school as it became increasingly known, came under the control of East Sussex County Council in 1948 and settled back into a peacetime regime after not only the strains of war but also five different Heads between 1941-46. Numbers fluctuated considerably from one hundred and twenty-six in 1947 to one hundred and forty-eight two years later, declining to one hundred and one by 1963 before climbing steadily to the numbers in the late 1990s of between one hundred and twenty and one hundred and forty. Facilities were progressively upgraded with major improvements to toilets, cloakrooms and staff facilities in 1957, a new kitchen extension in 1964 and electric central heating replacing coal stoves in 1971. In 2000 further improvements are planned including the replacement of the prefabricated classrooms, erected in 1972 and 1982, which is being financed through the sale of the allotments in Shrub Lane by the County Council.

The swimming pool was built in 1965, heated in 1969, roofed in 1971, renovated in 1983 and refurbished in 1998. Interest in agriculture fluctuated with a Rabbit Club being formed in 1950 to join the existing Young Farmers Club but in 1955 the long standing school gardens were ploughed up and grassed for a playing field. This may have been the result of recent sporting success for, in 1952, the school reached the final of the East Sussex Primary League Football Cup, losing to Barcombe 2 - 0, and in 1953 they won the Cricket final, beating Newick by six wickets. John Catt, cousin of the newsagents, had a remarkable average of 307 in school games and won his East Sussex cricket colours. The Parents Association was formed in 1945 with Mrs Gatland as chairman, Mrs Wrenn secretary and Mrs Catt a committee member, and in 1949 they donated an HMV650 wireless set to the school. In the same year Mrs Mary Longley (nee Ellis) retired after sixty years at the school as pupil, monitor, pupil teacher and then teacher. A visit took place in 1951 to the South Bank Exhibition and chest X-rays were introduced in 1956. By 1968 PC Dave Hedges was giving safety lectures and in 1972 Dr Hazel Walters and Sister Jean Holland were carrying out the regular health checks. In 1985 Margaret Waterhouse retired as "Lollypop Lady" after seventeen years on duty at the road crossing but continued as caretaker for another eleven years.

The popularity of religion and the number of people attending church has declined steadily during the 20th century. This has affected all denominations, with the Church of England closing churches, amalgamating livings and sharing priests, Non-conformists amalgamating different sects and closing churches and Catholics also having smaller congregations. The worst hit in Burwash have been the Non-conformists who have seen all their three chapels close. The first to go was the breakaway Calvinist chapel which closed in the 1920s and was later converted to a private residence, Chant Meadow, with all traces of the chapel disappearing. The last to go was the Congregational chapel next to Mount House which was sold for the Old Rectory Court development in 1968. Its membership had declined from thirty in 1932 to six in 1950, by which time it had neither minister nor lay preacher. Thus ended two hundred and fifty years of a strong Non-conformist presence in the village.

The Roman Catholic church, St Joseph's at Southover, continued to be administered by the Salesians who, in 1921, opened a boarding school which became very

St Joseph's Church and School

successful and required an extension of the buildings. This continued until 1951 when falling numbers and the requirement to comply with government building regulations resulted in the school closing and the staff and children being largely transferred to Cowley near Oxford. The buildings were used for theological studies and as an outdoor centre for a short time, then rented out as holiday flats and finally sold. St Joseph's reverted to being a Salesian novitiate but this closed in 1966. The Salesians still own the burial ground which remains open but the congregation moved to the new Church of Christ the King in 1968 and the grand old church at Southover was completely dismantled and disposed of with just one wooden archway being re-used in the hall at Christ the King.

St Bartholomew's has kept its own Rector but has followed the countrywide fashion of modernising its services to try to encourage young people to attend. The Rectory was sold in 1912 and the Rector, Rev. Martyn-Linnington who had previously been the Curate in the parish, moved temporarily to Ashlands until 1924 when the new Rectory was built near the church. Rev. Lionel Grant Meade arrived shortly afterwards (1925) and was succeeded by Rev. Sir Henry Denny Bt. in 1936, Rev. T Wingfield Heale in 1953, Rev. E Somerville Collie in 1957, Rev. John Howe Greene in 1969 and Rev. Patrick Durrant in 1976. In 1995 the Rev. Roy Vincent and his wife Hilary arrived and he was inducted in January 2000 by which time they had moved into yet another new Rectory.

Church of Christ the King

The development of housing down Shrub Lane had begun during Victorian times with the first houses in Greenfield Road being followed by one or two other houses and then the row of Bankside. After the 1914-18 war there was a slow but steady increase in the number of houses but these were generally built singly. A typical example was Nethercroft: in 1920 Anne Lucas, selling off the Franchise estate, sold the land to the Council who in turn sold it to W J Ellis, the local builder, who sold the completed building to the Misses Gladys and Annie Dunderdale for £75 in 1922. Gladys Dunderdale was a keen member of the British Red Cross Society, qualifying in Home Nursing in 1913 and serving for many years. It stayed in their family until 1961 and since then has had four owners.

Other houses followed but it was after the 1939-45 war that the demand for housing in the south east of England led to larger-scale developments. This started in Burwash with the construction of Rother View in 1961 on the site of the allotments, which then moved further down Shrub Lane. In 1999 the newer allotment site was sold for housing and the village is now without allotments for the first time for some two hundred years. Next came the building of Strand Meadow in 1966 to replace thirty-six prefabs erected after the 1939-45 war. Further houses have been added since then followed by Wealden View in about 1982, this replacing the old barn belonging to Square Farm that had stood on the site. Other individual houses have also been steadily added.

By the railway crossing there were a number of older houses, Crowhurst Bridge Cottages, housing staff of the Heathfield Water Company, which were destroyed in 1944 by a German V-I. One of those hit was the railway level crossing keeper's cottage and the keeper escaped injury only because he was in the privy at the bottom of the garden when the bomb struck. Three prefabs were erected in an orchard purchased from the Whittakers at Woodrising and were aptly named Orchard Cottages. The homeless Water Company employees, after a short time in temporary flats in Denes House and other emergency accommodation, moved into the prefabs where they stayed until new cottages were built at Crowhurst Bridge in 1957, at right angles to the original row. The prefabs were themselves replaced by new cottages in 1961 which were built immediately in front of them. On both sides of Shrub Lane more houses and bungalows were added to the few built in the 1930s such as Wild Thyme, earlier called Meadow Close. Another house hit by a German bomb was Oakside, which also seems to have been originally on Shrub Lane but after demolition was apparently rebuilt, largely from the original materials, in its current position. Since then it has been considerably extended by the current owners, Charles and Celia Merchant who both play an important part in St Bartholomew's congregation. The Blaikley family had sold Shrub Farm in 1923 to Weymss and Jane Whittaker.

Kildare

It was the Whittakers who changed the name to Woodrising, calling it after property owned by them in South Africa, and Jane Whittaker was an early member of the Monday Painters. Michael and Caroline Berger acquired the house in 1963 and considerably extended it in 1971 in keeping with the original, by adding the southern end.

Kildare, built in about 1890, was first owned by Amos and Hannah Elliott who ran a laundry there. Rainwater was collected for its purity, added to the well water and, after boiling, was poured into large wooden tubs where the laundry was washed and stirred with copper sticks before being lifted out for rinsing, starching and bluing. The huge ironing room contained a stove and irons. Wages were 3d. per hour. Once finished the laundry was delivered by horse and cart. Amos Elliott died in 1913 and the business was assumed in 1916 by Frederick Hunt. He was born in Birmingham, came to Hastings as a young man and earned his living pushing ladies along the seafront in bathchairs. He married the daughter of the owner of a Warrior Square laundry and they came to Burwash to start their own business. When his wife died Frederick married Flora Vigor in 1926 and they soon moved the laundry to its modern site. They lived in what is now the reception and office area of the laundry (called The Glen) before building Glendare next door and also acquiring Woodside Cottages on the other side. These latter were replaced by Chatterpie and The Leas in 1991. During the 1939-45 war there were searchlights in the field behind the laundry and a large part of the business was washing and mending clothes for the Canadian soldiers billeted in the village. Frederick Hunt died, aged eighty-four, in 1949

The Laundry with The Glen at the front

and Flora in 1955. The laundry was purchased by Bill Sear who later handed over to his son Jonathan who manages it today.

Kildare had been purchased by the Huntleys who turned it into a private house. James Huntley had left school at the age of eleven in 1884 to join the London, Brighton and South Coast Railway before later joining the East Sussex Police. In 1905 he was promoted Sergeant at Hurst Green before retiring to Burwash in 1915. He contributed much to local affairs: he was Parish Council Clerk from 1922-46, rate collector, cricketer and footballer for the village, twice winner of the cup for the best kept garden and once for the best kept allotment. During the 1939-45 war he was secretary to the Burwash Home Guard. He died in 1954 aged eighty-one and his daughter, Mrs. Burden, still lives in Bankside.

At the top of Shrub Lane, above the Victorian Bankside, the three pairs of cottages (Broads Cottages) owned by the Barnsley Trust, (named after the original donor of 1727) were gradually sold. Numbers 1 and 2 having been previously disposed of, Numbers 3 and 4 were sold in 1956 for £576 to William and Ethel Anderson of 3 Bell Alley and in 1963 Numbers 5 and 6 were sold to the Burwash District Housing Association for the Elderly for £2,700. The movement to form this Association had started the previous year when considerable concern was being expressed at the lack of housing available for older people, many of whom were living in cottages with no modern facilities. The concern was led by Jean Holland who had been district nurse, midwife and health visitor since about 1950. A public meeting was held, a committee appointed and the Association launched. Funds were raised and the cottages, which had been

Soanes before the corner was altered

home and office for district nurses for fifty years, were purchased and converted into four flats. Jean Holland continued to be a leading figure and almost single handed organised an antiques sale in 1970 at the village hall where 410 lots raised £3,100. This provided the first tranche of money that led to the purchase of land in Vicarage Lane, Burwash Common, and the building of six further homes that were opened in 1974. In 2000 there are a total of thirteen properties available for people of pensionable age for which there is always a ready demand.

One of the several village bakeries was for some time at Soanes Cottage, owned first by Matilda Bourner, confectioner, followed by "Pinch Plum" Hilder, so called because plums (and toffees) were cut in half if overweight on the scales. Later came the Russells who had their bakery at the back. They died within weeks of each other and although their daughter Joyce carried on for a while, she then moved and the business ceased in 1978.

The surviving Clifford sister, Miss Mabel, died in 1950 and Church House (formerly Hoppers Croft) was bought by Major Charles Verner in 1952. Verner, a keen woodworker, was a churchwarden from 1960-69 and when he died in 1975 his ex-batman and companion Jack Stepney stitched and presented kneelers for St Bartholomew's sanctuary rails. Jack Stepney died in 1993 and is buried at St Josephs. It was in 1952 that a further part of Church House garden, bordering Hoppers Croft Lane, was sold off and

Major Charles Verner (left) with some of his woodwork

Robins Corner built; opposite came Woodruffe and Buxley on the lane to Rother Close. These developments meant demolishing the stables that had been used by William Farley when he had been landlord at The Bell and fly proprietor up until 1923, and where he had kept his horses, harness, tackle and carriages. Further development took place with the bakery buildings and garages at the back of Soanes and Beeches being removed and Hawthorne and Woodcotes being built.

The Bell in the 1920s

At Burghurst (Adams Strake) solicitors Aitkens and Andrews became Andrews and Bennett and the house remained office or home to that firm and the families, and their successors the Careys, until 1998. Next door, Colemans, later called Rose Cottage, was knocked down and Barclays Bank was built in the 1950s. Guestling, now called Linden Cottage, had seen the Honeysetts followed by A E Ellis who was an ironmonger, hardware dealer and stone and monumental mason. By 1935 Linden was a private residence and was eventually purchased by Jim and Margaret Hobden in 1972. Oakbeam, Bower and Dudwell were all owned, from before the war until the 1950s, by Fred Farley who offered antiques, other furniture and ornaments, sweets and lemonade. Home-made humbugs were four for a farthing, for which price you could alternatively buy a Chicago Bar made out of black molasses and other secret ingredients.

Oakbeam becomes a private residence

After the Noakes had left the Old Granary and Yew Tree House in about 1920 it was owned until 1955 by Edwin Sweatman, grocer, draper and corn merchant who also had a shop in Battle. His manager here was Sidney Huggett who lived in Yew Tree with the Old Granary being the shop. In 1957 they were bought by the Tarrants who were followed by M & F Peebles (Fairway Stores). In 1972 the two houses were sold off separately, both as private residences, Yew Tree House being purchased by Tim and Prue Milling with Prue running Burwash Art Gallery on the premises from 1973-87. The last tradesman in Everton Cottages was the shoemaker Tompkinson who followed the tradition of Harry Spears and lived in the cottage which is now called Lobbs, perhaps being a reference to the well-known shoemaker of that name in St James's, London.

Swan Meadow (Swanne Mead and Laddes) had become the site of the annual Burwash cattle sales which had moved there after the 1914-18 war, having been held for centuries in the Bear car park and in the High Street between Mount House and the Bear. Traditionally there had been two fairs each year, now held on the 12th May and 4th October, and although they had been discontinued from time to time both dates had been reasonably regular fixtures since at least 1888. Wooden hurdles were used to erect

Sweatmans at the Old Granary

temporary pens and cattle and other produce were brought from all the surrounding districts to be sold. The village lads used to earn good pocket money driving the newly purchased cattle to their buyers' homes, often cross-country, and as far as Dallington or Ticehurst. Their additional reward would be cakes, bread pudding and perhaps a mug of beer when they arrived. Although village fairs and fetes continued, the main cattle sale ceased and in 1935 Swan Meadow became the home of the new Burwash football club and then also became the village cricket pitch when the old ground at Highfields was sold in 1947. The football club had a lease from Bass Brewery who had acquired the Rose & Crown and the field. All the players changed in the pub where they had their refreshments afterwards. In 1962 Burwash Playing Fields Association was formed. In 1975 Bass declined to renew the lease but offered to sell the field for £20,000, the price of building land. With only a few months to raise the money the Playing Fields Association, led by Bill Sear (by then the owner of the laundry with his wife Sheelagh) and Gwil Swift, obtained a grant of £10,000 from the National Playing Fields Association and raised enough of the remainder to make the deal. They worked tirelessly and when their annual fair raised £1,500 it was at once doubled by an anonymous local lady. A second hand prefabricated pavilion had been bought and erected for £700 and when the purchase of the field was completed the children's playground was added. The prefab was finally replaced in 1998 by a modern brick pavilion which was built at a cost of £155,000 assisted

The Burwash football team which won the East Sussex League Division 1 championship in 1967. Back row (l to r): L. Pickles, J. Waterhouse, M. Norries, G. Farmer, M. Catt, E. Workman, R Shilling Front row: J. Jenner, T. Noon, R. Funnell, D. Lusted, M. Farley.

by a large grant from the Sports Council Lottery Fund. Tennis courts were also added and a tennis club was started. Swan Meadow is now the venue for cricket and football matches, is used by the school for games and contains the improved children's playground. It also sees the annual village fete, held on the August Bank Holiday, the successor to centuries of fairs. Most village organisations have a stall, as one of their main annual fund raising ventures, and there are hundreds of visitors from all over Sussex to this essentially local event. The Playing Fields Association charges stall holders a small fee as part of their own fund raising activities to maintain and improve facilities. They also charge user fees for other events and run a lottery where about two hundred and fifty members of the 100-Plus Club subscribe £1 each month in the hope of winning a prize. Among the main organisers and motivators of the playing fields and associated events are Steve Mintram (the village policeman), Eddie Workman (who also runs marathons for charity), Steve Bennett (who runs the lottery) and they have many other supporters and helpers.

The fire station had moved to Ham Lane from the barn behind the Bell in 1939 when the new station was built and Charles Brook was appointed Station Master. They

144 *Chapter Six*

The fire fighting team

also received a new Dennis fire engine to replace the previous one which had been a converted Studebaker police car; before that the appliance had been horse-drawn. During the 1939-45 war there were up to three fire engines at Burwash in order to deal with the number of bombs falling in the area. On the outbreak of war the old private fire companies became part of the National Fire Service which was itself succeeded by control passing to local authorities and the Burwash unit then became part of East Sussex Fire Brigade. The officer in charge for part of the post-war period was Gordon Farmer (serving from 1956-91), who received the BEM for his services.

At the corner of Ham Lane Dr John Hancock had his surgery in Jarvis's house from about 1902 when he and Dr Curteis were the two village doctors until Hancock retired in about 1915. Fred (F J) Jarvis died in 1950 and his son Jeff took over the Burwash shop while Jeff's older brother Nelson ran the Etchingham shop. In due

The new Fire Station

course Jeff's sons Nigel (in 1984) and Graham in (1990) took over Etchingham and Burwash respectively and the family can look back at one hundred and thirty years of continuous business in Burwash. The Jarvis family gave up Ham Place Farm in 1950 when Fred died, while Ham Place itself had disappeared and been replaced by the Oast. Next door to the butchers shop the Blacksmiths Arms had ceased to be a pub soon after the 1914-18 war and the last publican, Henry Blackford, died in 1928. The Post Office was, for some years, in Gideon House and was run by Francis (Frank) Daunt. Frank was however keener on farming, at Court Lodge, and so his young wife Alma (Fred Jarvis's sister) took over the day-to-day running of the Post Office and transferred it back across the road to its present site once the Blacksmiths Arms closed. By then there were three deliveries a day at 6 am, 12 noon and 7.30 pm and despatches at 10.30 am, 5.30 pm and 9.45 pm, as well as collections from the seven letter boxes in the parish.

Farleys Corn Stores remained little altered throughout the first half of the century. Buckley and Pettit had acquired it from the previous owner Brook who had bought it in 1878. The business sold seeds, corn, coal, cattle feed and a wide range of other goods . When Frank (second son of Charlie the garage owner) and Joan Farley acquired the stores in 1952 it had become run down with a furniture shop and corn chandlers being either side of the house in the middle. They converted the downstairs part of the house into one shop, resulting in the three interconnecting sections that exist today, with their living quarters being above them. William Ellis' grocers shop (Chilston) stayed in business until about 1935 when the premises were acquired as the offices of the Heathfield and District Water Company. They were absorbed in 1959 by the Eastbourne Water Company and the office was closed with the staff being made redundant. The house was purchased by Lady Chilston in about 1960 who modernised it, turned it into a private residence and gave it its name. The current owners, Jim and Betty Reid, acquired it

Chilston House

in 1970 and have created a large and colourful garden to complement the house.

Noakes the butchers sold in about 1920 to F Vigor who retired in 1948 and this building ultimately became Chateaubriand Antiques. Next door, in the other part of this old house, Charlie Brown had his greengrocers shop for many years. He gave this up in 1951 when Tom and Marjorie Workman took it over. Eddie Workman came into his parents shop in 1963 and in 1969 bought Noakes' old clock shop from Hicks who had moved his greengrocers business there (from Gideon) after old Albert Noakes died in 1958. The shop had long since ceased to be a clock and watchmakers and had been H W Pagden and Son, tailors, for many years before Hicks. Noakes lived in the other half of the house and had installed electricity only towards the end: he used to come in from the Rose & Crown, switch on the light, light his candle, and switch off the electricity again. He was heard to say "marvellous stuff this electricity". With Albert Noakes' death ended a family's association with the village which had been continuous for over five hundred years. The earliest records of the 16th century contain numerous references to Anoke, Anokes, Noke and Noakes, and it is likely that many were part of the same family. Their descendants formed three branches by the 19th century, the farmers, the grocers and the clockmakers. In addition they had been pillars of the local churches, both St Bartholomew's and the non-conformist chapel, and often Overseers of the Poor. In 1984 the Workmans moved their greengrocers business into Noakes Cottage but kept their old

Rover, Noakes and Villiers

premises going as a florists before also moving that in with the greengrocers and converting their original premises entirely into a private residence. In 1997 they closed their greengrocers. In between their two shops was Hazeldens toys, following the tradition of Martha Fleming, but subsequently having a variety of trades, including Watsons estate agents, a café and now Broadview Kitchens, and Villiers, which has been a private residence for many years. On the other side of Noakes Cottage, Rover Cottage had ceased to be the post office early in the century and was for some time Farley's sweet shop and then a tea-room before it too eventually became a residence.

Shadwell Row had gradually become residential and all the houses had been modernised except for the end cottage (Revenue Cottage) where Albert Catt ran his newsagents shop. Before the war he also sold fish as a supplementary trade. By 1938 he and his wife Margaret (nee Woodall) had turned it solely into a newspaper shop and this continued until the early 1960s, when it was burned down. By reputation it was still unaltered and unmodernised from previous centuries but the fire allowed restoration and improvements to be made and it became a private residence. After Catt's newsagents shop was burned down they moved their business across the alleyway and remained there until

Catts Stores 1960

about 1970 with their son Bert and his wife Nell in charge. Before that this shop was occupied by the other Pagdens (Thomas Pagden and Son, Tailors) where Charlie Gardener could be seen sitting sewing cross-legged on a stool in the window. They were followed by Mrs Saunders' haberdashers. After the Catts came two further owners before the business was acquired by Teskey and Barbara O'Neil in 1987. They modernised and enlarged the shop and later also extended their business into Hurst Green. Down the lane between this shop and Catts was the Burwash Gospel Mission formed in about 1944 by Mrs Saunders' husband Henry and continued by their sons until the mid-1960s when it ceased through lack of support. The mission was housed in an old stable block which was then purchased by the Careys who demolished it and built the present offices of Andrews and Bennett in 1969, thus enabling the business to be moved out of their residence.

Fullers Stores was owned by the family until they were replaced by International Stores in the 1960s followed by Spar and then the present Village Stores.

The White House had been acquired in 1910 by Dr A W S Curteis who moved to The Ivy in 1921. After several owners it was once again owned by a lawyer when it was purchased in 1978 by Michael Stonor and his wife Sara (who became a churchwarden of St Bartholomew's in 1995). Tudor House was a barbers, complete with barbers pole, run

The Village Stores

by Tissard in the 1930s and Ford into the 1970s after which Simon and Joan Feltham opened their successful restaurant until 1998. Hilder's Bakery had been acquired by H L Petry and it was then run by his son until the 1960s when it became Penelope Claire and then Just So, and now Abbot Antiques. Next door Mr and Mrs Vickery ran their luncheons, teas and part time antiques business in Lime Tree until 1992, having succeeded the old coopers business.

C Waterhouse and Sons had been started as builders and undertakers in 1926 by Charles Waterhouse after he had served his apprenticeship in the trade with Finlayson of the Bear. Waterhouse employed up to ten people and the dead were laid out in their homes while he personally made and polished the coffins in his yard. He only ceased making the coffins himself in 1964. He died in 1987 and his daughter Dorothy, who had trained as a nurse and then helped out her parents, took over the business. In 2000 they handle over two hundred funerals a year and have efficient modern premises behind their offices. Spring and Autumn cottages were originally one house while Peartony was built in what was once the alleyway entrance to Waterhouses yard.

The Wrenns had been successful shopkeepers and had three separate businesses on their premises, a grocer, a draper and an ironmongers and china shop. They also acquired Wren Cottage where they lived. Herbert and Carrie ran the business until Herbert's death in 1938 whereafter Carrie continued it until she died in 1947. Their three sons Ted, George and Ernest

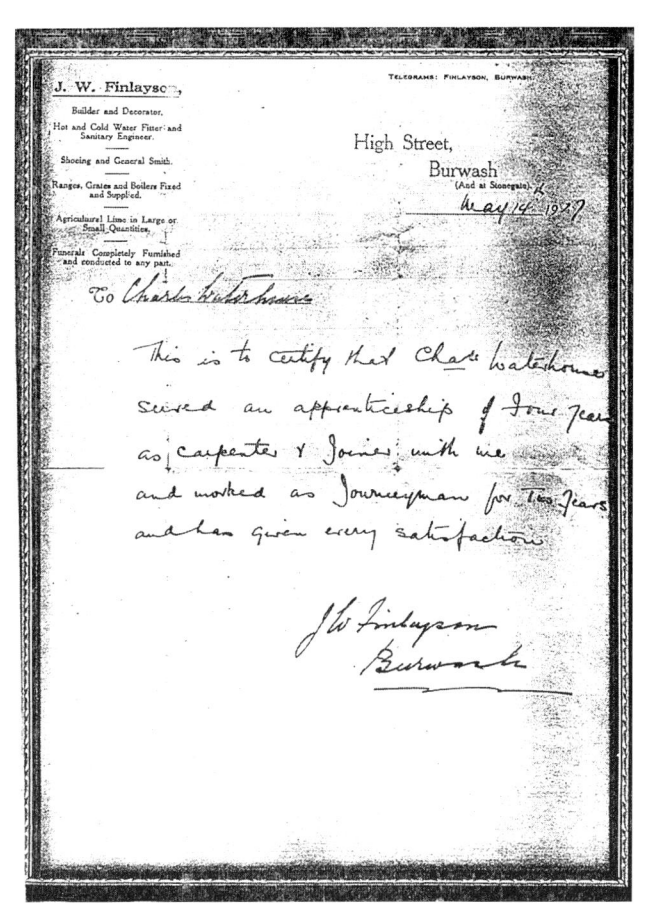

Charles Waterhouse's reference

continued the business for a few years and then sold them and Wren Cottage to Major Geirnaert. He lived in the cottage but the shops were gradually sold off. The ironmongers became first French's TV (of Robertsbridge), then Gee Jay

Cheriton, Wren and the three shops

Burwash in the late 20th century

Builders and now Burwash Home Improvements. The drapers has had a variety of owners, while the old grocers was acquired by the Leaves from Collyers in 1965 and is now a hairdressers (Chaplins). Next door, the White Hart ceased to be a pub and became Cheriton in 1968.

On the south side, the Misses Russell had purchased Ashlands, following Ellen Gould, but this small estate was broken up in 1951, when the Misses Russell left and the cottage, the main house and Weeping Birch (built 1925) were purchased separately. The principal house and land were acquired by Alan and Constance Sellick who stayed there until Constance died in 1986, having been pre-deceased by Alan in 1975. One of Constance Sellick's lasting actions was to donate the land to enable the Red Cross hut to be built at the top of the Highfields Estate. This estate had been built in 1947 on the site of the old cricket ground and one of the village allotments.

The original garage near Highfields was built by Madge Brothers in 1922 selling petrol and carrying out car repairs. The business was bought in 1924 by John Oakley and remained in the family ownership until 1997.

Novar, Providence and Wayside have for many years been three separate residences. Novar was variously a market garden shop, a book shop, library, toy shop and offices, until it was purchased in 1968 by Edward and Jenny Le Besque. Avon and Garrymore replaced the old row of cottages in the early part of the century when Rose Cottages were probably also built on what was a clear gap between the existing rows of houses. Next door Wrenns Cottages replaced the old row of cottages in the late 1950s. The older buildings protruded into the street, but they were now lined up with Cobblers to allow a footpath. Cobblers survived unaltered until about 1976 when there was a bad fire there and the occupant, known as Danilo, died from burns because of the difficulty the firemen had in getting him out of his bed as the bedclothes were nailed to the frame.

Wrenns Cottages on the right before redevelopment

The air raid shelter was removed from the slope by the car park in the 1950s and at about the same time Cyril Moore's wooden fish shop was demolished. He sold both wet fish and fish and chips, and was a popular local supplier. In 1992 the new surgery was opened at the back of the car park at which time the Doctors' practice moved there from Rockhurst with Dr Jane Woodgate being joined by Dr Bruce Packham.

The Bear Hotel added the motel in 1970 and is now one of the only three pubs remaining, together with the Bell and the Rose & Crown. Successively the Blacksmiths Arms, White Hart and Admiral Vernon have been converted and all the other houses supplying ale officially or unofficially have disappeared. Most pubs now remain open most or all of the day as the restrictive licensing laws have been repealed or amended, and they have become places where families go rather than being the traditional preserve of a largely male hard drinking clientele.

Next to Kimberley Mr Goodsell ran a sweet shop in Daisy Tea Rooms (Gregwood) until he was succeeded by Gordon and Dot White who continued until the late 1970s. Gideon had been the Post Office since the early part of the century when the Woodalls had moved it there from Rover Cottage. Frederick Woodall, son of John and Fanny (nee Fleming), who had succeeded to the Post Office, and his wife Nora, brought up their large family of seven sons and two daughters there until they moved. It was Frederick's sister Margaret who was married to Albert Catt across the street. The Woodalls were followed as Postmaster in Gideon by Frank and Alma Daunt and after they took the Post Office to its current site Gideon became Elizabeth's Wool Shop and then Hicks greengrocers. When his lease expired in 1961 Hicks also moved across the road, to Noakes Cottage, and Gideon became a residence.

The first bicycle had been ridden in 1867 in London and by 1900 they had arrived in Burwash's bumpy street. William Woodall started his bicycle repair and sales agency in Popes Cottage and a shed attached to the back and side, across the passageway from his brother Frederick's family. William was killed in the 1914-18 war but the business was carried on by his widow Sally and their son Harry. The business added radio repairs to its trade and continued until Popes Cottage became owned by Kay Blundell. Kay

Kay Blundell

Blundell was a talented artist under her maiden name of Kay Nixon, a distant relative of the US President Nixon, and she illustrated many of Enid Blyton's books. In 1987 the house was converted into two parts, one of which is now Popes Antiques.

Gas Showroom, Bicycle Repairs and Post Office in 1920s

The Burwash Gas Company remained at Sadlers until electricity arrived in Burwash in 1936 and the company went bankrupt. Sadly the manager, Herbie Taylor (who was also Hon. Secretary of the Institute), took it so badly that he committed suicide on the railway line. During the war the shop was a café and then in 1984 became Sadlers estate agents under Brian and Linda Matthews. In 1997 it reverted to a private house but retained the name.

Chaunt House ceased to be a chemists in the 1970s. Spot McConley and his bottles of coloured potions had been followed by John Lauder who extended the range to include cosmetics, perfumes, veterinary and agricultural products and photographic requisites. In 1972 came Mr and Mrs

Same view in 1999

Davenport who were both pharmacists but they ended the chemists business in 1979 and sold in 1981. They were followed for a short period by Mrs Scott-Becket and then by Milly's Tea Room which opened in 1982 and closed in 1998.

Central Cottage and Forge

Victoria Terrace still had no modern conveniences when Mrs Ballard, mother of Dolly Tester, moved in on her marriage in 1928. Water came in 1937, electricity in 1939, and sanitation a little later.

Dave Hedges brought a blacksmiths business back to Burwash in 1985 after a gap of nearly fifty years when he opened his forge on retiring from the police force. He had completed seven years training before he joined the police, and this traditional trade now supplies ironwork of all sorts as would have done its predecessors. Before this the site had been a garage since

The old Rectory 1968

1918 when Charlie Farley built it and supplied petrol, oils, motor repairs and car hire. He owned the first motor car in Burwash. His son Charles carried on the business from 1947, after serving in the RAF as an engine fitter, until 1980. Next door Central Cottage was converted from two small cottages into the single dwelling by Charlie Farley senior and his son lives there today.

Portland Terrace 1968

In 1968 a bitter local battle ensued over a plan by Battle Rural District Council to demolish all but two of the Victorian Portland Terrace houses, the whole of the 15th century Portland cottages, including the old Rectory, and the by now defunct Congregational church. Mr Tarrant, the grocer and Parish Councillor, was in favour of replacement. "The cottages aren't anything more than sheds", "they are unfit for

Old Rectory Court and the surviving piece of Portland Terrace 1999

Determined residents in 1968

human habitation". But eighty-two-year-old Allan Hepden would "barricade the doors and windows. I'm hanging on till the last brick falls" and Alec Parks "only has one leg but this house is ideal for me". The Council won, demolition took place and in 1969 Old Rectory Court was built to provide accommodation for older residents.

Mount House is still in the ownership of the Maude-Roxby's. After Wilfred died in 1953 and Dulcie in 1961 the house was inherited by their oldest daughter Jean. Next door in Mount House Cottage lives her sister-in-law Margaret, widow of her brother Peter who died in 1986; her other brother John died in 1989. The Maude-Roxby's can trace their ancestry back to Thomas de Roxeby in 1337, the name becoming Roxby in 1732 and Maude-Roxby through marriage in 1830. Another name change in the family took place in the 1914-18 war when Jean's aunts Rita and Gertrude abandoned the Germanic sounding Schroeter and adopted Jefferson, their mother's name. Gertrude had served in France and Rita on the land.

After the last Fielden had left Rampyndene in 1945 there were several changes of ownership before it was bought by Robert and Alice Ransom in 1973. Today it is the monthly scene of great activity as the Parish magazine is printed and collated there by a small army of volunteers. An annual plant sale is held in the garden in aid of the Burwash Horticultural Society, of which Robert Ransom is Chairman and Sir Henry Fielden President. This Society also hold well patronised Spring and Summer Shows in the Village Hall where the prizes are fought for by well known local gardeners. These shows go back many years as in 1857 there was an annual exhibition for carrots, turnips, parsnips and cabbages grown in cottage gardens and there was also an annual cottage garden competition. However, they became discontinued in the 1939-45 war and were not re-started until the Queen's jubilee in 1977, when a show was held in the Village Hall and the horticultural society was resurrected with Eric Godley as secretary.

Dr Curteis had moved his residence and surgery from the White House to the Ivy when he purchased the whole property from Henry Wemyss Fielden in 1921 and he remained there until he died in 1943. His widow and then his daughter (Patience) lived there afterwards, first selling Ivy Cottage to Douglas and Madelaine Trew in 1977 and then Ivy House was sold to the Osborns on Miss Curteis' death in 1982. The property remains as two residences today. Miss Patience Curteis left her mark on the village by her generous endowment of St Bartholomew's permanent restoration fund.

Down Bell Alley little changed except for the building of Court Barn Farmhouse in 1914 by Robert Jarvis for £450, who then farmed hops, fruit, and had a dairy. The Jarvis's sold in 1958 and the house was purchased in 1969 by Douglas Cook when the farm was broken up and sold off in units. The oast and the farm buildings by the duck pond also became separate residences at that time and a few more houses were added to the eastern side of the lane. Little Holton was built in 1930 by Lieutenant Colonel James Sawyer when he moved from Holton House in Spring Lane and he lived there until his death in 1953. He had served in the Royal Medical Corps in the 1914-18 war and on moving to Burwash became a leading figure in the Scouting movement, building a large hut in his garden for the use of the local troop. The scouts grew in strength and by 1937 had over seventy Rovers, Scouts and Cubs who in addition to their usual activities put on a three day variety show with sea shanties by the Rover chorus, "Shivering Shocks" by Clemence Dane, "Golden West" and a recitation of Tennyson's "Revenge". Colonel Sawyer also carried out medical research and produced a thesis on muscular dystrophy based on his knowledge of the large Vigor family who had thirteen cases spread over three generations. The thesis provoked considerable comment and interest.

The east end of the village also saw changes. After Miss Hayley's death Garstons had several owners before becoming flats in 1983 with four houses being built in its garden soon afterwards. The Police Station was sold in 1955 to Mrs Nellie Jane Lee, a close friend of district nurse Jean Holland, and renamed Keystones for a short period. The cottages next door had alternated frequently between being shops and houses, and also in numbers of dwellings, before becoming Glebe, Jasmine and Northview: despite the many alterations over the centuries much of the old framework has survived. In 1998 the Admiral Vernon also became a private residence (Admiral House) when it was restored after a fire. Two new houses were also built in the old pub car park in 1999. The new Rectory had been built

Old Police House

Northview, Jasmine and Glebe Cottages at The Square

Admiral Vernon 1997

in 1924 behind the Admiral Vernon with a typically large garden. This was first divided when the three houses in Rectory Close were built. In 1998 the Diocese once again decided to extract some value from their land and sold two further plots for houses, constructed a new smaller Rectory on a third plot and will later sell the Rectory, now known as Acer House.

Youngs Garden, had been acquired by the Bowens in 1922, passed to their daughter in 1940 and then eventually to the present owners Jonathan and Ann Sparke. Beyond Meadowlands (Little Tott) two more houses were built this century, being Tott Close, originally built in 1910 and extended since, and Kingfishers.

Tott Cottages had seen the return in 1934 of one of their wandering residents, George Pope, coming back to his home after twenty-two varied years in the navy. He had fought throughout the 1914-18 war and took part in battles against Chinese pirates when his ship was in action supporting the Cantonese army; he was also in the evacuation of Odessa in the Black Sea when his ship was shelled by the Bolsheviks.

The Georgian Rectory (re-named The Glebe) had been purchased in 1912 by Bernard Spring Rice, brother of Cecil Spring Rice who wrote "I vow to thee my country".

Bernard added a billiard room extension and a bay window. He married Cicely Alexander daughter of William Cleverly Alexander, of Heathfield Park, who was also Chairman of Alexanders Discount Company, the family firm of City billbrokers and bankers. Alexander had commissioned Whistler to paint portraits of his children and it took the artist two years and seventy sittings to complete his work of six-year-old Cicely. When Bernard Spring Rice died in 1956 he left The Glebe to Cecil's daughter Mary who was married to Sir Raynor Arthur who had been Governor of the Bahamas and the Falkland Islands. Their son Tom and his wife Angela now live in the house.

The Glebe

To the south, in Fontridge Lane, some new houses have been added and existing ones such as Old Brick and Grandturzle have been extended. Old Brick had for centuries been the home of well-to-do yeomen farmers, generally farming several hundred acres. In 1932 this 16th-century house with now just one hundred acres was restored and in the 1980s it was extended by Colin Spencer Wills who also acquired land on both sides of Fontridge Lane to build again a considerable estate. Grandturzel, previously Grandtwizzle, Grantwyssell or Grandwiste, had similarly been a farmhouse for many years, having been mentioned from the 16th century. It came into the Ashburnham family in the 19th century being owned by Sir Anchitel Piers Ashburnham-Clement and his wife Ellen in

1895. It was purchased in 1963 by Frank (later Sir Frank Sanderson Bt.) and Margot Sanderson who enlarged and modernised the house and in 1992 added Little Grandturzle to the estate. Towards the end of the 19th century the old Gliddish or Glydwich was burnt down. The site in the wood was abandoned and a new Glydwich Hall was built higher up on the ridge fronting onto Fontridge Lane. The building was erected in two phases, about thirty years apart, and after the 1939-45 war was joined next door by Glydwich Place.

On the road to Burwash Common new houses were slowly added to those built during Victorian times and alterations and extensions took place to those already there. In Rye Green Lane, Orchards was doubled in size by its present owners Arland and Sylvia Kingston in 1973 at which time Arland was regional director for the National Trust in East Sussex and Kent. During the 20th century Coppards, Millfield and Carlton, Winsun Ridge and Long Acre were added as was Windmill Cottage. Coppers Hill (originally Rotherhurst) had its top floor and turret removed and, after an abortive plan to turn it into flats, became a single residence again; in 1962 its former stables were sold off as Martlets. Other houses added in the second half of the 20th century include Witherhurst, Rocks Meadow and Oakhouse while Rockhurst was built in the early part of the century. It was bought by Dr Marjorie Hayward in 1940, four years after she had established her practice in the village. She took over as village doctor from Dr Curteis and she practised at Rockhurst until she retired in 1955. She then moved to Crathie where she sometimes played the church organ when the Queen was in the congregation. She in turn was followed by Drs Peter and Margaret Main whose tenure was disturbed by Peter being called up to serve in the Suez invasion; they left after only two years. In 1957 Drs Glyn and Hazel Walters purchased Rockhurst and began their long tenure. The Walters took in Dr Jane Woodgate in 1986 and she practised there until the Walters' retirement in 1992 when she moved to the new surgery. The National Health Service had been introduced in 1948 during Dr Hayward's time, providing medical treatment on an equal basis for all, and replacing the Lloyd George insurance scheme introduced in 1910 to give basic medicine to those earning little or nothing. The Lloyd George cards, some with Dr Hancock's name (around 1915) on them survived until the Walters introduced more modern systems. The Walters were also the first practice in the County to have a practice nurse allocated to them in 1970, largely because they were prepared to offer free facilities.

The Red House on the corner of Batemans Lane was sold in 1922, when Henry Noakes died, as the family had now moved away and the clock business closed. It became known as Bounders in 1925 and Pippins in 1948; it was purchased by Gwil and Margaret Swift in 1957. Gwil was to become chairman of the Parish Council from 1963-1974 and a leading member of the Playing Fields Association.

William Brown's forge and coachbuilders had moved from near Novar to the site which is now a Shell garage in the early part of the century. Over the years their business evolved with demand and they would make, or repair, anything from wagon wheels to iron gates, toboggans and other metal ware. They sold the business to Peter Glass who opened County Services Garage there and although since then it has changed brand from time to time it continues to sell petrol. It is however very noticeable that the garages of the 1930s, 1940s, 1950s and 1960s used to sell petrol as well as providing a full range of repair and motor supply services, whereas the increasing reliability of modern cars and tyres means that virtually no petrol station offers any repair service; instead they sell a range of groceries and other products. Next to the petrol station are a further four fairly modern houses which together with those on the other side of the road have gently extended the village westwards.

Beyond Burwash Common, at the top of the eastern end of Swife Lane, can be found a wooden and corrugated iron hut in the small copse. This was Alice Rowley's tea shop, which was owned by Alice's uncle in the 1920s when she came to give him temporary assistance. She stayed and ran it until 1970, with lorry drivers coming miles to buy her cheese sandwiches, cakes and tea. Only men were served and she was presented with a coffee set and salver by them when she finally retired. Also at Burwash Common near Mill House Farm was the Burwash post mill which was still operating until the 1920s but was then gradually dismantled.

In Spring Lane the break-up of the Franchise estate followed the death of Henry Lucas in 1912. The estate he had inherited from his uncle Henry now all went to his sister Anne, who lived at the Franchise with her cousins Jane, Anne, Mary and Rebecca McKnight. In 1913 the McKnight sisters purchased Dawes House and thirty acres running as far as Mottynsden Lane from Anne Lucas for £500. This included the nine hole golf course which dated back to about 1875 and on which was held an annual competition for a cup donated in 1909 by E H Dormer, the Honorary Secretary, who rented Mount House at that time. Winners included Dormer (1913), his successor as Hon. Secretary Lt. Colonel Hanley DSO MC (1926 and 1932), the Rev. R L Martyn-Linnington (1912), Wilfred Maude-Roxby (1935) and John Maude-Roxby (1936). The last two were father and son. The club closed in 1937 when the remaining two McKnights built St Giles on the site of the club house and moved in there shortly before the war. They lived there until after the war when it was purchased by the MacDonalds. They built Giles Cottage next door in 1975 in what had been the vegetable garden and Mrs MacDonald moved into this cottage on her Brigadier husband's death. Dawes House itself was occupied by the Canadian Army during the 1939-45 war and then was purchased by the Misses Dixon when they moved there from Holton House in about 1970. It was the surviving Miss Dixon who one day walked into the Holy Cross Priory near Heathfield and offered them

The golf course from Dawes

the Dawes estate. This was gratefully accepted and, on Miss Dixon's death, the house was converted into flats and St Annes Green bungalows were built.

Below Dawes House, Dawes Farm, together with Square Farm in Shrub Lane, was purchased by the Morris brothers, Harry and William, as part of the sale of the Franchise. The Morris's also rented part of Mottynsden and thus farmed virtually all the land between Spring Lane and Shrub Lane and beyond. When the golf course closed the Morris's rented this as additional grazing. Dawes Farm was sold in 1945 when Harry retired and was soon bought by John Stephenson whose widow still lives there. Part of the Morris's enterprise was a dairy herd and they were well known for their daily village milk round with milk being measured straight out of brass bound churns into housewives' jugs for $4^{1}/2$d. a pint.

Not included in the 1912 sale to the McKnights were Holton Cottages and Half Mile Cottage which had been sold to Lt. Colonel Sutherland Harris next door at Burwash Place (Firs or Frys) and renamed Frys Cottages. What is now Half Mile Cottage had the "ability to pass and repass to the well in the field behind" but "the well and tackle to be kept in good repair". Both these pairs of cottages were disposed of when the Lacys sold Burwash Place estate in 1947. Half Mile Cottage became one residence and was then extended by Rodney and Christine Smith when they acquired it in 1996. The rest of the Burwash Place estate was broken up into parcels at the 1947 sale but the older name lives on in the house which itself dates back to the 17th or 18th century and was formerly called Burwash Place Cottages and is now Little Frys. Burwash Place has had a variety of uses, being an educational outdoor pursuits centre and an old people's home before being restored to private residence again in 1999.

Mottynsden was purchased by Lt. Commander S L M Vereker in 1932 and he and his wife lived there until 1967 when they sold the manor house and moved down their drive into the lodge, retaining most of the land. Commander Vereker played a considerable part in the village, particularly as a school governor and church warden and he returned to the Navy during the 1939-45 war, retiring as a Captain.

Holton House was acquired by Lt. Colonel James Sawyer in 1919 and he then sold it to Mrs. Dixon in 1931 when he moved to Bell Alley. At this time the house was lit by petrol gas which "could be switched on as for electricity". Mrs Dixon died and her two daughters lived there until they moved to Dawes House. It was purchased by Captain Vereker's son David and his wife Jane in 1974 and they added Holton Farm to it in 1979 creating a mixed farm of fruit and sheep and including much of the Mottynsden land. David Vereker is a Parish and District councillor and a churchwarden.

As well as the demise of the Catholic and Salesian establishments at Southover, Southover itself was hit by a bomb during the 1939-45 war and little remains of the grand old house. The staff and tenants buildings have now been sold off.

As with so many historic villages Burwash seems to have its share of ghosts from the past. At Mount House a carter is seen occasionally in the Tithe Barn. He first appeared some years ago, when a new car was delivered to the house, and stood in the doorway of the barn; it obviously mystified the old man who stood, whip in hand, with his wide straw hat, bearded face, long smock and gaiters. Doubtless he decided that the new object was inoffensive as he has not reappeared for some time. Neither has the lawyer's clerk who was seen one summer's day at Youngs Garden, running out of the front door, leaping onto his horse which was awaiting him at the mounting block still to be seen on the road, and riding at a gallop down to Etchingham. He was clad in black jacket and breeches, leggings and buckled shoes. Perhaps he dates back to Philcox's days. There is another persistent and itinerant spirit which has been seen at both Youngs Garden and Mount House, as well as elsewhere in this area. She is a gypsy girl who appears when a family moves house, doubtless to inspect the premises and approve their condition. In the High Street, in Swan House, once said to have been an inn of doubtful repute, a lady in blue has been seen on several occasions. She appears in the upstairs rooms and at times moves into the adjacent house which at one time was part of the inn. Opposite at Popes Cottage lives an interfering gremlin who temporarily removes things until spoken to kindly, whereupon they are returned or found elsewhere. He is also known to dislike television and pulled the plug out of the wall on a newly installed set. In Sheepstreet Lane, which connects Burwash, Ticehurst and Etchingham, a gypsy caravan has been seen on several occasions in the evening, pulled by a plodding horse being led by its owner, a swarthy gypsy man. As soon as the caravan reaches its viewer, it disappears. Another old legend concerns a man hanged for murder who haunts Glydwish Wood (presumably Daniel Leaney) where his mournful cries can be heard on misty evenings and which Kipling said he would not enter because of them.

Also lost in the mists of history are the origins of the now defunct Burwash Band or brass band. It is however quite likely that a collection of musicians in the village had gathered together to play over the centuries, particularly at village fetes, fairs and similar events. There was certainly a brass band in Victorian times as in 1880 their rules had included:

> *Rules for the Burwash Brass Band*
>
> 1st That the hours of practice shall be from ½ past 7 till ½ past 9 on Mondays and Thursdays. any member failing to attend shall be find 2.
>
> 2nd Any member swaring or smoking or useing any abuseing language shall be find 1 for each offence.
>
> 3th Any member caught blowing is instaument going home from practice shall be find 2 for each offence

Burwash Band 1900
Top left standing: Alf Isted, Harry Eastwood, Tom Hook, Dick Godley, Darkey Jenner (four unknown)
2nd row: Mr Cork, Igens Pennells, C Sweatman, Dick Pope, Neo Jenner, Jim Pope,
Huggy Brabon (side drum)
Front row: Bow Farley, Fred Woodall, Bert Jenner, Spen Glazier

In 1886 they were described as "a somewhat draggletailed display ..... who blew really very creditable blasts".

By the 1930s the band had become known as the Thirsty Eight and although stories indicate that they were certainly thirsty they were not always eight and in the 1950s were shown with fifteen members on a parade. They used to play fairly regularly, particularly at the Admiral Vernon and the Rose & Crown and for dances at the Village Hall. Among the leaders were Dick (Gooseneck) Godley (brass), Bill Brown (tenor horn), and Len Hicks (base drum); the Treasurer was the landlord of the Rose & Crown, Ted Willis. The Woodall family were also well represented with postmaster Frederick on the cymbals or clarinet, his son George also playing the clarinet and being bandmaster at one time, and Margaret's husband Albert Catt also playing. They were perhaps at their best, or most vocal, at Christmas time when they would set out on Christmas Eve and play carols round the village all evening and sometimes continue, after suitable refreshment, until the early hours. Probably their greatest moment came at Christmas

Burwash Band 1969

1945 when they played for the radio programme "Wherever you may be", which preceded the King's first post victory Christmas speech. Not only were they heard by many people throughout this country but they were also listened to by W J Newick, an ex-resident, who was living in Subiaco, Western Australia. Sadly the band went into decline and packed up for lack of members in about 1970 when their uniforms and equipment were sold with the proceeds going to the playing fields.

Another musical inhabitant was Albert "Laddie" Richardson, the Singing Sexton, who was born in 1905, and who for years sang his traditional Sussex folk songs for radio and for gramophone records. In between the wars he was sexton and gravedigger as well as being the Rector's gardener and after the war he was a milkman and worked as a mechanic at Oakleys Garage before dying in 1976.

In 1973 the Parish Council decided to have a new village sign. They commissioned Jim Smith and he designed and made the sign that currently stands opposite Popes antique shop. The central feature is the ancient local craft of iron working and it is topped by the East Sussex County Council arms, granted in 1937, flanked by the Pelham and de Burghersh arms representing the two oldest families associated with the village. Soon afterwards, in 1978, Burwash won the competition for the best kept village

168   *Chapter Six*

The village sign

in Sussex and in 1993 and 1996 for the best kept small village and these plaques are attached.

⚜

By the end of the 20th century Burwash has become a very different village from the one that had seen the last days of Queen Victoria a hundred years earlier. Gone are most of the shops and local trades, gone is the peaceful High Street with its horses and carts and carriages, and gone is the regular local market. In its place is a busy main road and a High Street that is largely residential. Few of the inhabitants earn their living from the land or local trade and many work in London, Tunbridge Wells or other nearby towns, or are retired. But the actual buildings have been preserved, with few new buildings or major alterations in the centre of the village. Above all the surrounding countryside is largely unaltered and remains a rural farming landscape with many of the farms and fields still as our forebears would have known them. The population numbers three thousand, one hundred and twelve and a healthy range of ages and occupations means that, in addition to the churches and the school, the village has a wide range of clubs, societies and other organisations.

Burwash on the hill

The millennium itself passed quietly with most people spending the evening with family and friends. A beacon was lit on Swan Meadow to celebrate the start of the next one thousand years.

Sources and Acknowledgements

I drew on a wide range of sources including published works, private papers and original documents. Many of these I used several times, in different chapters. I am most grateful for the amount of information that was made readily available and I list my sources below.

GENERAL HISTORY

A History of Britain and the British People, Volumes I-III - Arthur Bryant; Collins (1984)
The Timber-Frame House in England - Trudy West; David & Charles (1971)
The Oxford History of England, Volumes 1 - 15; Clarendon Press
English Social History, Chaucer to Queen Victoria - G M Trevylan; Longmans (1944)
A History of the English Speaking People, Volumes I - IV - Winston S Churchill; Cassell (1956)
Story of England, four volumes - Arthur Bryant; Collins (1953)
Domesday Book - a Guide - R Welldon Finn; Phillimore (1973)
Britain and her Buildings, Book II 1485-1939, - John Kirkman; Butler & Tanner Ltd (1948)

SUSSEX - including works that have specific mention of Burwash

Victoria History of Sussex, Volume IX - L F Salzman, Oxford University Press
A History of Sussex - J R Armstrong; Phillimore (1961)(including maps and drawings)
Sussex - Ian Nairn and Nikolaus Pevsner (The Buildings of England); Penguin (1965)
The Iron Industry of the Weald - Henry Cleere and David Crossley; Merton Priory Press (1995)
Sussex Schools in the 18th Century - John Caffyn; Sussex Record Society Volume 81 (1998)
The Religious Census of Sussex 1851 - John A Vickers; Sussex Record Society Volume 75 (1989)
Chichester Diocesan Surveys 1686 and 1724 - Wyn K Ford; Sussex Record Society Volume 78 (1994)
History of East Sussex Police 1840-1967 - R V Kyrke (1967)
A History of the Royal Sussex Regiment 1701-1953 - G D Martineau; Moore & Tillyer Ltd (1953)
A History of the Southern Railway - C F Dendy Marshall, Curwen Press (1936)
Kellys Directories of Sussex 1867, 1878, 1887, 1895, 1899, 1915, 1927, 1938
Captain Swing - E J Hobsbawm and George Rude; Lawrence & Wishart (1969)

Sources and Acknowledgements

Sussex in the Great Civil War and the Interregnum 1642-1660 - Charles Thomas-Stanford, Chiswick Press (1910)
Roman Ways in the Weald - I D Margary; Phoenix House (1948)
The Place Names of Sussex, Part II - A Mawer and F M Stenton; Cambridge University Press (1930)
Sussex Archaeological Collections (generally but particularly Volume XXI - Charles Francis Trower - Burwash) - The Sussex Archaeological Society; George P Bacon
The County Books Series - Sussex - Esther Maynard; Robert Hale (1947)
Brickmaking in Sussex - M Beswick; Middleton Press (1993)
History of Sussex, Volumes I and II - Mark Anthony Lower, George P Bacon (1870)
Heathfield Park - Roy Pryce; printed for the author by the Authors' Publishing Guild (1996)
A County Community in Peace and War: Sussex 1600-1660 - Anthony Fletcher; Longman (1975)
Windmills in Sussex - G M Fowell; Walkers Galleries Ltd London (1930)
Watermills of Sussex, Volume I East Sussex - Derek Stidder and Colin Smith; Baron (1997)
Some Early Pelhams - Hon. Mrs Arthur Pelham and David McLean; Cambridge (1931)
Historic Buildings in Eastern Sussex, Volume 1 (Nos.1-6)(1977-80) - David and Barbara Martin; The Rape of Hastings Architectural Survey
Historic Buildings in Eastern Sussex, Volume 2 (Nos.1+2)(1980) - David and Barbara Martin; The Rape of Hastings Architectural Survey
Historic Buildings in Eastern Sussex, Volume 3 (Nos.1-7)(1982) 'Old Farm Buildings in Eastern Sussex (1450-1750)' - David and Barbara Martin; The Rape of Hastings Architectural Survey
The War in East Sussex - Sussex Express and County Herald (1945)
A Detective in Sussex - Donald Maxwell; The Bodley Head (1932)
Kipling's Sussex - R Thurston Hopkins; Simpkin (1921)
Footpaths of the Kent-Sussex Border - Joseph Braddock; Chatterton (1947)
The Development of Roads in Surrey and Sussex Weald 1700-1900 - Fuller
Chichester Diocese Clergy List - Rev. George Hennessy BA; St Peter's Press (1900)
The Dictionary of National Biography - Oxford (since 1917)
Smuggling and Smugglers in Sussex - W J Smith; Brighton 19th C.
Highways and Byways in Sussex - E V Lucas; Macmillan (1928)
County Genealogies - William Berry; Sherwood Gilbert & Piper (1830)
Alumni Cantabrigienses; Cambridge (1951)
Alumni Oxonienses; Parker & Co. (1891)

Burwash and District

Victorian Village - Diaries of Rev. John Coker Egerton 1857-1888; Ed. Roger Wells; Alan Sutton (1992)

Sussex Folk and Sussex Ways - Rev. John Coker Egerton - Ed. Henry Wace DD; Methuen & Co. Ltd. (1924)

Burwash and the Sussex Weald - James Goodwin; printed for the author by The Courier Printing & Publishing Co. Ltd. (1950's)

Individual surveys on houses including Medieval Burwash (Shadwell Row, Chateaubriand, Bower, Old Rectory): Swan, Cygnet and Lime: Yew Tree and Old Granary: Bell Inn: Hoppers Croft (Ham Lane): Villiers, Glebe Cottage etc: Green Hill: Tudor House: Rampyndene: Tott Farm Cottages: Great Tott: including drawings of the Old Rectory (3), Green Hill and Chateaubriand and a map of Tottgreene - David Martin; Robertsbridge & District Archaeological Society

Articles and pictures in the *Sussex Express*, *Sussex Advertiser* and *Sussex Agricultural Express*

Burghersh - Church and Village of Burwash - Clement Woodbine Parish, (1949)
A Walk in Burwash - Burwash W.I; East Sussex CC and Buwash WI (1978)
The Village Sign - Jim Smith; Robertsbridge & District Archaeological Society; Errys
You Can't Beat Burwash - M.M.; Catts Bookshop
Burwash When I was a Boy - Eric Godley; Sadlers
Notes on Hollyhurst and Burwash Weald - Sophia Trower's Memoirs (1872)

East Sussex Record Office

A wide variety of original and filmed documents relating to both Burwash and Sussex including:
Burwash Parish records from 1558 for baptisms, marriages and deaths (PAR 284 1/1-5)
Land Tax 1693-4, 1707-79, 1780-1832, 1833-1930 (XA 31/6-7)
Tithe Apportionment 1839 (TD/E 157)
Poor Rate 1701-17, 1755-6, 1767-98, 1828-35 (PAR 284/30)
Church Rate 1674-1740 (PAR 284/9)
Window Tax 1747 (RAP 15/21)
Census 1841, 1851, 1861, 1871, 1881, 1891 (XA 19/2, 9/10, 2/3, 17/3, 27/8, 54/78-9)
Archdeaconary of Lewes Index of Wills 1660-1858 and pre-1660 wills
Churchwardens Accounts 1674-1740 (PAR 284/9)
Overseers of the Poor Rates and Accounts 1701-1836, 1701-98, 1828-35 (PAR 284 30/1, 31/1)
Ashburnham Court Records 1643-1950 (ASH 148/154)
1840 Report of the Turnpike Commissioners

Additional manuscripts generally, but particularly AMS 5744 Coney Family of Burwash 1318-1801
Sussex Archaeological Society manuscripts
Non-conformist Registers (NC3)
A number of maps including OS1878, 1900 and 1910.

CENTRE FOR KENTISH STUDIES

Documents relating to the Hussey family's property in Burwash including Rampyndene.

FRONTISPIECE
The village sign by Jim Smith (1973)

DUSTCOVER
Taken from a print by Charles Higham

ENDPAPERS
Ordnance Survey 1999 (front)
Ordnance Survey 1910 (back)

Index

The index covers the complete text with the exception of the sources and acknowledgements. References to illustrations are given in *italic*. The alphabetical arrangement is word by word, in which a group of letters followed by a space is filed before the same group of letters followed by a letter, e.g. 'Barn Cottage' comes before 'Barnard'.

Act of Uniformity (1662) 39
Acts of Parliament
  Act of Uniformity (1662) 39
  County Police Act (1839) 81
  Education Acts (1870 and 1902) 86
  Marriages Act (1836) 91
  Poor Law Act (1601) 59
  Poor Law Reform Act (1834) 59, 69
  Public Library Acts (1892 and 1894) 91
  Reform Act (1867) 121
  Representation of the People Act (1928) 121
  Sussex Turnpike Act (1765) 62
Adams Strake (Burghurst) 15-16, 48, *48*, 65, 98, 140
Admiral Vernon Inn (Admiral House) 67, 81, 106, 107, 113, *114*, 152, 157, *159*
Agricultural Labour Union 90
agriculture 58-59, 120
air raids 129-130
alcoholism 106
Allen, Robert 26
allotments 108, 133, 135
Anabaptists 40; *see also* Baptists
Anderson-Morshead, Angela 74
Ansett, George 85
archaeological sites in Sussex *viii* (map)
army 88-89
Ashburnham family 5
Ashlands 23, 105, 116, 151
assurance (insurance), 19th century 121
Attersole, Wail 30
Austen, Edward 53

Baker, John 61
Baker, William 65
Baldock, John 50
Baldock, Thomas 41, 50, 61
Band, Burwash 165-167, *166*, *167*
Bankside 97, *97*, 135
Baptists 64; *see also* Baptists

Barn Cottage 118
Barnard, Richard 65
Barnsley, George 43
Barrow, John 73
Barton, William 110
Batemans 23, 117
Bear Inn (Hotel) 20, 52, 53, 57, 106, 107, *107*, 152
Beeches 14, *14*
Bell Alley (School Hill) 112, 157
Bell Inn (Five Bells) 15, 52-53, 106, 140, *140*, 152
Bellcroft 112
bells, church 33, 36
bible, Geneva 28
bicycles 152
Biggars, Robert 64
Bines Farm, Witherenden 86
Black Death 6, 7; *see also* plague
Blackford, George 90
Blackford, Henry 107, 145
Blacksmiths Arms *101*, 106, 107, 145, 152
bloomeries 8-9
Blundell, Kay 152-153, *152*
Blundell, Thomas 63, 64
Blunden, John 59, 84, 101
Blunden, William 98
Boer War (1899-1902) 88
bombs in Sussex *129* (map), *130* (map)
Borders Farm 25
Bough Farm 59
Bower *15*, 16, 140
Bowles, John 64
Bowles, Robert 68
Bowmans Farm 25
Breach, John 55
Brede 69
'breeches' bible 28
Brickhouse Farm (Old Brick) 25, 49, 50, 64, 116, 160
brickworks 59

Brightling 39, 61
Brightling View 112
Broads Cottages 97, *98*, 138
Bronze Age vii
Brook, Charles 143
Brook, Fred 126-127
Brook, James 56
Brooksmarle 4, 5, 23, 100
Brown family 109
Brown, John 105
 coachbuilder's business *106*
Brown, Joseph 105-106
Buckles (Hollyhurst), Burwash Common 95, 129
Burgess, John 90
Burghersh family 4
Burghurst 4
Burghurst (Adams Strake) 15-16, 48, *48*, 65, 98, 140
Burrell, William 34
Burwash *150* (map), *169*
 (1625) *10* (map)
 (c. 1750) *54* (map)
 (1839) *96* (map)
 (1910) *99* (map)
 origin of name 4
Burwash Band 165-167, *166*, *167*
Burwash Common vii, 63, 93, 95, *95*
Burwash District Housing Association for the Elderly 138
Burwash Gas Company 84, 109, 153
Burwash Gospel Mission 148
Burwash Horticultural Society 156-157
Burwash Place (Frys) 120, 163-164
Burwash Playing Fields Association 142, 143
Busbridge, John 30, 61
Busbridge, Robert (17th century) 30
Busbridge, Robert (18th century) 53-54, 55, 56
Buss, William 64, 91
Butler, John 43, 46
Button, Richard 66
Byne family 24

Calvinist chapel 91, 133
Calvinists 64, 91
Carly, Margaret 68
cars, introduction of 126-127
Carter, Robert 53
Catt, Albert 147, 166
 Catts Stores (1960) *147*
cattle sales 108, *108*, 141-142
Central Cottage *154*, 155
Chandler, Thomas 69
chapel 44, 63, 64
Charity School 42-43, 53, 65-66, 73, 85, 87
Chateaubriand *17*, 18, 89, 100

Chaunt House 109, 110, *110*, 153-154
Cheriton (White Hart Inn) 81, 104, *105*, 106, *150*, 152
Chestnut 20
Chilston 100, *101*, 145, *145*
Chime 23, *23*
choir, church 93, *94* (programme), 95
Church House (Hoppers Croft) 14-15, 17, 49, *49*, 50, 98, 139
Church of Christ the King 134, *135*
church, Norman 2, *31* (plan)
Civil War (1642-1649) 29, 30
clock, church 34, 35-36, 54
Cobblers 19-20, 106
Cohen, Algernon 109-110
Colemans (Rose Cottage) 53, 99, 140
Collier, George 89
Collins family 24
Collins, Edward 33, 44
Collins (Colyns), John (16th century) 9
Collins, John (18th century) 65
Collins, Thomas 30
Colyns (Collins), John 9
Combs House *see* Denes House
Combs, James Weston 73, 109, 112
Commonwealth War Graves Commission 124
Coney (Conys) family 22, 24
Coney, Bicknell 46
Coney, John 33, 34, 43, 45, 46
Coney, Samuel 43
Coney, Thomas 46
Congregational chapel (Independent chapel) 44, 91, *92*, 133, 155; *see also* Calvinists
Congregational Independent Sunday School 104
Conley, Thomas 110
Constable, John 72, 73
Constable, William (church warden in 1735) 34
Constable, William (born 1745) 65, 66, 73
constables 81
Coppard, John 116-117
Coppard, William 102, 121
Copper, James 102
Coppers Hill 118, 161
Cornford, William 64
Cornwall, Alfred 88-89
Coronation Cottages 127
Cottages, The *22*, 23
Cottingdon, Sarah 64
County Police Act (1839) 81
Court Barn Farm 100, 157
Court House, Hurst Green 115, *115*
Courtail, John 63
Cox, Alfred 85, 121
crafts 120-121
cricket 105, 142, 143

Crossingham, John 79
Crowhurst Bridge 42
Crowhurst Bridge Cottages 136
Crowhurst Bridge Farm 12-13, *13*, 44
Crowhurst, Robert 68
Cruttenden family 13, 14, 24
Cruttenden, Anthony 29, 30
Cruttenden, Elizabeth 44
Cruttenden, John (17th century) 33
Cruttenden, John (18th century) 43, 56
Cruttenden, John (19th century) 115
Cruttenden, Nathaniel 52, 57
Cruttenden, Thomas 61
Curteis, Arthur William Statter 103, 148, 157
Curteis, Whitfield 63, 66
Cygnet *15*, 16

Dame School 87
Dann, Henry 104
Daunt, Francis (Frank) 145
Daw, Samuel 121
Dawes Farm 51, 163
Dawes House 51, 131, 162-163
Dean, Edward 44
Denes House (Combs House) v-vi, 47, 48, 71-75, *72*, *74*
destitution 27, 42, 55, 56, 59, 69
dissenters, religious 39-40, 44, 63-64, 133
Ditlers (Dudwell) Mill 23-24
Ditton, John 83
doctors of medicine 161
  Baldock, Thomas 41, 50, 61
  Barton, William 110
  Cohen, Algernon 109-110
  Combs, James Weston 73, 109, 112
  Curteis, Arthur William Statter 103, 148, 157
  Evans, Thomas Abel 61, 68, 109
  Green, Arthur 110
  Hancock, John 144
  Hines, Joseph Cox 110
  Parker, William 41
  Walters, Hazel 133
Dodswell, John 54
Domesday Inquest 1-2
dragoons 68, 69
Dray, Thomas 92
drunkenness 106
Dudwell House 114, 115, 140
Dudwell Mill 23-24, 25, 117
Dunderdale, Gladys 135
Dyke, Mary 43
Dyke, Thomas 57

Eastwood, Thomas 90
education 28-29, 65-66, 85-87

Education Acts (1870 and 1902) 86
Edwards School 65
Edwards, Richard Swinfer 65
Egerton, Helen 74, 75
Egerton, John Coker 35, 91, 93, 111
electoral reform 121
Elliott, Amos 137
Ellis, John 54, 99
Ellis, Richard 64
Ellis, Thomas 24
Ellis, William 91, 92, 100
  grocer's business *101*
Elphick, William 54
emigration 90
Empire Day 87
enclosure 26-27
Etchingham 81, 82
evacuees 129
Evans, Thomas Abel 61, 68, 109
Everton Cottages 16-17, 100, 104, 141

fairs 3, 141-142, 143
Fairview 112
Farley, Charlie 127, 155
Farley, Fred 140
Farley, William 107
Farley, William 140
Farleys Corn Stores 145
Farmer, Gordon 144
farming 58-59, 120
farms 24-25
  Bines Farm, Witherenden 86
  Bough Farm 59
  Brickhouse Farm 25, 49, 50, 64, 116, 160
  Court Barn Farm 100, 157
  Crowhurst Bridge Farm 12-13, *13*, 44
  Dawes Farm 51, 163
  Fishers Farm 25, 116
  Glydwish Farm 25, 161
  Holton Farm 107, 164
  Mill Park Farm 117
  Palmers Farm, Wadhurst 43, 65-66
  Platts Farm 49
  Shrub Farm (Woodrising) 97, *97*, 136-137
  Square Farm 23, 44, 114, *115*, 163
  Tott Farm (Great Tott) 13-14, 115
  Witherhurst Farm 118
  see also farming
fete 143
feudal system 1
Fielden, John Leyland 111-112
financial transactions, 18th century 53
fire fighters *144*
fire station 143-144, *144*
First World War 88, 122

Fishers Farm 25, 116
Five Bells (Bell Inn) 15, 52-53, 106, 140, *140*, 152
Flack, Fanny 87
Fleming, Ellen 89
Fleming, James 57, 66, 101
Fleming, John 57
Fleming, Martha 101
Flurry, John 51
flying bombs in Sussex *129* (map)
Fontridge Farm 25
Fontridge House 14, 51
football club 142
football team (1967) *143*
forges 154, *154*, 161-162
Foster, Edward 52
Fosters 4, 5
Franchise (Frenches) 24, 57, 64, 119-120, 162
Franchise Bill (1885) 121
French, Edward 61
French, John 61
Frenches (Franchise) 24, 57, 64, 119-120, 162
Friends, James 13
Froy Challenge Spade 127
Frys (Burwash Place) 120, 163-164
Frys Cottages 163
Fuller, Bentham 84, 102-103
Fuller, George 91
Fuller, John 91, 103
Funnell, Thomas 122

Garstons 112-113, *113*, 157
gas supply 84
Geneva bible 28
ghosts 164-165
Gibbs, Andrew 114, 115
Gideon House 87, *109*, 145, 152
Gillham, Thomas 121
Girdlers, Worshipful Company of 56
Glaisyers Farm 25
Glebe, The 44, 51, 116, 159-160, *160*
Glebe Cottage 113, 157, *158*
Glen, The 137, *137*
Glydwish (Gliddish or Glydwich) Farm 25, 161
Goldham, Thomas 30, 39
Goldsmith, Henry 14-15
Goldsmith, Walker 50, 66
golf course 162, 163, *163*
Gould, Joseph 34, 36, 79, 93, 116
Grandturzle (Grandtwizzle) Farm 25, 116, 160-161
Great Tott (Tott Farm) 13-14, 115
Green Hill Farm 25, *25*
Green, Arthur 110
Green, John 64
Grove Villa (St. Anthony's) 50, *50*, 51, 99
Guestling (Linden Cottage) 53, 98, 140

Half Mile Cottage 120, 163
hall houses 10, *11*, 12, *12*
Halt Down (Holton) 23
Ham Lane 17
Ham Place 100
Hancock, John 144
Harris, Arthur Sutherland 92, 120, 124, 125
haunted houses 164-165
Haviland family 119
Hawkesworth, Joseph 30
Hawkhurst gang 67, 68
Hawkins, Albert 81, 107
Hayward, Marjorie 161
Heathfield and District Water Company 145
Heathfield Water Company 136
Heathfield, Henry 57
Hedges, Dave 36, 133, 154
Henshurst (Parkhill) 25
Hepden family 22, 24
Hicks, James 81
Hicks, Thomas 55
High Street 10, *74*, *151*, *153*(West End) *104*
Highfields 105
Highway 18-19
Hilder, Edward 65
Hilder, John 103
Hines, Joseph Cox 110
Holland, Jean 133, 138, 139
Hollyhurst (Buckles), Burwash Common 95, 129
Holman, Abraham 56
Holman, Isaac 56
Holmshurst 24
Holt Down (Holton) 51, 119, 164
Holton Cottages 120, 163
Holton Farm 107, 164
Home Guard 129
Honeysett, Edwin 83
Hoppers Croft (Church House) 14-15, 17, 49, *49*, 50, 98, 139
houses
  13th century 3, *3*
  14th century 10, *11*, 12, *12*; see also Chateaubriand, Highway, Timbers
  15th century *11*, 12; see also Adams Strake, Bell Inn, Green Hill Farm, Shadwell, Smugglers, Sones Cottage, Yew Tree House
  16th century see Bower, Cygnet, Hoppers Croft, Lime Cottage, Oak Beam, Paygate Cottage, Swan Inn, Willards Hill House
  17th century see Admiral Vernon Inn, Batemans, Glebe Cottage, Jasmine Cottage, Novar, Old Granary, Providence, Rampyndene, St. Nicholas Cottage, Wayside
  18th century see Barn Cottage, Dudwell, Fontridge House, The Glebe, Grove Villa, Holt Down

(Holton), Mount House, Northview
   Cottage, Rampyndene, Tott Cottages, White
   House, Witherhurst
  19th century 96-98; *see also* Ashlands, Garstons,
   Police House, Prospect Cottages
  20th century 135, 159
  see also prefabs
Hughes, Angela Louisa 74
Hughes, Isobel 36
Hundreds x, *x* (map)
Hunt, Frederick 137
Huntley, James 138
Hussey family 47, 111
Hussey, Thomas 34, 43, 47

Independent chapel (Congregational chapel) 44, 91,
   92, 133, 155
industry and trade 53-57, 89-90, 120-121
inns
  Admiral Vernon Inn (Admiral House) 67, 81,
     106, 107, 113, *114*, 152, 157, *159*
  Bear Inn (Hotel) 20, 52, 53, 57, 106, 107, *107*,
     152
  Bell Inn (Five Bells) 15, 52-53, 106, 140, *140*,
     152
  Blacksmiths Arms *101*, 106, 107, 145, 152
  Rose & Crown 17, 52, *52*, 106, 142, 152
  Swan Inn *15*, 16
  Wheel Inn 68
  White Hart Inn (Cheriton) 81, 104, *105*, 106,
     150, 152
Inskip, Elizabeth 53
Institute, Village 92-93, *93*, 129
insurance, 19th century 121
Irelands Cottages 97-98, *98*
Iron Age vii
iron industry 7-10, *8* (map), 58
Isted, Harry 90
Ivy, The 47, *47*, 72, 73, 74, 112, 157

Jarvis family 100, 144-145
Jasmine Cottage 113, 157, *158*
Jenkins, John 41
Jenner, Amos 81
Jenner, Nick 56
Johnson, Richard 53
Jordan, George 33, 34, 43, 44-45, 63

Kestrels 19-20
Kildare *136*, 137, 138
Kimberley 108
Kingdom of the South Saxons ix
Kingfishers 159
Kipling, Rudyard 117
Knowles, Philip 81

Lade, John 64
Lancaster, William 30
Langham family 24
laundry 137-138, *137*
Laurelhurst 117
Lawrence, Edward 33
Lawrence, John 33
Leadbetter, Thomas 100
Leaney, Daniel 68-69, 165
library 91-93
Lime Cottage *15*, 16
Lime Tree *19*, 19, 103, *103*
Linden Cottage (Guestling) 53, 98, 140
Little Frys 164
Little Tott (Meadowlands) 14, 115, 116
Little Worge Farm 25
Longley, Mary 133
Lusted, Ernest 107

Mackenzie, William 66
Mainwaring, Stephen 89
Mainwaring, William 81
Manktelow, Richard 57, 102
Mann, Daniel 44, 63
manor house 3-4
markets 3; *see also* fairs
Marriages Act (1836) 91
Marten, Margaret 43
Martyn-Linnington, R. L. 36, 93
Maskell, Charlotte 109-110
Mather, William 91, 111
Maude, Charles Frewin 36, 93
Maude-Roxby family 156
Maude-Roxby, Wilfred 111, 125
Maye (May) family 17
Mayfield gang 67
Maynard, Charles 90
Maynard, Henry 82
Maynard, John 108
Meadowlands (Little Tott) 14, 115, 116
medicine, doctors of *see* doctors of medicine
Mepham family 119
Mepham, John 118-119
Mepham, Walter 122
Mepham, William 64
Mesolithic Age vii
Mill Park Farm 117
mills
  Dudwell Mill 23-24
  Park Mill 23
  post mill 162
Morphew (Morpheus or Morfey), William 72
Morris, Joseph 79
motor cars, introduction of 126-127
Mottynsden 4, 5, 24, 164

Mount House 21-22, *45*, 45-46, 51, 61, 109, 110, 111, 156, 164
Mugridge, Ann 65
Mugridge, Henry 54, 55

name of Burwash, origin of 4
Nash, Thomas 111
National Lottery 59-60
National School 66, 85-87, *85*, 127, 132-133
National Vaccination Establishment 61
Neolithic Age vii
Nepecker, John 53
Nethercroft 135
Nevitt, Thomas 56
New Stone Age vii
Nicholson, Charles 36
Noakes Cottage 101, *102*, *146*, 146-147
Noakes family 146
Noakes, Edward 101
Noakes, Henry 118
Noakes, John 65, 99, 101
Noakes, John Buss 64, 91, 99
Noakes, John Simmons 91, 92, 99
Noakes, Lawrence 61
Noakes, Robert 56
Noakes, Walter 99
Nokes, David 40
nonconformity (religion) 39-40, 44, 63-64, 133
Norfolk Militia 68
Northview Cottage 113, 157, *158*
Novar 19, *106*, 151

Oakbeam *15*, 16, 140, *141*
Oakdown 95
Oakley, Albert 127
Old Brick (Brickhouse) 25, 49, 50, 64, 116, 160
Old Granary 16, *16*, 53, 99,141, *142*
Old House *22*, 23
Old Rectory *20*, 20-21, *21*, 63, *154*, 155
Old Rectory Court *155*, 156
Old Stone Age vii
Old Thatch 23, *23*
Oliver, Albert 122
Oliver, Joseph 68
Orchards 118, 161
organ, church 35, 101

Pagden family 108-109
Pagden, Emma 87
Pagden, Henry 87
Page, Mary 43
Paine, Richard 103
Paine, Thomas 44
Palmers Farm, Wadhurst 43, 65-66
Pankhurst, John 88

Parham, Thomas 72
Parish, Charles Woodbine 36
Park Mill 23
Park, John 100
Parker, William 41
Parsons, John 106-107
Paygate Cottage 24, 119
Peckham, Thomas 34
Peerless, John 82
Pelham family 4, 5
Pelham, Thomas 30
Pennells, Edward 88
Perrymans 23, 25
phantoms 164-165
Philcox, James (18th century) 48-49, 50, 72, 73
Philcox, James (died 1896) 36, 49, 74, 79
Pickering, Peter 43
Pilbeam, Edward 64
plague 42; *see also* Black Death
planning regulations, 18th century 58
Platts Farm 49
Polhill family 24
Polhill, Edward (17th century) 29, 30
Polhill, Edward (18th century) 44
Polhill, William 44, 53
police 81-83
Police House (Station) 82, *82*, *83* (plan), 157, *158*
Poor Law Act (1601) 59
Poor Law Reform Act (1834) 59, 69
poor rate 27, 42, 55, 56, 69
Pope, George 159
Pope, Thomas 55
Pope, William 89
Popes Cottage 152-153, 164
population 168
Porchester Cottages 118
Portland Terrace 155, *155*, 156
post mill 162
Post Office 145, 152, *153*
postal system 84, 145
Potten, Neri 68
poverty 27, 42, 55, 56, 59, 69
prefabs 135, 136
Press, John 64, 91
Prospect Cottages 114, 119
Providence 19, 151
public houses *see* inns
Public Library Acts (1892 and 1894) 91
Puck of Pook's Hill 117
Pump Court 16
Puritanism 30

railways *79* (map), 81, 82
  South Eastern Railway Company 78
Rampyndene *46*, 47, 51, *51*, 111, 156

Rapes 1, *2* (map)
Rectory (The Glebe) 44, 51, 116, 159-160, *160*
Red House 161
Reeves, Lucy 65
Reform Act (1867) 121
Reform Bill (1832) 121
Relf John 97
religious dissenters 39-40, 44, 63-64, 133
Representation of the People Act (1928) 121
Revenue Cottage 19, 102, 147, *147*
Rice, Bernard Spring 159-160
Richardson, Albert "Laddie" 167
riots, Swing 69
roads viii, 27, 61-63, 115; *see also* turnpike system
Robertsbridge Abbey 26
Rochester, Traiton 121
Rocks, The 118
Rocksmead 118
Roman Catholic school 87, 96, 133-134, *134*
Roman Sussex vii-viii, *ix* (map)
Rose & Crown Inn 17, 52, *52*, 106, 142, 152
Rother View 135
Rover Cottage 57, 101, *102*, *146*, 147
Rowley, Alice 162
Royal Sussex Regiment 88, 89
Russell, Benjamin 68
Russell, Francis 66
Russell, Hannah 68-69
Russell, William 107
Rye Green 23, 25, 117

Sadlers 20, 153
Salesians 96, 133-134
Saville, William 26
Sawyer, James 157
Sawyer, John 89
Sawyer, Joseph 99
Saxons ix-x
Schoeter, John Conrad 117
School Hill (Bell Alley) 112, 157
School Hill Cottages 112
schools
    Charity School 42-43, 53, 65-66, 73, 85, 87
    Congregational Independent Sunday School 104
    Dame School 87
    Edwards School 65
    National School 66, 85-87, *85*, 127, 132-133
    Roman Catholic school 87, 96, 133-134, *134*
    St. Philips School 86, 95
    see also education
Schroeter, John 111
Scouts 157
Sear, Bill 142
Second World War 127-131
Self, James 86, 127

Shadwell Row 18-19, *18*, 147
Shadwell, Thomas 57, 102
Shadwell, William 43, 47, 71-72
shipbuilding 7
shops 145-148
Shovers Green 64
Shrub Farm (Woodrising) 97, *97*, 136-137
Shrub, The 13, *14*
Siggs, Richard 64
sign, village *iv*, 167, *168*
Smugglers Cottage 18-19, 102
smuggling 67-68
Snape Furnace, Kent 27
Soane, George 98
Soanes Cottages 98, 139
Socknersh 9, 24
Sones Cottage 14, *14*
South African War (1899-1902) 88
South Eastern Railway Company 78
Southover 95, 96, 119, 129, 131, 164
Southside 109
Spears, Harry 100
Spencer, David 26
Square Farm 23, 44, 114, *115*, 163
Square, The 14, *114*
St. Bartholomew's Church v, 28, 31-37, *32*, *34*
    (plan), *35*, *37*
  Norman period 2, *31* (plan)
  18th century 63
  19th century 90-91, 93
  20th century 134
St. Giles 4, 5, 24, 51
St. Joseph's Church 95-96, 124, 133-134, *134*
St. Nicholas Cottage 24
St. Philip's Church 95, 124
St. Philip's School 86, 95
St. Wilfred ix-x
Stapleton, Thomas 26
Stepney, Jack 139
Stonegate 63
Stores, The 148, *148*
Strand Meadow 135
Suffolk, H. 92
suffrage 121
Summerhayes, William 119
Sussex Advertiser 69
Sussex Regiment *see* Royal Sussex Regiment
Sussex Turnpike Act (1765) 62
Sussex
  early vii, *viii* (map)
  Roman vii-viii, *ix* (map)
Swan House 164
Swan Inn *15*, 16
Swan Meadow 141, 142-143, 169
Swan, John 30

Sweatman, Edwin 141, *142*
Swing riots 69

taverns *see* inns
taxation 59
Taylor, Charles 100, 111
Taylor, Herbie 153
Taylor, William 33
telephone system 84
Thompson, William 64, 104, 106
Thunder, Margaret 15
Ticehurst 59, 69, 73
Ticehurst & District Water & Gas Co. 84
Ticehurst Lunatic Asylum 110
Tilley, Sarah 36, 113
Tilley, W. J. 35, 120
Timbers 18-19
Tisehurst, John 43
tollgates 63, 79, *80* (plan), 119
Tott Close 159
Tott Cottages 14, 115, *116*, 159
Tott Farm 115
Tott Farm (Great Tott) 13-14
Tottgreene (1550) 13, *13* (map)
Tournay family 98
Tournay, Ann 66
Tourney, Robert 50
trade and industry 53-57, 89-90, 120-121
Trower sisters 95, 103
Tudor House *18*, 19, *103*, 148-149
Tunbridge Wells, Kent 81
turnpike system 61-63, *62* (map), 78-79; *see also* tollgates
Turzes 4, 5
Twort, Thomas 90, 102
Twort, William 102

Venness, Samuel 57
Vereker, S. L. M. 164
Verner, Charles 139, *139*
Verrall, H. G. 127
Vigor family 157
Vigor, John (19th century) 100
Vigor, John (18th century) 65
Vigor, Robert 107
Vigor, Thomas 100
Village Institute 92-93, *93*, 129
village sign *iv*, 167, *168*
Villiers 18, 101, *102*, *146*, 147
Vines Cottage 112
voting rights 121

Wadhurst 63
Waghorn, William 64
Walker, John 52
Walter, Dean of Burwash 71
Walters, Hazel 133
War Memorial 124-125, *124*, *125*, *140*
Waterer, Thomas 71
Waterhouse, Charles 149
   reference *149*
Waterhouse, Margaret 133
Waterhouse, Thomas 67
Waterhouse, William 57
Waters, Walter 43
Wayside 19, 151
Wealden View 135
Webb, John 44
Weller, Katherine 106
Wesleyan chapel 91
Westdown Farm 25
Weston, Henry 83
Wheel Inn 68
White Hart Inn (Cheriton) 81, 104, *105*, 106, 152
White House 50, *50*, 51, 103, 148
Willards Hill House 29
Williams, William 48, 65
Willow 20
Wills, Colin Spencer 37
Wilmshert, John 28
Wilson, Edward 71, 72
Windmill Cottages 118
Witherhurst Farm 51, 118
Wood, Benjamin 66, 106
Wood, Harbart 56
Woodall, John 84, 102
Woodall, William 152
Woodknowle
Woodknowle 4, 5, 24
Woodruffe, William 122
workhouse 59
Working Men's Institute and Reading Room 91-93
World War I 88, 122
World War II 127-131
Worshipful Company of Girdlers 56
Wren Cottage 104, *105*, *150*
Wrenn family 149-150
Wrenn, Herbert 104
Wrenns Cottages 151, *151*

Yeomans Cottage 24
Yew Tree House 16, *16*, 53, 99, 141
Youngs Garden 23, 48-49, *49*, 73, 74, 159, 164

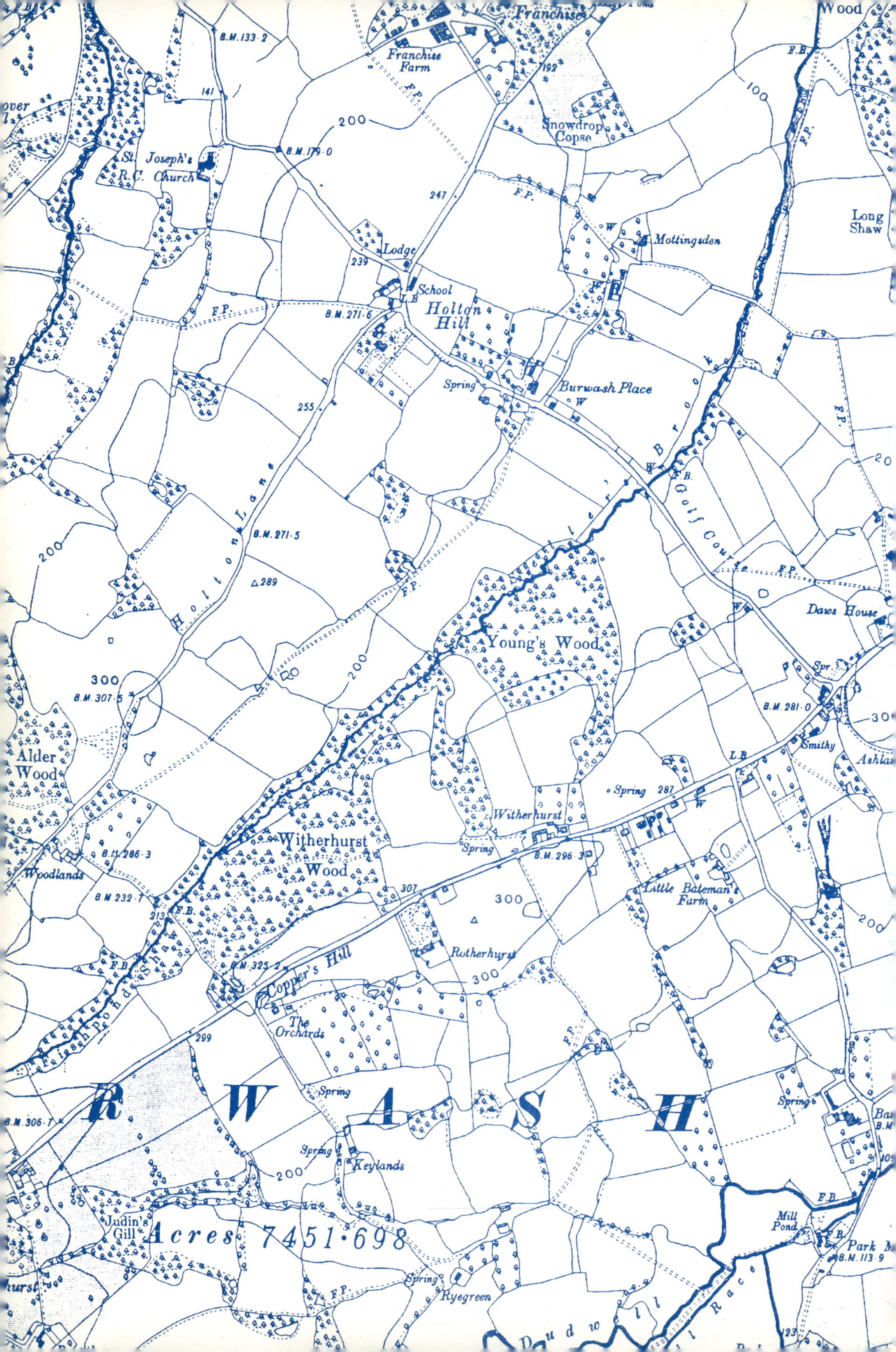
Franchise
Wood
B.M. 133·2
Franchise Farm
F.P.
141
F.B.
192
100
Snowdrop Copse
200
B.M. 179·0
St. Joseph's R.C. Church
247
F.P.
Long Shaw
Mottingsden
Lodge
239
School
L.B
Holton Hill
B.M. 271·6
F.P.
Spring
Burwash Place
W
255
Brook
Golf Course
Holton Lane
B.M. 271·5
289
200
F.P.
Young's Wood
Daws House
Spr.
300
B.M. 307·5
B.M. 281·0
Smithy
Alder Wood
L.B
Spring 287
Witherhurst
Witherhurst Wood
Spring
B.M. 296·3
B.M. 286·3
Woodlands
B.M. 232·7
307
300
Little Bateman's Farm
213
200
Rotherhurst
B.M. 325·2
Copper's Hill
300
The Orchards
299
R W A S H
Spring
B.M. 306·7
Spring
Keylands
200
Judin's Gill
Acres 7451·698
Mill Pond
F.B.
B.M. 113·9
Spring
Ryegreen
Race
123